Joseph F. Smith

Joseph F. Smith, 1838-1918

Joseph F. Smith

Patriarch and Preacher,
Prophet of God

Francis M. Gibbons

Deseret Book

Salt Lake City, Utah

To Suzanne, Mark, Ruth, and Daniel

©1984 Deseret Book Company
All rights reserved
Printed in the United States of America
ISBN 0-87747-988-7
Library of Congress Catalog Card Number 84-70071

First printing March 1984

Contents

Contents

Key to Abbreviations

BFRLS	Snow, *Biography and Family Record of Lorenzo Snow*
CHC	Roberts, *A Comprehensive History of the Church*
CR	*Conference Report*
GD	Smith, J. F., *Gospel Doctrine*
HC	Smith, J., *History of the Church*
IE	*Improvement Era*
JD	*Journal of Discourses*
JFS	Smith, J. Fielding, *Life of Joseph F. Smith*
POC	Nibley, *Presidents of the Church*

Chapter One

What's in a Name?

T he clipped accent immediately identified the woman as English. And her decisive air suggested she was not one easily deterred or discouraged. But the adversities this immigrant now faced were to test her mettle to the limit and plumb the depths of her British resolve.

Her name was Mary Fielding. She was a native of Honeydon (or Honidon), Bedfordshire, England. Migrating to Canada in 1834 at age thirty-three, this energetic woman, whose finely chiseled features made her stand out in a crowd, had crossed the Atlantic in search of material gain but instead had found spiritual wealth in the message of Mormonism. It was brought to her by Parley P. Pratt, an apostle of The Church of Jesus Christ of Latter-day Saints, who, on a mission to Toronto, Canada, in 1836, converted a large group of Bible students, which included Mary; her brother, Joseph; and her sister, Mercy Rachel. The leader of her study group, John Taylor, who was converted at the same time, was later to play a leading role in the drama of Mormonism, serving as the third president of the Church.

Impelled by a spirit of "gathering," which seized most early converts, Mary soon moved to Kirtland, Ohio, where a large concentration of Latter-day Saints resided. There she met, fell in love with, and married a tall, handsome widower, Hyrum Smith, whose first wife, Jerusha, had died a few days after giving birth to her sixth child. The marriage took place

December 24, 1837, in Kirtland. Soon after, the Smiths were forced to migrate westward, settling in Far West, a Mormon community located in the verdant, rolling countryside of northwestern Missouri. It was in this place, near the first of November 1838, that Mary Fielding Smith faced her first Gethsemane.

By now, Mary was within a few weeks of giving birth to her first child. The rustic dwelling the Smiths occupied was small and drafty, hardly large enough to house a childless couple comfortably, let alone to accommodate parents and five children (one of Jerusha's had died), including a year-old baby in diapers. It is easy to surmise that during the years Mary looked forward to motherhood, she never dreamed of a state of instant and overwhelming domesticity such as this, even in her wildest flights of fancy.

However, the pervasive and constant poverty and domestic clutter of Mary's life at Far West were overshadowed by a brooding fear that infected the entire Mormon community. This fear, which had simmered for months, was brought to a boil by Governor Lilburn W. Boggs's callous order to exterminate the Latter-day Saints. The Far West Saints were terrified when, on October 30, 1838, nineteen Mormons were killed and twelve were wounded by a mob, emboldened by the governor's order, at nearby Haun's Mill. Soon after, Colonel George Hinkle, a nominal Church member and commander of the Caldwell County Militia, negotiated an agreement with Governor Boggs's generals under which the leaders of the Church at Far West were to be surrendered, tried, and punished. This agreement also required the Saints to relinquish their arms, to forfeit their property in order to indemnify their enemies, and to leave the state as soon as directed by the commander in chief.

Two days after the Haun's Mill massacre, Mary's husband was arrested under the Hinkle agreement, was summarily tried by a court martial, and, as a warning to the Saints, was ordered to be shot the following day on the public square. (HC 3:190.) It was believed that the execution of such a prominent Mormon would quell any insubordination or resistance among the other Saints. Patriarch to the Church and elder

2

brother of the Prophet Joseph Smith, Hyrum was the scion of a distinguished New England family that traced its ancestry to Robert Smith, a Briton who migrated to America in 1638.

Later recision of the execution order did little to ease the pressure upon the expectant mother, who was uncertain whether it would be revived and who was unnerved by reports of rape and plunder committed by undisciplined members of the militia. (CHC 1:484; HC 3:191.)

On November 2, 1838, the day following the court martial, Hyrum, his brother Joseph, Sidney Rigdon, Parley P. Pratt, Lyman Wight, Amasa Lyman, and George W. Robinson, who had been arrested earlier, were taken to the Far West public square, where they were allowed to visit momentarily with their families before being herded into wagons for a trip to Independence, where it was expected they would be tried by a military tribunal and, perhaps, executed.

As Mary bid him farewell, there was no assurance she would ever see Hyrum alive again. And, left alone in Far West without his protection, she was exposed to the dangers of an army out of control, worsened by mob elements of the kind responsible for the Haun's Mill tragedy who had been drawn magnetically to Far West by news of its surrender. It was on November 13, 1838, amidst the tension and fear created by these conditions, that Mary Fielding Smith's first child and only son was born. The name selected for the infant—Joseph Fielding Smith—had special significance; throughout his life it would be a reminder to him of his identity and mission.

The *Joseph*, given in recognition of his distinguished uncle, the Prophet Joseph Smith, and his grandfather, the first patriarch to the Church, would remind him of his father's ancestry, a hardy line of Puritan-Yankees who had struggled and achieved on American soil for two centuries. And the *Fielding* would remind him of his mother's ancestry, a doughty, independent, and persevering line of Englishmen, fixed in their ways, and positive, even dogmatic sometimes, in their opinions and outlook.

If there is truth in the psychological maxim that even a small infant imbibes impressions and attitudes from its environment that are influential throughout its life, we may un-

3

derstand better some of the qualities that emerged in the character of the mature Joseph Fielding Smith as the result of the experiences and life-style of his parents during his infancy.

The fact that this was Mary's first child, delivered when she was more than thirty-seven years old, coupled with the turmoil and tragedy that surrounded the infant's birth, put Mary in bed, where she was to remain for almost four months, practically an invalid. Had it not been for her sister Mercy, who was married to Robert B. Thompson, Mary and her children would have been in dire circumstances. But Mercy stepped in during this emergency to care for the children and to nurse Mary back to health.

But the new mother's convalescence was terribly slow, made so in part by concern for her husband's welfare. The stressful circumstances under which he had been taken into custody and the overt and implied threats made against his life thereafter had created a morbid fear in Mary that she would lose her husband and would be left a widow with six children to rear alone. That it had been said she would never again see Hyrum alive when he left Far West with the other prisoners seems to have greatly intensified her fears. It is inferred that the apprehension thus created was the impelling force that caused her to accompany Emma Smith, her sister-in-law, to Liberty, Missouri, in January 1839 to visit their husbands, who were incarcerated there. Since Mary was still unable to move about with comfort, a bed was made for her in the bottom of a wagon. In this condition, she made the bumpy trip to Liberty, where she seems to have been reassured somewhat to see Hyrum alive and as well as his depressing circumstances would allow.

Back in Far West, where she found her children safe under the care of Mercy, Mary faced a cruel dilemma. Pursuant to the Hinkle agreement, the Missouri officials had ordered the Mormons to leave the state. To ignore the order would have placed her in jeopardy, exposed to the wrath of men who seemed devoid of compassion. And to obey it would force upon her another long, wearing trip toward an uncertain destination in neighboring Illinois and toward a still less-certain life as a refugee in a strange land.

The decision to migrate to Illinois was made clear to Mary when Brigham Young, who led the Church as the president of the Twelve while the Prophet was in jail, directed the Saints to leave Missouri. Obedient to that direction, she collected her meager possessions, with Mercy's help, and in February 1839 was moved to Quincy, Illinois, lying on a bed in the bottom of a springless wagon with the infant Joseph F. cradled nearby.

The scene at Quincy, where Mary and her children would remain for three months, was chaotic. The facilities of this small river town were severely overtaxed by the hundreds of Mormons who streamed across the Mississippi to avoid the wrath of Governor Boggs and his militia. Most of them lived in wagons, tents, or hurriedly erected lean-to shelters. A skimpy diet, poor sanitation facilities, and exposure to the elements brought on a whole compendium of respiratory and intestinal illnesses that made the Mormon camp seem like a huge open-air infirmary. It was in the midst of these squalid conditions that the Smith's baby spent some of the critical months of his early infancy.

However, conditions took a turn for the better in March as spring broke and as Mary arose from her sickbed. And then a month later, life took on an even rosier hue when on April 22 Hyrum arrived in Quincy with the Prophet, the brothers having been released from Liberty jail with the connivance of their captors. In May, Hyrum moved his family upriver to the swampy, mosquito-infested village of Commerce, later named Nauvoo the Beautiful, where he established the last home of his short, turbulent life, a home that his widow and children would evacuate under military duress as they had been evacuated from inhospitable Missouri.

Notwithstanding the pitiable conditions under which Hyrum and Mary set up housekeeping in Commerce, they seemed to move forward with optimism and purpose. Hyrum, as one of the Church leaders, was heavily involved in every aspect of the building of Nauvoo. This imposed on Mary a heavy burden to care for the children and manage the household. Notwithstanding, she found time to participate in the affairs of the community and the Church. One project in which she played a leading role was the Sisters Penny Subscription, a fund-raiser in which several hundred dollars were collected to help build the Nauvoo Temple. The name of the drive suggests the slow, tedious way in which the funds were raised, penny by penny, from the extraordinarily tight budgets of the Nauvoo sisters. And the success of the drive also suggests the dogged perseverance of its principal mover, a quality that would appear again and again in her son.

By June 1839, Mary and Hyrum had been married for eighteen months. During that short period, they had been driven from two homes. Hyrum had been imprisoned for six months, Mary had been bedridden for four, and now, without financial resources, they were struggling to establish another home for themselves and their six children. Against this background, the following excerpt from a letter Mary wrote to her brother in June 1839 provides important insight into the spirit of the family in which a future prophet was being reared: "It is now a little more than a month since the Lord, in his marvelous power, returned my dear husband, with the rest of the brethren to their families in tolerable health," she wrote to Joseph Fielding in England. "We are now living in Commerce, on the bank of the great Mississippi river. The situation is very pleasant; you would be much pleased to see it. How long we may be permitted to enjoy it I know not; but the Lord knows what is best for us. I feel but little concerned about where I am, if I can but keep my mind staid upon God; for you know, in this, there is perfect peace." (POC, p. 225.) This statement takes on added significance when it is seen that the forepart of the letter details matter-of-factly the turmoil through which the writer had passed in Missouri. The letter also breathes the love Mary had for her husband and for her infant son, whom she referred to fondly as "my dear little Joseph F.," and appreciation for her sister, Mercy, who had nursed her baby when she was unable to do so.

Chapter Two

An Abbreviated Childhood

I mprisonment is an attractive alternative to one sentenced to the gallows. So also Commerce seemed attractive to Mary when compared to the miseries of Ohio or Missouri. She apparently overlooked the mosquito-infested swampland on the verge of the river, the scruffy buildings, the steamy summers, and the piercing cold of the Nauvoo winters. Instead, she seemed to see only the beautiful verdure of the area, the graceful Mississippi snaking its way around the town's promontory, the fertile soil, and the aggressive spirit of enterprise that actuated the Saints in their new home. Therefore, compared in the scale of Mary's likes and dislikes, Commerce far outweighed either of the Smiths' previous homes. Moreover, now that her husband had returned to her side and the anxieties of the Missouri persecutions had been left behind, she enjoyed a sense of peace and contentment; and, because Hyrum stood in the front rank of Church leadership, she occupied a place of status and privilege she had never known before. Therefore, it is undoubtedly true that Mary Fielding Smith felt exceedingly happy and secure in Commerce, or Nauvoo. And it follows that these feelings would have been transmitted to her children, including Joseph F. and the seventh child, Martha Ann, who was born May 14, 1841.

For a period of five years, then, from June 1839, when his parents moved to Nauvoo, until June 1844, when his father was martyred, Joseph F. lived a peaceful, secure life. In reality, these years spanned the entire period of his childhood which, for all practical purposes, ended with the fusillade that cut down his father and uncle in the nearby Carthage jail on June 27, 1844. But though they were short, these years of childhood were critical in forming the attitudes and character of the mature Joseph F. Smith.

Through these years, he was exposed daily to the direct influence of a great man, Hyrum Smith, who after the death of Joseph Smith, Sr., in September 1840, was not only the Patriarch to the Church but was also the patriarch to the Smith family. Joseph the Prophet always regarded his elder brother in this light, deferring to him in family matters while taking the lead when Church doctrine or procedures were involved. This unusual relationship was demonstrated when the brothers were in the Liberty jail. There Joseph insisted that Hyrum sit at the head of the prison dining table as a symbol of his family patriarchal status.

Also during these years, Joseph F. enjoyed the love and special tutorship of his mother, who, relieved of the burdens of providing for and protecting the family, was able to devote most of her time to the care and instruction of her children. Being more mature than most mothers of infants or young children, Mary brought special skills to the task of mothering and teaching. While Joseph F. enjoyed the companionship of his mother for eight years after his father's death, his life was hardly the same as before. With the father gone, the whole chemistry of family relationships was changed. The boy became a man overnight. His status was altered from one of dependency to one of partnership. And with that change came responsibilities and anxieties that were previously shouldered by the parents alone and that seldom, if ever, were even known by the child.

And finally during the childhood years before his father's death, Joseph F. enjoyed the special status and privileges accorded to a child of the second leading figure in the Church. The boy could not have failed to note the respect paid to his father and the efforts of others to please and to serve him. All this would have had the tendency to demonstrate to an im-

pressionable child that his was a family of worth and importance and beyond the realm of the ordinary.

So the boy was raised in an atmosphere of love, acceptance, and special privilege. And he was raised according to
the strict teachings of Christian morality. All these facets of his
upbringing are clearly reflected in an anecdote he later related
to his own son and namesake. "On one occasion," wrote
Joseph Fielding Smith, his son, "Joseph F. . . . who was then
about five years of age, found in his father's desk a sum of several dollars. . . . Childlike he put it in his pocket and went out
to play, happy in hearing the dollars jingle in his pocket. To
his great consternation one of the neighbors took him to his
mother in great excitement because the boy had stolen the
money from its secreted place. Never, said he, would he
forget the fright that was given him when he was told that he
was a thief. What he did was a perfectly innocent act that any
normal child might have done. However the impression remained with him all his days." (JFS, p. 128.)

Joseph F. was a few months less than six years old when
his father was murdered at Carthage. He was too young,
therefore, to have understood the political intrigue, the
bigotry, and the religious persecution that preceded the
tragedy. These he would learn about later. But he was old
enough to understand the meaning of his father's death and
to remember vividly in later years the terrible impact it had
upon him. In 1906, when he was sixty-eight years old, President Joseph F. Smith visited Nauvoo with a party from Salt
Lake City. As the group visited various places of historic interest in the city, President Smith shared with them his personal
recollections of the events that preceded and followed the
martyrdom of his father and uncle. Stopping on one of
Nauvoo's streets, he declared, "This is the exact spot where I
stood when the brethren came riding up on their way to
Carthage. Without getting off his horse father leaned over in
his saddle and picked me up off the ground. He kissed me
goodbye and put me down again and I saw him ride away."
Joseph F. never saw his father alive again. Later he told the
group, "I remember the night of the murder when one of the
brethren came from Carthage and knocked on our window

after dark and called to my mother 'Sister Smith, your husband has been killed!'" His mother's screams on hearing the news and her moaning and crying through the night could never be erased from the impressionable boy's memory.

So young was he at the time, Joseph F. could not articulate his feelings nor grasp at once the full significance of what had happened. But it is inferred that when he saw the bodies of his father and uncle lying in state in Joseph Smith's Nauvoo home, the radical change the martyrdom had wrought in the lives of the Smith family began to be impressed upon him. "In this room," Joseph F. told his party during his 1906 visit, "the bodies of the martyrs lay in their coffins, after they had been brought from Carthage and dressed for burial. I remember my mother lifting me up to look upon the faces of my father and the Prophet, for the last time." (POC, pp. 228-29.)

Aside from the sadness of losing a beloved husband and parent, Hyrum's death left Mary and the children in economic chaos. Without insurance, pension, or a significant estate, and with their breadwinner gone, the family faced a bleak future, made worse by the unsettled economy and the volatile political conditions following the martyrdom. There being no well-developed welfare program at the time, Widow Smith had to rely on her own initiative and the liberality of neighbors and relatives for sustenance. And her independence and self-reliance practically eliminated the last-mentioned source of help.

So, with Hyrum Smith's burial, his family found itself cast adrift on an uncharted sea of trial and uncertainty. As it turned out, the powerful external forces that threatened to disrupt if not destroy the family produced an even more powerful internal force that welded the family together in an extraordinary way. The catalyst that produced such unity was Mary Fielding Smith, whose background and training had equipped her well for the task she now faced. Being forty-three years of age and accustomed to caring for herself during most of her adult life, Mary seemed not to be overwhelmed by the uncertain future. And her innate self-confidence seems also to have been bolstered by the teachings of her adopted religion, whose first principle is faith in the Lord. Whatever the source, Mary showed a great deal of spunk and initiative following her husband's death. She assumed the direction of her large family with a sure hand. And the extra burden Hyrum's death imposed on her required that she shift part of the load to the children old enough to carry it. Although he was not yet six, Joseph F. proved to be willing and reliable, and his mother began to use him and to depend on him more and more. By the summer of 1846, Mary's son had grown larger and stronger and in the two years following his father's death had learned to work hard and consistently. The skills he had acquired would soon prove to be an even greater help to his mother, who had been looking with anxiety toward the possibility of moving her family west.

The death of Hyrum and Joseph had done nothing to resolve the deep-rooted conflicts between the Saints and their gentile neighbors. There was a brief period following the martyrdom when the enemies of the Church seemed to recoil from the enormity of what had happened. But after a short respite, the old problems and enmities surfaced again, and these, riled up by a hard core of bitter and malignant enemies, generated tremendous pressure on the Mormons to leave Illinois. So strong had these pressures become by mid-February 1846 that Brigham Young and a company of Saints hurriedly departed from Nauvoo, ferrying the wide Mississippi, which was intermittently frozen over that winter. Attracted by the bustle and excitement, young Joseph F. was drawn to the river's edge, where he watched the beginnings of the great Mormon exodus with boyish fascination and, perhaps, some sense of foreboding.

As the ferocity of a predator is intensified by the first smell and taste of blood from its prey, so the besiegers of Nauvoo were aroused to greater fury by Brigham's departure. They used every known device to hasten the exit of the remaining Latter-day Saints. By summer, when it appeared their objective could be attained in no other way, they prepared a military attack. Although Mary was not fully prepared to leave, she loaded her children and a few household belongings on a flatboat and crossed the river to Montrose to avoid the assault that seemed imminent. While encamped beneath the trees on the Montrose side of the river, young Joseph F. heard the roar of the guns bombarding Nauvoo, the only home he could remember. Those sounds and the terror they evoked would remain with him throughout life, as would a sense of outrage toward those he considered responsible for the fall of Nauvoo.

Cut adrift from the last moorings that tied her to the life of security and privilege she had enjoyed as the wife of Hyrum Smith, Mary launched a new career of improvisation from her temporary base in Montrose. Leaving the children alone, she traveled downriver to Keokuk, carrying in her purse documents of title to her real property in Hancock County, Illinois. There she entered into negotiations with several merchants, which culminated in an exchange of the real property for wagons, oxen, horses, cows, and supplies needed for the long journey ahead. Back at Montrose, all the Smiths and their gear were loaded on the wagons which, with the animals other than the ox teams tethered behind, and with Widow Smith firmly in command, creaked and jolted west across the prairies of Iowa toward the Missouri River. And beyond was a less definite objective, vaguely referred to by the Saints as "the Rockies" or merely "the mountains." At the reins of one wagon was a budding young teamster, Joseph Fielding Smith, age seven years, seven months.

Passing through the Mormon outposts of Garden Grove and Mt. Pisgah, the travelers pressed on to the encampment of the Saints on the Missouri, later named Winter Quarters. There they established a semipermanent camp, where they were to remain for almost two years.

Given the poverty, the illness, the uncertainty, and the endless toil that characterized life at Winter Quarters, one could be misled into painting this segment of Joseph F.'s life in gray hues. In truth, however, this was an interesting and exciting period for the boy. He was in good health while there; his diet, though not fancy, was adequate; he was near family and friends; and he was among powerful men who had known and who admired his father. In these circumstances, then, which were calculated to give him a sense of security, Joseph F. settled down into a routine of work and play—with the emphasis on work. His play consisted of games with his friends, fishing, swimming, and horseback riding. And his work centered in his role as the family's chief herdsman. This was a necessary and demanding task, necessary because the whole family depended on its animals for both food and transportation, and demanding because the lack of fences and the dangers of rustling required the herdsman to be constantly alert. Yet there were many hours when the animals were relatively secure that would have afforded the opportunity for reflection and meditative prayer. And given his temperament and training and knowing of the spiritual stature he attained in maturity, it is a safe assumption that Joseph F. Smith, the boy, often used his leisure moments as a herdsman for this purpose. And viewing this era of his life through the perspective of more than a century, it is interesting to compare this boy with ruddy-cheeked David, another young herdsman, whose habits of reflection, discipline, courage, and dependability trace largely to his youthful occupation as a sheepherder.

Against this background, it is little wonder that the two stories about Joseph F.'s experiences at Winter Quarters that he related most frequently as an adult involved the family livestock.

In late 1847, when Joseph F. was about nine, he accompanied his mother and his uncle Joseph Fielding down the Missouri to purchase provisions and clothing for Mary's large family. They drove two wagons, each having two yoke of oxen. Loading the wagons with groceries and dry goods purchased at Savannah, and with flour, meal, corn, bacon, and other provisions purchased at St. Joseph, they started north in rainy weather that practically converted the dirt road into a quagmire. One evening the party camped in an open prairie near a spring creek located more than half a mile from the river but in plain view of it. Across the river they could see several men with a herd of beef cattle heading south, presumably toward the cattle markets in Savannah and St. Joseph. Usually they unyoked their oxen and turned them loose to feed. On this occasion, however, fearing their animals might get intermixed with the other cattle and driven off, they left them yoked. The next morning, their best team of oxen was nowhere in sight. Joseph F. and his uncle immediately began to search for the lost team. They spent the entire morning looking, but without success. Returning to the camp, dejected and wet to the skin from the dew on the tall grasses through which he had been searching, Joseph F. saw and heard something that made a deep impression on his boyish mind and that had a profound influence on him throughout life. His own words tell it best: "In this pitiable plight I was the first to return to our wagons, and as I approached I saw my mother kneeling down in prayer. I halted for a moment and then drew gently near enough to hear her pleading with the Lord not to suffer us to be left in this helpless condition, but to lead us to recover our lost team, that we might continue our travels in safety. When she arose from her knees I was standing nearby. The first expression I caught upon her precious face was a lovely smile, which discouraged as I was, gave me renewed hope and an assurance I had not felt before. A few moments later Uncle Joseph Fielding came to the camp, wet with the dews, faint, fatigued and thoroughly disheartened. His first words were: 'Well, Mary, the cattle are gone!' Mother replied in a voice which fairly rang with cheerfulness, 'Never mind; your breakfast has been waiting for hours, and now, while you and Joseph are eating, I will just take a walk out and see if I can find the cattle.' My uncle held up his hands in blank astonishment. . . . 'Why, Mary!' he exclaimed, 'What do you mean? We have been all over this country, all through the timber and through the herd of cattle, and our oxen are gone—they are not to be found. I believe they have been driven off, and it is useless for you to attempt to do such a thing as to hunt for them.' 'Never mind me,' said mother, 'get your breakfast and I will see,' and she started towards the river, following down spring creek. Before she was out of speaking distance the man in charge of the herd of beef cattle rode up from the opposite side of the creek and called out: 'Madam, I saw your oxen over in that direction this morning about daybreak,' pointing in the opposite direction from that in which mother was going. We heard plainly what he said, but mother went right on, and did not even turn her head to look at him. . . . My mother continued straight down the little stream of water, until she stood almost on the bank of the river, and then she beckoned to us. . . . I outran my uncle and came first to the spot where my mother stood. There I saw our oxen fastened to a clump of willows growing in the bottom of a deep gulch which had been washed out of the sandy bank of the river by the little spring creek, perfectly concealed from view." (JFS, pp. 132-33.)

This example of a mother's faith and of God's promptness in answering her prayer had a lasting effect on the son. He referred to it often as an adult. Not infrequently he would share it with his family as he endeavored to teach the principles of prayer and faith. A son quoted him as saying, "It was one of the first practical and positive demonstrations of the efficacy of prayer I had ever witnessed. It made an indelible impression upon my mind, and has been a source of comfort, assurance and guidance to me throughout all my life." (Ibid., pp. 133-34.)

The other incident, which followed soon after, occurred when Joseph F. and a friend, Thomas Burdick, were tending livestock at the herd grounds two miles from Winter Quarters. As the animals grazed peacefully nearby, Joseph F. and Thomas amused themselves by running races with their horses and jumping them across ditches. Suddenly the boys were startled by a band of paint-daubed Indians on horseback, naked except for breach cloths, who galloped toward the livestock, intending to rustle them. Thomas immediately headed for home shouting, "Indians, Indians," while Joseph F. wheeled his horse toward the herd in order to stampede it in the direction of the village. Succeeding in this by loud shouts and violent waving of his arms, Joseph F. then turned his attention to evading the Indians. "I got the lead in the direction of home," he reported later. "I could outrun them, but my horse was getting tired or out of wind and the Indians kept doubling on me, coming in ahead of me and checking my speed, till finally, reaching the head of the spring again, I met, or overtook, a platoon which kept their horses so close together and veering to right and left as I endeavored to dodge them, that I could not force my horse through. I was thus compelled to slacken speed and the Indians behind overtook me; one Indian rode upon the left side and one on the right side of me, and each took me by an arm and leg and lifted me from my horse; they then slackened their speed until my horse run from under me, then they chucked me down with great violence to the ground. Several horses from behind jumped over me, but did not hurt me." (JFS, p. 136-37.)

Picking himself up from the dust, Joseph F. was relieved to see a number of the elders, armed with pitchforks, appear on the scene. They had been alerted by Thomas's cries. Their appearance caused the Indians to leave hastily, taking with them the horse Joseph was riding and a few strays. However, the main part of the herd evaded the Indians because of Joseph F.'s quick thinking and courage and the timely appearance of the pitchfork brigade.

Some time elapsed before Joseph F. learned that the herd was safe. In the dust and commotion created by the stampeding livestock and the mounted Indian raiders, he could not be sure that the animals had escaped. During this period of uncertainty, Joseph F. was worried that he might have failed in his duty to protect the herd and, worse, that its loss might prevent the Smiths from going west the following spring. However, a few hours later, the herd was found by Thomas Burdick's brother, Alden, who had gone to the grazing site to meet his brother and the Smith boy, and in finding them and the herd gone, had commenced a search that at last had led him to the animals.

Chapter Three

The Orphan

T he hopes lighted in young Joseph F. on his learning that the family livestock had escaped the marauding Indians were dimmed by the harshness of the following winter, which killed several of Mary Smith's choice animals. Despite this, she was determined to go on to what the Mormon refugees now called the Valley. So in the spring of 1848, she loaded her brood of children in the wagons she had purchased at Keokuk and, with her sister Mercy (whose husband Robert B. Thompson had died in Nauvoo), Mercy's daughter Mary Jane, and several others, started for the Elkhorn crossing, where the next pioneer company was to be organized. So depleted was the family livestock by the ravages of the past winter, it was necessary to couple the wagons in pairs with but two yoke of oxen for each pair. The reins of one such rig were in the hands of nine-year-old Joseph F. Smith, by now a journeyman teamster.

The twenty-seven mile trip to the Elkhorn was negotiated by Mary's company in three days, a longer period than was usually required. The delay resulted from the double-loading that made it necessary to uncouple the wagons at each hill and pull them up separately. The yoking and unyoking of the oxen this complication entailed gave Joseph F. enough experience in teamstering to last a lifetime. It also engendered in him an appreciation, even a love, for the patient and powerful animals who were the means of transporting his family to the

17

Promised Land. At a pioneer celebration in 1917, a year before his death, the reflective prophet shared with an audience at Ogden, Utah, his feelings toward these animals who were so important to him and his family at the time: "My team consisted of two pairs, or yokes, of oxen," he told the Ogden Saints. "My leaders' names were Thom and Joe—we raised them from calves and they were both white. My wheel team were named Broad and Berry. Broad was light brindle with a few white spots on his body, and he had long, broad, pointed horns, from which he got his name. Berry was red and boney and short horned. Thom was trim built, active, young, and more intelligent than many a man. Many times while traveling sandy or rough roads, long, thirsty drives, my oxen lowing with the heat and fatigue, I would put my arms around Thom's neck, and cry bitter tears! That was all I could do. Thom was my favorite and best and most willing and obedient servant and friend. He was choice." (JFS, p. 155-56.)

As we shall see soon, the boy's inclination to ascribe human qualities to his favorite ox was shared by his mother, who, under the compulsion of dire necessity, would seek priesthood blessings for her ailing animals.

The Smiths' arrival at the Elkhorn opened a disagreeable chapter in their lives. At the center of their difficulty stood a man who was never identified by name but only by one or the other of two titles, either the "supervisor of cattle" in the Camp of Israel or "captain of the company" with which Mary made the trip to the Valley. Widow Smith first met her nemesis while he was acting in his role as supervisor of cattle. After examining her gear and animals, he gruffly told Mary she could not make the trip that spring but would have to wait until the next year. "If you start out in this manner," he said, "you will be a burden on the company the whole way, and I will have to carry you along or leave you on the way." The supervisor was both surprised and irritated by the spunky little widow's answer. "Father———," she replied, "I will beat you to the valley and will ask no help from you either." Apparently unaccustomed to uppity remarks of this kind from a woman, the supervisor turned on his heel and left, repeating his prediction that Mary Smith would be a nuisance were she to come along. (JFS, p. 148.)

If the supervisor expected Mary to dissolve in tears or meekly accept his direction, he had much to learn about her character and temperament. Mary promptly returned to Winter Quarters with her brother Joseph Fielding, using a single wagon and her two best yoke of oxen to save time. There she purchased on credit, or hired, enough animals to meet the supervisor's exacting requirements, and she returned to the Elkhorn crossing with an air of triumph. It is inferred that neither Mary Smith nor the supervisor of cattle greeted with enthusiasm Heber C. Kimball's decision to assign Mary to the company the supervisor was to lead across the plains.

On the trail, the conflict between the dogmatic captain and the recalcitrant widow was not eased when Mary adamantly refused to allow nine-year-old Joseph F. to stand watch at night in rotation with the grown men in the company. While the protective mother was willing to allow her son to work like an adult during the day, teamstering and herding, she felt his growing body required more rest than the men. And no amount of grousing or criticism from the captain could shake her resolve not to allow Joseph F. to stand night watch. The tension her refusal created, added to the strained relationship that existed from their first encounter, put the captain and Mary on constant guard. Each was suspicious of the other's actions and motives. And these attitudes were readily perceived by the widow's son, who took an instant dislike to the captain and who often read a malignant purpose in his conduct. This story Joseph F. later told his son illustrates the contentious relationship between Mary and the captain, and the son's perception of it: "With Widow Smith," Joseph F. told his son, "in addition to other dependents not of the family, was one Jane Wilson, a subject of great care and attention. She was subject to fits and fond of snuff. Her mother, a nice old lady, was travelling in Bishop Newel K. Whitney's company. All went well with Widow Smith until the company reached the fork of the Platte River. At this point they came in sight of the advanced company, and Jane Wilson, being out of snuff, started out ahead to overtake her mother and get some snuff, expecting to return to her own train of wagons in the evening. The companies were so near Jane thought they would both camp together that night. The captain of Widow Smith's company, knowing that Jane had gone ahead, concluded to camp in the middle of the day, and the result was that the advanced company pulled further away as they traveled during the afternoon. Late in the afternoon Captain ——— came into the center of the circle of the camp, and called the camp together, and when all had assembled he inquired in a very excited and noisy manner, 'Is all right in the camp!' This he repeated several times and then asked each group if all was right with them, and each answered 'Yes.' Then, turning to Widow Smith, he asked if all was right with her. She answered, 'All is right with me.' When she spoke he exclaimed: 'All is right, is it, and a poor woman lost!'" (JFS, pp. 149-50.) Mary then explained to the captain that Jane Wilson was not lost but had gone to her mother, whereupon he answered angrily, "I rebuke you, Widow Smith, in the name of the Lord! She is lost and must be sent for at once." (Ibid.) Yielding to his demand, Mary sent the elder son John ahead on the trail; he found Jane safe with her mother.

In requital for the captain's hostility toward her, Mary seemed to treat him with aloofness and disdain. She always responded to his abuse with civility, though without warmth, never questioning his authority and, except as to the issue of Joseph F. standing watch, always complying with his orders, no matter how harsh or unreasonable. The captain doubtless knew he did not stand high in Mary's estimation, and her outward show of obedience and submission seemed to rankle and annoy him all the more. And given the obvious competitiveness and drive of this pair, it is a fair assumption that the widow's boast that she would beat the captain to the valley without his help always lurked below the surface of their outward relationship, coloring and agitating it.

These intense feelings did not appear again until the travelers were midway between the Platte and Sweetwater rivers. There, one of Mary's strongest oxen, weary of the constant burden it bore, laid down in its yoke as if ready to die. When her wagon stopped, the entire column came to a halt to ascertain the root of the delay. The captain was among those who crowded around the fallen animal. While others offered assistance or condolences, he took the occasion to denounce Mary before the entire company. "There," he said pointedly, "I told you you would have to be helped and that you would be a burden on the company." (JFS, p. 150.) Whatever sense of vindication the captain derived from Mary's misfortune was short-lived. Relying on the unseen power that had led her to the oxen lost on her trip down the Missouri, Mary felt impressed to ask her brother, Joseph Fielding, and James Lawson to administer to the fallen ox. Feeling, perhaps, a certain awkwardness in employing for this purpose priesthood authority customarily used in blessing human beings, the two elders heeded the widow's request, using consecrated oil she provided. After the animal had been anointed in the usual way, the pair laid their hands on its great horned head and blessed it as if it were human. Soon it struggled to its feet and, after being fed and watered, took its place to resume the journey. Not long after, a second ox laid down in its yoke, exhausted, and still later a third ox did the same. Following the earlier procedure, these animals were also anointed and blessed with the same result. Joseph F. later reported that these unusual and seemingly miraculous events, which were a source of joy and thanksgiving to Mary, her family, and her friends, "brought great chagrin to the countenance of the captain of the company." (JFS, p. 150.)

The tide of events, which until then appeared to be running in Mary's favor, suddenly turned against her at Rattlesnake Bend on the Sweetwater. There one of her oxen, Old Bully, died from exhaustion and old age. Even though this animal was old and for some time had not pulled its share of the load, it was sorely missed if for no other reason than the affection the family had for it. To bury an ox on the pioneer trail aroused emotions not unlike those that attended the burial of a family member. However, compared to the misfortune that soon overtook the captain, the Smith family's loss of Old Bully was negligible. At the last crossing of the Sweetwater, the captain's favorite mule and three oxen laid down one night and died without warning and for no apparent reason other than the wear and tear exacted by the trail. Grief and sorrow at such a loss under those circumstances is understandable. But the captain's implication that Mary caused the death of his animals is not, except when viewed as an example of his paranoid dislike for her. Although Joseph F. was not yet ten years old, he was enraged by the captain's slur against his mother, and he showed the fiery temperament that, when unbridled, was one of his greatest weaknesses, but when controlled and channeled, was one of his greatest strengths.

"It was well for him," Joseph F. later said of the incident, "that I was only a stripling of nine years of age, and not a man, even four years would have cost the old man dearly regardless of his age, and perhaps a cause of regret to me. My temper was beyond boiling, it was 'white hot', for I knew his insinuation was directed or aimed at my mother, as well as I know that such a thing was beyond her power even had she been capable of such a deed. All of which he knew as well as I, and all the camp. At this moment I resolved on revenge for this and the many other insults and abuses he had heaped upon my mother, and perhaps could have carried out my resolution, had not death come timely to my relief and taken him away, while I was yet a child." (JFS, p. 151.)

In later years, Joseph F.'s fury at the conduct of the captain, who should have aided and sheltered his widowed mother and not harassed her as he did, was mellowed. But on the trail and for a long time thereafter, he loathed the man. While he never practiced revenge upon him as he had once thought of doing, he derived much satisfaction from an incident that rang down the curtain on the Smith family odyssey, a satisfaction tinged with an aura of revenge.

The scene was set on September 23, 1848, as the company prepared to pass over Little Mountain into Parley's Canyon and thence into the valley. The day before, the travelers had been treated to their first view of the Promised Land from the summit of East Mountain. After drinking in the sights of their new home, which until then they had seen only through the eyes of others or through the dim medium of imagination, they rough-locked the hind wheels of their wagons with chains and dragged them down the mountain, using only one instead of two yoke of oxen for each wagon. Spending the night at the foot of Little Mountain, a night made sleepless by the excitement and anticipation that gripped everyone, the Smiths arose early to prepare for the last leg of their journey. Excitement soon turned to disappointment on finding that some of their cattle had strayed during the night, and disappointment became anger and frustration on discovering that the captain intended to go ahead without them. Remembering his mother's prediction that she would beat the captain into the valley without help, Joseph F. watched with chagrin as the company made its way slowly up the east side of Little Mountain under a clear sky. As the column neared the summit, however, an early autumn squall blew in suddenly from the northwest, bringing with it heavy winds and a brief, torrential rain. Not knowing that the storm would end as abruptly as it began, the captain ordered the teams unhitched and the wheels of the wagons blocked. In the confusion that ensued, many of the teams and some of the unyoked cattle wandered away from the column into the brush that grew densely on all sides. In the meantime, the Smiths' strays had been found. Once the teams were yoked and hitched and the other cattle tethered behind the wagons, Mary was asked whether her party would delay its departure until the scattered cattle of the company had been collected. "They have not waited for us," she answered defiantly, "and I see no necessity for us to wait for them." (JFS, p. 155.) With that, Mary's wagons crossed Little Mountain, passing the captain and his company, who were still scrounging for strays; moved down Parley's Canyon; and entered the Valley, reaching the Old Fort Saturday night, September 23, 1848.

The next morning, the Smiths attended a worship service in the Old Bowery, where they heard several of the leading brethren speak, including presidents Young and Kimball and Erastus Snow. Then in the afternoon, they welcomed the captain and the rest of his company, who straggled in after spending a restless night atop Little Mountain. "The prediction of the widow was actually fulfilled," Joseph F. later reported with obvious elation, "we beat them into the valley, and we asked no help from them either!" (JFS, p. 155.)

Mary Smith and her family moved to a small farm plot on Mill Creek in the south part of the valley. There, with the aid of her sons and brother, she built a modest cabin and continued to exhibit the qualities of industry, independence, and frugality for which she was noted. By degrees, at times almost imperceptibly, the Smiths began to prosper according to the austere standards of Mormon pioneer life. Outsiders, who saw only the widow's poverty, may have pitied and patronized her. Such as these, however, would have been ignorant of the faith and optimism that fueled her daily labors. Mary was not merely scratching out an existence on virgin farmland in an arid mountain valley. She was gaining vital experience in an essential phase of her eternal progression. She was also a partner in the process of training a prophet. It is hinted that she knew her son was destined to play a leading role in the Church in the years ahead. Knowing this, she doubtless spared no effort in schooling and disciplining him for the task. And the other children, equally important to her, also required special attention in their development.

So Mary had a well-defined and appreciated role to play, one she looked forward to playing for years to come. This was not to be, however. She became ill in the summer of 1852. A combination of overwork and a skimpy diet weakened her body and left her prey to the numerous diseases that abounded in the Valley. These took their toll in the Smith family when on September 21, 1852, Mary Fielding Smith quietly passed away. She was only fifty-one at the time. An obituary in the *Deseret News* on December 11, 1852, summarized her life and accomplishments. "By the massacre of Carthage, June 27, 1844," it read in part, "she was left the sole guardian of a large family of children and dependants, for whom, by her indefatigable exertions, she provided the means of support, and removal, from Nauvoo to this peaceful valley of the mountains. And after providing for their future wants here, she has been called to leave them and a numerous circle of kindred and friends. . . . Her last illness, of about two months' continuance, she bore with her usual fortitude and patience; and only wished to live to do good to her family, and those around her. She has entered into rest; and may the examples she set, during her sojourn on earth, not be forgotten by those she left behind, to follow after."

Chapter Four

The First Mission

The last wish expressed in Mary's obituary was granted. The son never forgot his mother nor the example of faith and integrity she set for her children. Frequently, through a long life, he told stories about her and about the things he had learned from her. These stories reveal the bond of love and confidence that bound the two together, a bond whose severance was one of the most painful experiences of Joseph F.'s life. When his mother died, the boy was not yet fourteen. He had been toughened and matured, it is true, by the exodus and the taming of his mother's small farm. But he was still a boy in many ways and was deeply affected by his mother's passing.

In this extremity, the law of compensation came into play. The event that orphaned him also made him a surrogate father to his younger sister, Martha Ann. With both of their parents gone, young Joseph F. assumed a major responsibility for Martha's care and protection. The zeal with which the brother fulfilled his new parental responsibility to his sister is shown in a confrontation he had with their schoolteacher. "My little sister Martha was called up to be punished," he told his friend Charles W. Nibley. "I saw the school teacher bring out the leather strap, and he told the child to hold out her hand. I just spoke up loudly and said, 'Don't whip her with that', and at that he came at me and was going to whip me;

26

but instead of whipping me, I licked him, good and plenty."
(POC, p. 236.)

This incident, which occurred in the boy's fifteenth year,
seems to have ended his formal education. And whether because of it or in spite of it, he was soon launched on an
ecclesiastical career, a career whose mortal phase would carry
him to the pinnacle of Mormon leadership and would end
only in death.

Like the Indian raid on his herd at Winter Quarters,
Joseph F.'s call to the ministry came suddenly and without
forewarning. He first learned about it as he sat at ease in the
1854 April general conference. He had enjoyed the remarks of
Heber C. Kimball and Jedediah M. Grant, counselors in the
First Presidency, who, in turn, had expounded on the principle of obedience and on the terrible judgments that awaited
the nations and individuals who reject God. Then President
Brigham Young came to the pulpit. The youth was jolted out
of his ease when the Lion of the Lord, in reading the names of
brethren who were being called on missions, said, "And to
the Pacific Isles ———, ———, ———, and Joseph Fielding
Smith."

Whether or not he was aware of it, young Joseph F.'s call
to the Pacific began the process of molding and disciplining
that would ultimately fashion him into a man of prophetic
stature. The shaping process continued on April 24, 1854,
when he received his endowment and was ordained an elder
by his cousin, George A. Smith, who had been a member of
the Quorum of the Twelve Apostles for fifteen years. He was
then set apart for his mission by two other members of the
Twelve, Parley P. Pratt and Orson Hyde, who promised
Joseph F. he would learn the Hawaiian language both by
study and by the gifts of the Spirit.

Twenty other missionaries were called to the Pacific at the
same time as Elder Smith. They commenced their journey on
May 27, 1854, leaving in wagon train on the southern route.
From Salt Lake to Parowan, the party was under the direction
of President Brigham Young, who, in company with several
other leading brethren, was on his way to inspect and counsel
Mormon communities in the southern part of what is now the

state of Utah. At Cedar City, just a few miles south of Parowan, the missionaries, under the direction of Parley P. Pratt, angled off in a southwesterly direction toward the desert between Cedar City and San Bernardino, California, their immediate destination.

At fifteen, Joseph F. Smith was the youngest of these missionaries. In point of experience and maturity, however, he ranked much higher in the company. Ability and temperament would have moved him even further up the scale. And these, combined with the motivational fires that burned within, would have elevated him almost to the top rank. Joseph F.'s drive to excel derived from his parents—from his father's impeccable Mormon pedigree and from his mother's tenacity and competitiveness.

There was no more revered name in the Church than Joseph Smith. Indeed, that name stood high above all others, and identified the man who according to latter-day scriptures had, except for Christ, done more for the human race than anyone else. The fact this young missionary was the blood nephew of the Prophet and the son of the Prophet's older brother automatically set him apart in a circle of distinction. And the example of his mother's faith, perseverance, and independence could have had no effect other than to give the boy a self-image of the most positive kind, an image that, as we shall see later on, was readily perceived by others. So on the threshhold of his ecclesiastical career, an aura of success and destiny surrounded young Joseph F. Smith. But the distinction and achievement that loomed ahead could hardly mitigate the realities that faced the growing boy as his wagon bumped its way across the desert toward San Bernardino.

Orphaned, and separated from his brothers and sisters for the first time, Joseph F. doubtless felt occasional pangs of loneliness as he contemplated several years of labor among an unfamiliar people in a strange environment. Perhaps these feelings were eased to an extent by the presence in his group of two relatives, Silas Smith (a son of Asael) and his son Silas S. Smith.

To his loneliness were added periodic fear and tension

caused by the bands of Indians that followed his party intermittently and that used implied threats of violence to coerce
food from the missionaries. To placate them, the missionaries
shared their meager supplies with them, so when they
reached Cajon Pass, they had practically no food left. However, by tightening their belts and scrounging, they were able
to reach San Bernardino, where they were hospitably received by Elders Charles C. Rich and Amasa Lyman of the
Twelve, who headed the Church's colonizing effort in Southern California.

At that day, Mormon missionaries traveled without purse
or scrip and usually received no subsidy from home. Thus,
they had the dual responsibility in the field to proselyte and to
acquire the means to cover their own expenses, which usually
came from donations or their own labors. Because the Saints
at San Bernardino were subsisting not far above the poverty
level themselves, it was necessary that the missionaries find
temporary employment to earn money for their passage to
San Francisco and from there to their assignments in the
Pacific.

Elder Smith and his friend William W. Cluff found work in
the nearby mountains making shingles for a Latter-day Saint
named Morse. In the meantime, Elder Parley P. Pratt went on
to San Pedro on the California coast, where he made tentative
arrangements for the passage of the missionaries to San Francisco. He then took a coastal steamer to San Francisco, where
he was met by President Henry Tanner of the California Mission.

When Joseph F. and his companions had saved what they
considered to be enough to get them to their fields of labor,
they left San Bernardino, using animals they had purchased
from a group of Latter-day Saint missionaries returning to
Utah from Australia. At San Pedro, they sold their animals,
using the cash to help pay the cost of ship passage to San
Francisco. There they found Elder Pratt and President Tanner
negotiating for the purchase of a ship to transport missionaries to and from their fields of labor in the Pacific. On its
face, the idea had merit as an economy because of the large

numbers of missionaries who were constantly shuttling back and forth. It was reasoned that the savings in fares would soon pay for the ship.

This plan had two major flaws. First, the ship Elder Pratt and President Tanner finally acquired was not seaworthy. And second, the missionaries, who were expected to man the ship, proved to have no aptitude or liking for seamanship. The captain of the vessel, whose many years at sea had honed his autocratic ways to a fine edge and had enlarged his vocabulary of invective beyond anything the brethren had heard, found that he was wholly out of tune with the Mormon elders. Not accustomed to obeying blasphemous and arrogant commands, the elders bridled at the captain's domineering leadership. His response was to treat their conduct as insubordination, punishable according to the strict codes of the sea. Thus, some of the more independent and forthright missionaries, among whom Joseph F. Smith was presumably a notable standout, faced possible flogging or imprisonment in irons. Foreseeing nothing but difficulty and discord in the future, Elder Pratt soon abandoned the idea of a Church-owned vessel and canceled the contract of purchase, which resulted in a forfeiture of the money already paid under it. This included money Joseph F. and the other Pacific missionaries had earned at San Bernardino. Finding themselves penniless again, they sought employment in the San Francisco Bay Area to raise additional money for their passage to their fields of labor. Having no special skills other than as a herdsman and farmer, and apparently lacking the strength or desire to work on the docks, Joseph F. found employment as a farmhand. He worked at this occupation from July until September, earning enough money (when supplemented by a small refund from the ship fiasco) to purchase a ticket to the Hawaiian Islands.

All was in readiness by September 8, 1854, when Joseph F. and eight companions embarked on the clipper ship *Vaquero*, destined for Honolulu. What was projected as an eight-day cruise on the placid Pacific turned into a nineteen-day nightmare during which the *Vaquero* was alternately becalmed and then buffeted by violent winds. The savagery of the storm was aggravated by a surly controversy between the captain and his crew, the latter urging that the ship's sails be furled during the storm and the former insisting that they remain unfurled. The result of the captain's obstinancy was that all sails except the mainsail were whipped loose. In the shouting and confusion that followed, the crew finally managed to bring the vast expanse of flapping canvas under control and to lash it to the masts. As the *Vaquero* neared Oahu, the storm abated, enabling the crew to bring some order out of the chaos and to allow the proud clipper to sail into Pearl Harbor with a semblance of dignity.

One can imagine the excitement and relief with which Joseph F. and his land-bred companions saw Diamond Head loom up out of the Pacific. Overcrowded conditions aboard the clipper had made it necessary for the missionaries to be billeted in the forecastle with the crew. There they were treated to the bucking gyrations and nausea that only the forecastle of a ship can provide during a storm at sea. And they were also treated to the crew's profanities, which they found degrading and incompatible with their callings as representatives of the Savior.

The young missionary was enthralled by the distinctive sights, sounds, and smells of Polynesia as he alighted on the dock on Oahu. The exuberant friendliness of the natives appealed to him instantly. He was struck, too, by the luxuriance of the vegetation, made even more pleasant by contrast with the sparse vegetation of the deserts through which he had passed en route to San Bernardino. And he was impressed by the towering magnificence of the volcanic mountains that loomed up behind Honolulu and were covered with a restful verdure.

Chapter Five

Iosepa

After a brief welcome and orientation by the mission leaders, the novice missionaries were assigned to their fields of labor. Joseph F. was assigned to work on the islands of Molokai and Maui, both of which lie southeast of Oahu. Joseph F.'s cousin Silas also was assigned to Maui. As the pair departed from Honolulu on an interisland craft, young Joseph F. suddenly became ill, running a high fever with accompanying nausea. They landed first on Maui, the island said to resemble the head and bust of a woman, which consists of two extinct volcanoes connected by a low isthmus. That Maui resembles a woman in form seems to have had some symbolic significance for the ailing missionary, as it was here that he came under the maternal care of Sister Mary J. Hammond, who nursed him back to health after a month's illness. Sister Hammond, the only white woman then serving on Maui, was the wife of Elder Francis A. Hammond. This pair had been laboring on the island for some time. By their many acts of Christian charity toward Joseph F., they gained his love and respect, which he expressed often in later years.

Once he had recovered sufficiently from the "Island illness," the new elder was assigned to labor in Kula, a community located on the isthmus of Maui near Wailuku, which consisted of a series of small scattered villages. In Kula lived the reputation of a missionary who had preceded Joseph F. there and with whom he would have a long and intimate association in the years ahead. This missionary, George Q. Cannon, who had commenced his Hawaiian labors in 1850, had left the islands two months before Elder Smith arrived in order to return to San Francisco to publish the Book of Mormon in Hawaiian.

As it was with Elder Cannon, Joseph F. Smith faced two main problems as he commenced his missionary labors in Kula: the Hawaiian food and the Hawaiian language. Since the missionaries lived with the people, it was essential that these two problems be solved promptly. The staple of the Hawaiian diet at that day was poi, which consisted of baked, mashed kalo root mixed with water to form a thick paste. Much of the new missionaries' distaste for poi came from their negative attitudes and preconceived notions. As these lie within the power of the individual, so does a like or dislike for poi. George Q. Cannon demonstrated this when he prayed that poi (which at first reminded him of a bookbinder's old, sour pastepot) would be made to taste sweet to him. So effective were Elder Cannon's prayers that he ultimately came to prefer poi over bread. It is unknown whether Elder Smith was aware of Elder Cannon's formula for developing a taste for poi. But it is known that he soon adjusted to the new diet and never criticized it or complained about it as some were inclined to do.

A facility with the new language came almost as easily as an acceptance of the new diet. Joseph F.'s native intelligence, his youth, his desire, and the special blessing he had received enabled him to acquire a working knowledge of Hawaiian within three months after he arrived in the islands. Before the new year dawned, his leader, Reddick N. Allred, had begun to call upon him both to conduct and to speak at meetings. And on April 14, 1855, a companion, John T. Caine, wrote in a letter to James Ferguson, "Some of the brethren who came here first (I mean of our company) have advanced considerably in the language, and are speaking publicly. Among them, the most forward in the language is Joseph [F.] Smith, son of Hyrum." (JFS, p. 173.)

Aside from his language skill, the new elder had two other

valuable assets that accounted largely for his success as a missionary: he loved the people and he was dedicated to the work. These qualities shone forth in a letter the young missionary wrote to his cousin, George A. Smith, on October 20, 1854. "This people are very kind and generous-hearted," wrote Joseph F. about those with whom he was working, "and will do all they can to assist us to learn the language, and to make us comfortable; that is, those who are not opposed to the work." His sense of loyalty and dedication were expressed in these words: "I am happy to say that I am ready to go through thick and thin for this cause in which I am engaged; and truly hope and pray that I may prove faithful to the end." We can also gauge the depth and sincerity of young Joseph F.'s testimony from these words contained in the same letter: "I know that the work in which I am engaged is the work of the living and true God, and I am ready to bear my testimony of the same, at any time, or at any place, or in whatsoever circumstances I may be placed; and hope and pray that I ever may prove faithful in serving the Lord, my God." (JFS, p. 176.)

Two other aspects of this letter are worthy of special note. First, the concise and lucid literary style belies the fact that the author was not yet sixteen years old and had had limited opportunity for formal schooling. The second is the objective and detached perspective the writer adopted, which was devoid of vanity and self-seeking. He had little to say about himself other than to bear testimony and to describe generally the nature of his work. But he had much good to say about his companions, about the people with whom he was working, and about the loved ones he had left behind.

The powerful intellect this letter reveals was more than matched by the deep spirituality this sixteen-year-old missionary began to exhibit. This spirituality manifested itself in many forms but perhaps most dramatically in the power to heal and in his dominance over evil spirits. "'Of the many gifts of the Spirit which were manifest through my administration," Joseph F. wrote in later years, "next to my acquirement of the language, the most prominent was perhaps the gift of healing, and by the power of God, the casting out of evil spirits which frequently occurred." (JFS, p. 179.)

He illustrated this once by telling an experience he had at Wailuku on Maui at the home of a couple with whom he was staying. One evening as the young missionary sat studying the scriptures, he heard the woman of the house utter a loud, terrifying scream. Rushing into the room, he found her, with her features contorted into the most ugly and fearful shape, standing in the center of the room while her husband crouched fearfully in a corner. While at first the missionary shared the husband's terror, he soon composed himself and then in a somewhat hesitant though commanding tone addressed the woman, saying, "In the name of the Lord Jesus Christ I rebuke you." Almost instantly the woman crumpled to the floor as if dead. The husband, thinking that his wife was in fact dead, began to wail and sob while implying that Joseph F. was at fault. The young missionary then rebuked the man in the same way, which finally brought quiet and a sense of peace to the home. At length the woman revived from her swoon and was able to go about her duties in the usual way.

As expected, this and other unusual experiences involving the young elder were noised about, which seemed to arouse feelings akin to awe among those with whom he labored. The difference in age between the missionary and his flock made no difference in the way they treated him. It seemed to matter little to them whether the elder was sixteen or sixty. What did matter was his effectiveness as a teacher and spiritual leader; judged by that standard, Joseph F.'s flock found him to be amply qualified.

While Elder Smith was still convalescing from his illness, he accompanied Francis A. Hammond on a trip from Maui to the nearby smaller island of Lanai. There the new elder joined in a significant rite by which Lanai was dedicated as a gathering place for the Hawaiian Saints. As a prelude to this symbolic event, Elder Thomas Karren had been appointed to direct the development of a farming community on Lanai. In furtherance of that plan, the soil was ploughed and prepared for the planting of potatoes, beans, corn, and a variety of other vegetables. The native Hawaiians, who until then had had little exposure to the practices of systematic farming, were highly entertained by what appeared to them to be a nonsensical act. Snickering among themselves, they pointed with amused condescension at the foolish Haolis as they struggled to cultivate the soil. However, the increased yields and the variety of the elders' crops this husbandry produced would, in the future, convert native laughter into applause.

These industrious elders added further substance to their call to the Hawaiian Saints to gather to Lanai by laying out a townsite divided into city lots so as to bring the members into a more compact social and cultural relationship. The finishing touch was added to their plan of gathering when the name *Joseph* was bestowed upon the city and the name *Ephraim* was given to the valley in which the city and the agricultural enterprise were located. From this time, the concept of gathering was vigorously preached by the elders on all the Hawaiian Islands. This proselyting effort was to set the stage for an event that occurred a decade later that would prove to be one of the most unusual and significant of Joseph F. Smith's long career.

Once he had fully recovered from his illness and had mastered the language, Elder Smith began to fulfill regular proselyting assignments. One of the first was to tour the island of Maui with a local elder named Pake, who was one of George Q. Cannon's converts. Years later, writing to his son Wesley, who was then serving on Maui, Joseph F. recalled this tour with Elder Pake, who, he wrote, was a "full-blooded native, and a good speaker." Continuing, he wrote, "We had one horse between us, and we would 'ride and tie'. It is 125 miles around east Maui, from Kula around to Kula again, and we then had small branches at numerous places. I had then been in the islands only a little over three months, but I could say anything in the Hawaiian language, and took my turn with Pake in preaching. I was only a little more than fifteen years and 9 or 10 months old." (JFS, p. 179.)

From April 6 to April 8, 1855, about two thousand Saints, drawn from forty-two branches on the islands of Maui, Molokai, and Lanai, met in conference at Wailuku. Young

Joseph F. was one of the principal speakers at this conference, exhibiting an unusual facility with his adopted language. A main item of business was to approve the expenditure of four hundred dollars to acquire a boat for interisland travel. Built with timber taken from Oahu and christened the *Lanai*, this twenty-one ton craft proved to be a cranky boat and, according to Elder Hammond, who was an experienced sea captain, was as ugly as anything he had ever seen afloat. When it was found that the Lanai was a financial albatross, it was sold for two hundred dollars, and good riddance. While it was operated by the elders for only a short time and never fulfilled the high expectations held out for it, the Lanai at least gave Joseph F. enough experience with navigating the treacherous surfs around the islands that he was able to speak with authority about them a decade later when he served as a guide for two apostles who were sent to Hawaii to straighten out a serious jurisdictional dispute that had arisen there through the pretentious claims of an apostate named Walter Murray Gibson.

Following the April conference on Maui, a young native elder named Lalawaia was assigned to labor as a junior companion to sixteen-year-old Joseph F. Smith. This young pair, filled with the exuberance of youth and the spirit of their evangelical calling, followed much the same route Joseph F. and Pake had followed a few months before, preaching and ministering to the people, calling them to repentance, and setting in order the affairs of the Church in the many small branches that dotted the island. An evidence of their effectiveness is the acrid opposition their work stirred up among the Protestant ministers on the island, who were troubled by the inroads being made on their membership by the Mormon elders. Consistent with the past, this opposition focused on imagined defects in the character of Mormon leaders and a distorted representation of Mormon doctrine. While this assault on the elders and the Church caused some attrition among the membership, in the long run it had a salubrious effect not unlike the invigorated growth of a plant following a pruning.

Elder Smith was called to preside over the entire island of Maui at a conference of the Hawaiian Mission held in July

1855. The meetings convened on Lanai, apparently to dramatize the concept of gathering and to underscore the fact that this island was to be the hub of the mission. That the strength added to Lanai by the process of gathering had an effect upon the other islands is clearly shown by this comment made by the new president on Maui: "The gathering at the island of Lanai," wrote Elder Smith, "has gleaned out most of the faithful and diligent brethren, and that, perhaps, is one cause why the Saints feel so discouraged on the other islands." (JFS, p. 183.)

It was inevitable that the discouragement among the Saints noted by the seventeen-year-old presiding officer on Maui would be reflected, to a lesser degree, in the attitudes of the missionaries. And this element, added to the manifestations of evil spirits, the attacks of hostile ministers, the cultural shock of living among a foreign people, and the physical illnesses that infected him from time to time, made Joseph F.'s task difficult and challenging. But it was this very exposure to difficulty and challenge that ultimately brought to Elder Smith some of his greatest joy. Frequently in later years he would reflect with a nostalgic sense of satisfaction upon the difficulties he had endured and upon the fact that he had survived and grown from them.

The work routine developed by the young missionary on Maui was followed with little variation during the remainder of his service in the islands. There was the usual fare of proselyting with its successes and disappointments. And, as a presiding officer, he had the customary administrative work in directing the affairs of the struggling branches, often aggravated by the loss of leaders who heeded the call to gather at Lanai.

An element of variety was introduced into the work by occasional transfers. In April 1856, for instance, Joseph F. was transferred to Hawaii, the largest of the islands, where he was assigned to preside over the Hilo conference; and six months later he became the leader of the Kohala conference on the same island.

During this period Elder Smith learned firsthand about the process by which the Hawaiian Islands had, in a sense, been raised up out of the sea, when he witnessed eruptions of the huge, active volcano on Hawaii, about sixty miles from Hilo. "I experienced the tremendous shocks of earthquake which immediately preceded the eruptions," Elder Smith wrote, "and subsequently visited the great lava flow which issued from the crater." (JFS, p. 184.) This lava flow continued for months, moving over fifty miles from the volcano, and for a while it threatened the city and bay of Hilo.

The last transfer came in the summer of 1857 when Elder Smith was assigned to preside in Molokai. Here, near the end of his mission, he was confronted with the last and greatest challenge of his mission, greater even than the illness he suffered at the beginning or than the unfortunate fire that occurred just before his transfer to Hilo, when most of his personal belongings were burned. This last challenge was another illness much more aggravated and lengthy than the one he suffered on Maui. It was marked by many of the same symptoms, however. His fever ran dangerously high and was so debilitating that he was unable to work for three months. In this instance, as on Maui, young Joseph F. was blessed to have a concerned and able nurse to care for him. Ma Mahuhii, a faithful Polynesian Saint, nursed the sick missionary as if he were her own son. Indeed, the affection that developed between this pair during Joseph's illness seemed to be as deep and enduring as any that binds a mother to her natural son. The quality of this relationship was shown years later when the missionary returned to the islands after he had become the president of the Church. With the president on this occasion was Bishop Charles W. Nibley, who gave this account of the meeting between Ma Mahuhii and her former patient: "One touching little incident I recall," wrote Bishop Nibley, "which occurred on our first trip to the Sandwich Islands. As we landed at the wharf in Honolulu, the native Saints were out in great numbers with their wreaths of leis, beautiful flowers of every variety and hue. We were loaded with them, he, of course, more than anyone else. The noted Hawaiian band was playing welcome as it often does to incoming steamship companies. But on this occasion the band had been instructed by the Mayor to go up to the 'Mormon' meetinghouse and there play selections during the festivities which the natives had arranged for. It was a beautiful sight to see the deep-seated love, the even tearful affection that these people had for him. In the midst of it all I noticed a poor old blind woman tottering under the weight of about ninety years, being led in. She had a few choice bananas in her hand. It was her all—her offering. She was calling 'Iosepa, Iosepa.' Instantly, when he saw her, he ran to her and clasped her in his arms, hugged her, and kissed her over and over again, patting her on the head saying 'Mama, Mama, my dear old Mama.'

"And with tears streaming down his cheeks he turned to me and said, 'Charlie, she nursed me when I was a boy, sick and without anyone to care for me. She took me in and was a mother to me.'" (IE, Jan. 1919, pp. 193-94.)

Appraising President Smith's first mission over the gulf of time and tabulating his achievements in terms of proselyting, administrative success, and personal growth, it is easy to look upon them as if they came about without difficulty, other than occasional bouts with evil spirits or the island sickness. However, a glance beyond these mountaintop experiences reveals valleys of discouragement and doubt. As able, effective, and mentally tough as he was, Joseph F. was still an orphan boy in his midteens, working in a strange land a long way from home. Moreover, his poverty and the primitive living conditions of the people among whom he worked combined for a time to give him a deep sense of degradation and inferiority. Under these circumstances the young missionary had a vivid dream that immediately lifted him out of his despondency and that served as a beacon throughout the remainder of his life. In the dream, Joseph saw himself hurrying to an appointment, carrying only a small bundle wrapped in a handkerchief. As a large mansion, which was his destination, came into view, he also saw a sign with the word *BATH* on it. Entering, he washed himself and, opening the bundle, found a pair of clean, white garments, which he put on. He then went to the door of the mansion and, upon knocking, was admitted by the Prophet Joseph Smith, who said to him reprovingly, "Joseph, you are late," to which the boy responded, "Yes, but I am clean—I am clean!" As the dream continued, the young missionary began to wonder whether the unfolding drama was indeed a dream or whether it was reality. An opportunity to check his perceptions came when, in the dream, the Prophet directed him to bring a child being held by Joseph F.'s mother. "I went to my mother," he wrote, "and picked up the child, and thought it was a fine baby boy. I carried it to the Prophet, and as I handed it to him I purposely thrust my hands up against his breast. I felt the warmth. . . . I saw a smile cross his countenance." Not quite satisfied with this attempt to confirm his perceptions, the boy was given another chance to do so when the Prophet, after blessing the baby with the assistance of Hyrum Smith and Brigham Young, summoned him to take it back to its mother. "I was determined to test whether this was a dream or a reality," he later recorded. "I wanted to know what it meant. So I purposely thrust myself up against the Prophet. I felt the warmth of his stomach. He smiled at me, as if he comprehended my purpose. He delivered the child to me and I returned it to my mother, laid it on her lap."

Reflecting upon this isolated event just a few months before he died, President Joseph F. Smith gave this appraisal of its impact on him: "When I awoke that morning I was a man," he said, "although only a boy. There was not anything in the world that I feared. I could meet any man or woman or child and look them in the face, feeling in my soul that I was a man every whit. That vision, that manifestation and witness that I enjoyed at that time has made me what I am, if I am anything that is good, or clean, or upright before the Lord, if there is anything good in me. That has helped me out in every trial and through every difficulty." (GD, pp. 542-43.)

When he had recovered from his serious illness on Molokai, Elder Smith went to the mission headquarters on Lanai. He worked there until he and the other missionaries were summoned to attend a mission-wide conference at Honolulu. There Joseph F. received word that President Young had released the missionaries who had been called to the islands in 1854. Aside from their length of service, these missionaries were called home because of the threatened invasion of Utah territory by Johnston's army.

On October 6, 1857, following the conference, Elder Smith and six other missionaries embarked on the *Yankee*, a clipper ship headed for San Francisco. A shortage of funds made it necessary to book passage for the missionaries in the hold of the *Yankee*, where the foul, fetid air impregnated everything the missionaries owned. Joseph F. described the putrid atmosphere of his quarters aboard ship in a letter written in 1907 to his son Willard R. while the son served a mission in Norway. The son had commented on the stuffy condition of the ship on which he had crossed the Atlantic and the trains in England and Scandinavia: "I never before smelt a smell like that smell smelt," he had written. Responding, the father implied that the smells of Scandinavia were hardly worth mentioning. Wrote the father to his son, "In all of these places, I have smelt a smell intensified many fold by tobacco smoke, from sailors' nasty pipes, from the aroma from the stalls of beef cattle, sheep and poultry, carried for the use of the passengers and crew. Now they carry all of these things in refrigeration, dressed and ready for the cook's galley. Things have changed since I was a boy and crossed the seas with the Divine message you bear. Experience is better possessed than to be gained. It is like a bruise, it feels better after it quits hurting." (JFS, pp. 187-88.)

At San Francisco, Elder Smith and his companion, Edward Partridge, found their island lightweight clothing insufficient to ward off the cold of the autumn fog that shrouded the Bay area. To their rescue came a Sandwich Island alumnus, George Q. Cannon, who was then publishing the *Western Standard* and who furnished them with good overcoats and a pair of blankets. Thus equipped, the pair made their way down the coast to Santa Cruz, where they joined a company of Saints headed for San Bernardino.

Joseph F. found the Mormon colony at San Bernardino in a state of high excitement and confusion. The combined impact of the Mountain Meadow Massacre and the threatened invasion of Johnston's army had caused President Brigham

Young to order the evacuation of this California outpost. By the time the released missionary arrived, many of the Saints had already departed for Utah Territory, and most of those who remained were preparing to leave. With such a sudden drain on manpower as the Mormon exodus from Southern California produced, it was relatively easy for Elder Smith to find temporary employment. He worked only long enough to replenish his wardrobe, to buy needed supplies to get him home, and to accumulate a modest nest-egg for use upon his arrival. He then signed on as a teamster for George Crisman, who was making up a wagon train destined for Salt Lake Valley.

Confidently taking the reins in hand, nineteen-year-old Joseph F. Smith, by now a veteran of wagon-train travel, clucked at his team and began the last leg of his journey home. Behind him lay almost four years of trying but triumphant missionary work, and ahead lay an uncertain future, made even more dubious by the threat of armed invasion of his home. Moreover, the tale of the fate of the Fancher party at the Mountain Meadow, the grisly details of which had been magnified over and over through biased retelling by enemies of the Church, had inflamed the non-Mormon population throughout Southern California, and the Latter-day Saints traveling through the area reaped the fruits of this animosity. Joseph F. tasted it once and found it acrid and disagreeable.

The incident occurred early one morning as breakfast was being prepared. Joseph F. had left the cooking area to tend the animals when a wagonload of profane drunks approached, shooting their guns, yelling wildly, and cursing the Mormons. When their wagon stopped, one of them, waving a pistol, came toward the fire, which the Mormons had left hurriedly to hide behind the nearby chaparral. At that moment, Joseph was returning to the campfire, having finished his chores, and was seen by the drunk. Although the missionary was terrified, he felt it would be unwise and useless to run under the circumstances, and so he advanced toward the gunman as if he found nothing out of the ordinary in his conduct. "Are you a ——— ——— ——— Mormon?" the stranger demanded. Mustering all the composure he could,

Joseph answered evenly while looking the man straight in the eye, "Yes, siree; dyed in the wool; true blue, through and through." Almost stunned by this wholly unexpected response, the gunman stopped, dropped his hands to his sides, and, after looking incredulously at Joseph for a moment, said in a subdued tone, "Well, you are the —————— pleasantest man I ever met! Shake. I am glad to see a fellow stand for his convictions." So saying, he turned and walked away. (GD, p. 532.)

An innate modesty prevented Joseph F. from ascribing heroic qualities to himself as a result of this incident. Indeed, he later was frank to admit the fear that gripped him at the time: "I dared not run," he reported. "I trembled for fear which I dared not show." (Ibid.) Yet the stressful circumstances surrounding this incident, the young man's instinctive reaction to it, and his modest appraisal of it afterward impart a heroic quality to the affair.

The long trip from San Bernardino to Salt Lake afforded Joseph F. the opportunity to reflect in a leisurely way on his future. The chaos introduced by the threatened invasion, which was the chief topic of conversation in all the Mormon communities along his line of travel, had the effect of both simplifying and complicating his immediate future. It was simple to foresee that an able-bodied, dedicated Latter-day Saint of nineteen, imbued with a sense of outrage at the woe heaped upon his people by an insensitive if not tyrannical officialdom, would find himself under arms in the Nauvoo Legion opposing the invasion. That much seemed clear. What was murky and unclear related to his personal life—to the imponderables of marriage, family, creating a home, and choosing an occupation. These issues had not loomed large in the mind of the fifteen-year-old boy who had left for the islands in 1854. However, they were of paramount importance to the man who returned in 1858, who was fully alive now to the eternal significance of fatherhood and family, and whose physical maturity had sharpened and intensified his desire and need for marital love and companionship.

Chapter Six

Interim

T he seasoned Polynesian missionary arrived home on February 24, 1858. The next day found him in the new office of President Brigham Young, which was located between the Lion House and the Beehive House. The Church leader received Elder Smith with fatherly warmth and, after embracing him and exchanging the usual pleasantries that ordinarily pass between friends who have been separated for some time, listened with absorbed interest to the young man's report. It is not difficult or unreasonable to surmise that as President Young listened to Joseph's report, he recalled his association with Hyrum Smith, the missionary's father, and with the Prophet, his uncle. And the Lion of the Lord's spirituality and unquestioned ability to judge men may also have seen in the young man an apostolic potential that would reach fruition in a few years, after he had had more seasoning.

Aside from commending him for his service and giving personal counsel, President Young, as expected, suggested that Joseph join the legion to help protect against the threatened invasion. The returned missionary promptly acted on this suggestion and was first assigned to military duty under the command of Col. Thomas Callister. From then until the following June, when peace was restored, Hyrum's son, by his own account, was constantly in the saddle "prospecting and exploring the country between Great

Salt Lake City and Fort Bridger." (POC, p. 240.) During this period, Joseph F. also served on picket guard duty with a squad of men under the leadership of the wily frontiersman Orrin Porter Rockwell, whose fame as one of Joseph Smith's bodyguards still lives on. The Rockwell men and others like them, called pickets, were essentially guerrillas whose object was to impede the federal troops by delaying, harassing tactics, but they operated under a prophetic command not to take human life.

Also during his brief military stint, Joseph F. assisted in the evacuation of Salt Lake City in line with President Young's threatened "scortched earth" policy; after the evacuation, he remained on duty in the deserted city under orders to help burn it down should the federal troops, on cessation of hostilities, fail to keep their pledge to march peacefully through the city to their camp beyond the Jordan.

When the dust from "Buchanan's Blunder" had finally settled and it became apparent that the Saints would be allowed to occupy Salt Lake City in peace, Joseph F. assisted his relatives to return to their Salt Lake homes from the Provo area. Among these relatives was a cousin, pert sixteen-year-old Levira Smith, who caught the returned missionary's eye. Aside from her personal charm, this young lady would have attracted a returned missionary, conscious of the need for a dedicated companion, because of her gold-plated family credentials. Levira was the daughter of Samuel Harrison Smith, one of the Prophet's younger brothers; he was also one of the eight witnesses to the Book of Mormon, one of the charter members of the Church, and one of its first missionaries. Samuel H. reportedly distributed the Book of Mormon that was instrumental in the conversion of some of the Young family. The apparent attraction Joseph F. instantly had for this beautiful young woman, who was a mere child when he left for the islands, would blossom into romance and then marriage within a year.

In the meantime, it was necessary for the young man to find employment before he could give any serious thought to matrimony. He found a temporary job as the sergeant-at-arms of the territorial legislature for the 1858–1859 term. Although Fillmore was then the territorial capital, the legislature met in Salt Lake City for convenience; thus, Joseph F. was able to remain close to his family, to his fiancée, and to the leaders of the Church while earning his livelihood.

During this interim period, the recently returned missionary maintained a high level of activity in ecclesiastical affairs. On March 20, 1858, he was ordained a seventy and inducted into the thirty-second quorum. He was destined to function in that role for only a short while, as on October 16, 1859, he was called to the high council of the Salt Lake Stake and ordained a high priest. In the meantime, Joseph F.'s attraction for Levira had blossomed into a courtship that culminated in marriage on April 5, 1859.

Given their family heritage, this couple doubtless knew from the outset of their marriage that their personal interests would always be subordinate to the demands of the Church. This subordination grew from the conviction that the Church is the earthly embodiment of the kingdom of God and that submitting to its mandates without restraint ultimately would yield the greatest blessings. But their faith lay deeper than an expectation of reward and was founded on a desire for the approval of God and his earthly agents. Such convictions and qualities of character are readily inferred from the willingness with which the newlyweds accepted a call to Joseph F. to fill another mission, a call that came just a year after their marriage. This assignment, which was extended at the April 1860 general conference, would send the twenty-one-year-old missionary veteran to the British Isles, the home of his ancestors.

As usual, the call came unexpectedly, and the missionary was given little time to arrange for his departure. This did not impose an undue hardship on Joseph F., as he had had little time to accumulate physical possessions, and Levira had not yet conceived. So the missionary's preparation consisted only of making arrangements for his wife to stay with relatives, packing his traveling gear, and receiving final instructions from the presiding brethren. This completed, Joseph F. left Salt Lake City on April 27, 1860, in a company led by Bishop Edwin D. Woolley. Among his traveling companions was

Samuel Harrison Bailey Smith, Levira's brother, who was, therefore, both Joseph's first cousin and his brother-in-law.

These cousins were enough alike in heritage, age, appearance, and experience to have been twins. Samuel was born in Missouri three months before Joseph F., came west with the Brigham Young company, was called as a missionary at age seventeen, was called home from Great Britain at the onset of the invasion, and was married just a short while before departing for his second mission to the British Isles. Both of the Smith cousins were tall, powerfully built men, cast in the physical mold of their ancestors. And they were "happy warriors" in the army of the Lord, diligent, active, and purposeful.

Each of the cousins drove a four-mule team from Salt Lake City to Des Moines, Iowa, retracing the well-worn trail they had followed west many years before. At the Missouri River near Florence, Nebraska, Joseph met his brother, John, who was destined to follow his father and grandfather into the patriarchal office and who had gone east to get their sister Lovina (Walker) and her family. It had been fourteen years since Joseph F. had seen his sister, and these three children of Hyrum, joined by their cousin Samuel, spent a pleasant evening visiting and reminiscing.

Gauging from a letter John had written to Joseph F. on April 18, 1860, a chief topic of conversation at this rendezvous on the Missouri was their cousin Joseph Smith III, who, only a few weeks before, had taken a fateful step that in the years ahead would create a deep schism between the families of the martyrs, Joseph and Hyrum. The step was taken on the thirtieth anniversary of the organization of the Church, April 6, 1860, when at Amboy, Illinois, Joseph Smith III was sustained as the first president of the Reorganized Church. John, who had talked to the Prophet Joseph Smith's namesake before the event, had written him a letter on April 3, 1860, warning about the motives of the small group of men who had been advising him. In this letter John told his cousin that from what he had learned, the plans of these men were "a speculation," that they did not care "a d——" for young Joseph, and that their object was "to make a tool" of him in order to carry out

48

their "schemes that they may get gain." (Buddy Youngreen, "Sons of the Martyrs' Nauvoo Reunion—1860," BYU Studies 20 [Summer 1980]: 355.)

Confirming an earlier letter he had written to his younger brother, John also told Joseph F. about what to expect were he to visit Nauvoo. He would find a "desolate looking place" with only the west wall of the once-magnificent temple still standing. He would also find many relatives there, descendants of the Prophet Joseph Smith, who would treat him well and whose religious views would coincide with his own except as to polygamy and the right of succession in the presidency. (Ibid., p. 356.)

Deciding to test the religious and familial waters at Nauvoo themselves, Joseph F. and Samuel left John and Lovina at the Missouri and, in ten days of arduous travel, leap-frogged across Iowa, arriving at Montrose on the west bank of the Mississippi in the late evening of June 19. Joseph arose early the next morning and walked to the riverbank to get an unobstructed view of his former home. In a letter written to Levira eight days later, the Britain-bound missionary told his wife about the nostalgic thoughts that flooded his memory as he gazed across the broad Mississippi at "poor old Nauvoo." Wrote he to his young bride, "It looked as natural to me as tho' I had lived there my life time. There stood our old Barn and Brick Office as they did 14 years ago. Uncle Joseph's Big Brick store looked as it did when I saw it last, in fact I could pick out nearly every spot that I had known in Childhood." (Ibid., p. 357.)

Crossing the river at 9:00 A.M., the missionaries landed near an old stone house on the east bank of the river and then took a walk through Nauvoo's quiet streets, which evoked more memories of long ago. "We walked down the River past the old steam mill," he wrote reflectively, "took a good look at the old printing Office where uncle Don Carlos lived." After minutely examining his father's homestead with its satellite building, the "office," and the barn and the brick outhouse, the visiting missionaries called at the "Old Homestead." This was the first home the Prophet Joseph Smith occupied in Commerce, where now lived his son, Joseph Smith III, the newly installed president of the Reorganized Church. Here the Utah visitors received a warm welcome from their Nauvoo cousin, who shook them warmly by the hand and, according to Joseph F.'s report, showed "unfeigned pleasure" at seeing them.

Across the street at the Smith Mansion, where they were soon taken, the Utah cousins received a mixed welcome. Frederick and Alexander, two more of the Prophet's sons, reacted in the same open and friendly way as had their elder brother. However, Major Bidamon, Emma's second husband, showed "no great pleasure" at seeing the young men. (Ibid.) And after dinner, when they were taken to Emma's room, she showed the same cold and distant attitude. As Frederick ushered the pair into his mother's presence, he asked, "Mother, do you know these young men?" Looking up, she said without hesitation, "Why, as I live, it is Joseph. Why, Joseph, I would have known you in hell, you look so much like your father." (JFS, p. 197.)

As the conversation developed during the visitors' short stay in Nauvoo, it seemed apparent that the coldness in Emma's behavior toward them came not from any dislike for them as individuals but from their affiliation with the church led by Brigham Young. There was never any genuine feeling of friendship between this pair. Emma seemed to regard Brigham as a Johnny-come-lately who had appeared on the scene some time after the Church was organized and who was not, therefore, privy to the early trials she had shared with her martyred husband. And Emma seemed to be offended by Brigham's assumption of authority after Joseph's death as much by his apparent intention to perpetuate the system of plural marriage Joseph had instituted as by her obvious feeling that the disciple could not hope to assume the role played so brilliantly by his mentor.

The cold indifference Emma and the Major showed toward the visitors was compensated for by the warmth and sincerity of Emma's sons. Joseph III, Alexander, and Frederick spoke freely with their Salt Lake cousins. Without rancor or condemnation, the prophet's sons rejected the leadership of the hierarchy in Utah solely on the grounds of polygamy, although Joseph III went so far as to assert that the Nauvoo Temple was destroyed because it had been defiled by the "authorities" and that because of their "sins and transgressions they were driven from Nauvoo." He also expressed the view that the Utah Saints were in "bondage" and that they were oppressed by the "authorities." (Youngreen, pp. 359-60.) Reciprocating this frankness, the Utah cousins raised questions about the motives and reliability of William Marks and whether the Prophet's sons were unduly influenced by the negative views of their mother. As to William Marks, Joseph III seemed unaware of the forebodings his father had had about him and was unwilling to attribute any false or questionable motives to him; and as to his mother, he disclaimed she had tried to influence him against President Young and his associates, although he impliedly acknowledged that she was adamant and unreasoning in her scornful contempt for them.

So, it was a standoff between the two sets of cousins, each believing its own views to be unassailable and each entertaining the opinion that the other was gullibly misled. But they did not impute qualities of insincerity to each other, and they parted the best of friends, extending heartfelt best wishes to each other. Emma, on the other hand, retained her reserved and distant attitude to the end. As the missionaries were about to leave Nauvoo, they called to pay their respects to her. "When we returned to the mansion to bid the folks 'good by,'" Joseph F. wrote in his letter to Levira, "Aunt Emma came to me and said, 'Joe—You are going a wandering are you?'" Answering that he supposed he would "wander" some before returning home, Emma asked whether he had done much of it. "I told her I had done some," Joseph F. wrote later. "She asked me then if I liked it better than I did to stay at home. I told her my natural feelings would be to stay at home.—and she turned away, and as she went towards the house said 'I hope the time will come when we can all stay at home!', giving me no time to say any more." (Ibid., p. 360.) Underscoring the enigmatic qualities of Emma's conduct and comments on this occasion, Samuel had this to say about her in a letter he wrote to his cousin George A. Smith on July 11,

1860: "Aunt Emma was pretty much the same as she use[d] to be. She has that same way about her which is very strange. I think, we all have our ways and especially *her*." (Ibid., p. 361.)

While the reception Joseph F. and his cousin Samuel received in Nauvoo from relatives ranged from cordial to cold, the reception received from practically all others was frigid, to say the least. The fourteen years since the exodus had done little to moderate the animosity the gentiles felt toward the Utah Mormons. The Salt Lake cousins began to feel the oppressive weight of that hatred as they moved eastward from the Missouri. And it became ever more pronounced and burdensome the nearer they came to Nauvoo. On the landing at Montrose before crossing the river, Joseph F. and Samuel heard the Mormons cursed for no apparent reason and heard the profanities of rough-looking men who boasted about the evil treatment to be given to any Mormon found in the area. These threats, coupled with vivid memories of the martyrdom, which had occurred sixteen years before, filled the young men with apprehension. So when questions were later asked about their identity, the missionaries were intentionally vague and imprecise. When a Catholic priest directly asked where they came from, he received the airy answer, "Oh! from the West." Pressing the issue, the priest inquired, "How far West?"

"From the Rocky Mountains."

Having backed them into a corner, the interrogator then asked the question that was impossible for the cousins to dodge or parry. "Are you 'Mormon' elders from Utah?" Joseph F. reported later that he was never so tempted to lie as he was on that occasion. Genuinely fearful for his safety, if not for his life, and confronted suddenly and unexpectedly with the need to make a hurried decision entailing serious moral implications, he wavered for a moment. Soon stifling the impulse to misrepresent, however, he figuratively squared his shoulders and answered, "Yes, sir, we are 'Mormon' missionaries on our way to England." (GD, p. 533.)

The feelings of self-congratulation and relief the young man must have felt at having told the truth were doubtless heightened when he discovered later that the Catholic priest was a guest at the Mansion House in Nauvoo. The damage to the Church and to the missionary's self-esteem that would have occurred had he lied is incalculable. As it was, young Joseph Fielding Smith, a developing prophet, was strengthened immeasurably in his habits of courage and truthfulness, and the stature of the church he represented was enhanced.

As the Smith cousins had traveled eastward from Des Moines, they had tried unsuccessfully to find temporary employment to earn money to pay their expenses to England. This raised a serious problem for the pair, as the likelihood of finding work in unfriendly Nauvoo was remote at best. In this emergency there occurred another of those unusual and providential events that characterized the life of President Smith. One day the cousins met an Iowan who asked who they were and where they were going. On learning they were Mormon missionaries on their way to England, he confided he had a sister there whom he wanted to emigrate and asked that they take money to her for this purpose. In the meantime, he authorized them to use the money for their personal needs, provided they replace it in time for the sister to come to the United States. This unexpected windfall enabled the missionaries to travel to their field of labor without the need to stop en route to earn expense money.

Leaving Nauvoo, the cousins traveled through Carthage, whose old stone jail aroused unpleasant and melancholy memories for Joseph F., and on to Colchester, McDonough County, which lies a few miles northeast of Carthage. There lived the Prophet Joseph Smith's three sisters. These aunts welcomed their nephews warmly, housed and fed them while they were in the vicinity, and were attentive listeners at the services they conducted. It would have been difficult for the aunts not to have been impressed by the self-confidence, eloquence, and fervor of these two young nephews, not yet twenty-two years old, who had already filled proselyting missions to the isles of the sea and who were on their way abroad to serve again. But such ability and achievement in men so young was nothing new to the Smith clan, whose most distinguished member, the Prophet Joseph Smith, had begun his extraordinary ministry at age fourteen. These aunts had been reared in the home that had produced this young prophet as well as the faithful and able fathers of the two visiting missionaries. Judging from Emma's reaction when she first saw Joseph F., the aunts likely were reminded again and again of their brothers Hyrum and Samuel as they listened to their nephews expound the principles that had meant so much to the entire family and that had contributed to the martyrdom of two beloved brothers.

From Colchester the cousins made their way to New York City by coach, steamer, and rail, with not a little walking in between. There, on July 14, 1860, they took passage on the steamship *Edinburgh* bound for Liverpool. On board with them were eleven other missionaries, including two members of the Twelve, Amasa M. Lyman and Charles C. Rich, the brethren who had greeted Joseph F. in San Bernardino en route to his Polynesian mission. Also among the missionaries was Amasa's son, Francis M. Lyman, who would one day be inducted into the Twelve and who would later be mortified by the erratic behavior of his father, who was destined to suffer the ignominy of excommunication for dabbling in spiritualism.

A seasoned voyager by now, Elder Smith seems not to have been unduly troubled by a crossing of the more turbulent Atlantic, nor is there any indication he found the smells of his ship any more or less pungent than those of the vessels on which he had plied the Pacific. That there were offensive odors and nauseous discomfort aboard the *Edinburgh* we may be sure, given the comparatively crude engineering of ships at that day and the limitations imposed by the lack of adequate refrigeration and sanitation facilities, and the violence of North Atlantic storms.

Chapter Seven

The Second Mission

T he missionaries were met at the Liverpool pierhead on the River Mersey by seasoned personnel who led them to the building that headquartered both the British and European missions located at 42 Islington, an address familiar to battalions of Mormon missionaries who passed through Liverpool during several decades, either going to or returning from their various fields of labor in Europe or the British Isles. A three-and-a-half-story brick building with a plain, dingy facade resembling nothing less than a small textile factory, 42 Islington from 1861 also housed the staff and equipment of the *Millennial Star*, the Latter-day Saints' muted but persistent voice in England, which, since its birth in Manchester in 1840 under the editorship of Parley P. Pratt, had striven to broadcast the message of Mormonism against the flood of invective and abuse that poured almost incessantly from a hostile British press. The editor of the *Star*, commenting on the group of missionaries that arrived on the *Edinburgh*, had this to say about the Smith cousins: "There was much food for thought and for me a precious morsel was the presence of the sons of Hyrum and Samuel Smith and nephews of Joseph, our Prophet. I could not be forgetful of the great dead, or be insensible of the presence of these their natural . . . [descendants]." (JFS, p. 199.)

Upon their arrival in Liverpool, Elders Amasa Lyman and Charles C. Rich jointly assumed the presidency of the British and European missions, replacing Nathaniel V. Jones and Jacob Gates, who had been serving as presidents protem since the release of Asa Calkins in May 1860. At this time, there were less than a hundred so-called traveling missionaries serving in Great Britain, most of whom had arrived or were to arrive that year. Because of the exigencies created by the Johnston invasion, only five foreign missionaries arrived in Great Britain from 1858 through 1859. Consequently, when in 1860 the Smith cousins arrived, the mission was building up to the proselyting strength it had enjoyed from 1852 to 1857, when about one hundred sixty-eight missionaries arrived in Liverpool from the United States. This process of building, added to the experience he had gained in Polynesia and his native leadership abilities, resulted in Joseph F. being appointed as the president of the Sheffield Conference by Elders Lyman and Rich soon after their arrival in England. So pleased were the apostles by the work of this twenty-two-year-old elder that within a short while thereafter he was appointed as a "pastor," in which capacity he directed the proselyting work in four large conferences, covering a large part of Great Britain. That the confidence and respect in which Elder Smith was held by his leaders was shared by his fellow missionaries and the Saints is suggested by this report made to the *Millennial Star* by Elder Thomas Taylor: "I find the Sheffield Saints are warm-hearted and full of good works, under the Presidency of Joseph F. Smith, who though young is like a father to them. He is esteemed very highly by the Saints, and by some who have not, for some reason or other, dared to own the Latter-day work by baptism, although they have in every other way." (JFS, p. 203.) Another fellow missionary, Jacob G. Bigler, added this observation of Elder Smith: "I went to Sheffield to visit the Saints who compose that Conference, and under the Presidency of Elder Joseph F. Smith, and attended one branch meeting, which was well-attended. I took much pleasure with Brother Joseph; he reminded me much, in his appearance, of his father, whose example he seeks to follow." (Ibid.)

This reaction toward Joseph F. Smith was typical of those who were acquainted with his ancestry and background. To see the living son of one of the martyrs, who resembled his parent in appearance and conduct, and to realize that the father was a chief actor in the spiritual events surrounding the restoration and early growth of the Church, added a new sense of reality and urgency to the work.

Fellow missionaries and members alike soon learned that Elder Smith was a diligent, no-nonsense, straight-arrow type. He insisted that his subordinates be as disciplined and orthodox as he always was. He brooked no sloth or laxity from anyone and was prompt to rebuke the backslider, sometimes under circumstances that dramatically demonstrated the conquest of zeal and forthrightness over diplomacy. Such an instance occurred at Leeds one Sunday when Joseph was offended by a member who reeked of alcohol. Venting his displeasure from the stand, the forceful young missionary announced in the hearing of all, "I wish those who are in the habit of drinking liquor to keep off the stand on the Sabbath, when their breath smells." Demonstrating the truth of his Uncle Joseph Smith's statement that "hit birds always flutter," he received a curt note from a brother that afternoon, along with his elder's license. The note said in part, "I have burnt up my hymn-book and all other works that I have, and will burn the Book of Mormon as soon as I can find it." (JFS, p. 200.)

The unusual linguistic ability Joseph F. demonstrated in quickly mastering the Hawaiian language while in the Sandwich Islands shone forth again during his first mission to Great Britain. This time, of course, it was focused upon his native tongue. The frequency with which he was called upon to speak, the precision and richness of the English language he heard spoken around him every day, the inherent linguistic talent he possessed, and the inner drive for excellence that seemed to goad him constantly toward higher achievement combined to make him one of the most fluent and effective public speakers the British Mission had produced. These qualities shone even more brightly against the background of his fiery, enthusiastic temperament, which flared up intermittently as it did when he chastised the alcoholic. This appraisal by a man who knew him well and who wrote a brief biographical sketch of Joseph F. Smith indicates the scope of his eloquence and the impact he had on an audience. "Of all men that I have ever heard speak," wrote Preston Nibley, "I think that he was the most eloquent and impressive. His voice was pleasant and appealing; he could speak with the utmost kindness and tenderness; but when aroused or angered, his rebuke to the sinner was terrible. Of all preachers of the Gospel, I always think of Joseph F. Smith as the greatest I ever heard." (POC, p. 241.)

The positive influence Elder Smith had on an audience through his preaching was also exerted during his individual teaching and counseling. In this setting, he appeared honest, sincere, accomplished, and dependable, qualities that made him an effective proselyter and enabled him to bring many converts into the Church. But all his skills were unavailing in the attempt to convert his mother's relatives who still lived in England. These devout people received their American cousin warmly and showed him every hospitality, but they treated his message with cold indifference. There seemed to be a widely held view among the English Fieldings that Joseph, Mary, and Mercy had been duped into joining the Church, which they looked upon as an opportunistic cult. These false perceptions of the Latter-day Saints were doubtless founded in part upon the libelous fulminations of the British press, which seldom missed an opportunity to blacken their name, and, in part, upon the Reverend James Fielding, a brother to Joseph, Mary, and Mercy.

It was in the Reverend Fielding's chapel in Preston on July 26, 1837, that the first sermons were preached by Mormon elders on British soil. Desiring to be hospitable to his long-absent brother, who was one of the first Mormon elders in England, and apparently assuming that the doctrines taught by the visitors could do no harm to his parishioners, the good reverend had flung open the doors of his chapel and had offered his pulpit to them. These privileges were promptly withdrawn, however, when James saw the unsettling effect of their preaching upon his flock and saw some of them follow the elders into the waters of the River Ribble to be baptized. From that moment the Reverend Fielding was wary of the Mormons and was prompt to denounce them with harsh criticisms that doubtless reached the ears of his family. These helped to turn the minds of the Fieldings away from the doctrines of the Restoration, and it was in this fixed and negative mold that Joseph F. found his English relatives when he tried unsuccessfully to convert them.

The disappointment Elder Smith must have felt in his failure to bring his mother's family into the Church was probably mitigated in part by the joy he felt in the conversion of many nonrelatives who thereby became his brothers and sisters in the gospel. That joy is illustrated by Joseph F.'s association with a Sheffield convert, William Fowler, who was a polisher and grinder in a local cutlery works. In his odd moments, however, Brother Fowler enjoyed writing poetry and lyrics and one Sunday brought to meeting one of his compositions, a song, with the request that the choir learn to sing it. The first words of the opening stanza, "We thank thee, O God, for a prophet," soon became the title of the song whose popularity was almost instantaneous in Great Britain. That popularity soon spread to the headquarters of the Church in Utah, where it was later included in the official Church hymnal, thereby ensuring the extension and perpetuation of its popularity. Had the author of this classic Latter-day Saint hymn lived to the present day, he doubtless would have been amazed at the powerful and ever-growing impact of his words as they are repeated over and over in many tongues around the world, words written in the obscurity of a humble Sheffield home. And had he foreseen the results of this volunteer offering, the lyricist doubtless would have considered them a sufficient compensation for having been discharged at the cutlery works because of his Mormon affiliations.

The increase in the number of British missionaries in 1860 and the ability and zeal of men like Joseph F. Smith were soon reflected in the accelerated rate at which converts like William Fowler were baptized. During 1859 there were 1,064 baptisms in the mission compared to 1,928 in 1860 and 2,067 in 1861. Because of the integral role of Church publications in the conversion process, the Church leaders sought to strengthen this aspect of the work in the British Isles at this time by sending there a skilled editor who took the helm of the *Millennial Star* in January 1861, just a few months after Joseph F.'s arrival. This was thirty-three-year-old George Q. Cannon, Elder Smith's predecessor on Maui and the kindly editor of the *Western Standard*, who had given Elders Smith and Partridge the overcoats that protected them from the dank San Francisco fog as they returned from Hawaii. Elder Cannon had been ordained an apostle by President Brigham Young in August 1860 and inducted into the Twelve; five months later he found himself in Liverpool, the city of his birth, directing the staff of the *Star* at 42 Islington. This native of Liverpool, whose roots extended deep into the Isle of Man, whence his ancestors came, was to play a leading role in the life of Joseph F. Smith for a period of almost forty years. During that time, this pair would serve as counselors to four presidents of the Church, Brigham Young, John Taylor, Wilford Woodruff, and Lorenzo Snow. And this tandem service, which to date has not been duplicated by any other pair of counselors in Church history (although President N. Eldon Tanner singly served as a counselor to four presidents) bound them together in the bonds of brotherhood and mutual admiration. Being eleven years older than Joseph F. and having preceded him into the Twelve, Elder Cannon was to be senior to the Patriarch's son in the hierarchy of the priesthood during the remainder of his life except for a short period during 1866–1867 when Elder Smith served as a counselor to the First Presidency while Elder Cannon remained in the Twelve. These roles were reversed when Joseph F. was released as a counselor in 1867 and when George Q. was called as a counselor to the First Presidency in 1874. Later, under Presidents Taylor, Woodruff, and Snow, Elder Cannon served as first and Elder Smith as second counselor.

This long period of tutelage under George Q. Cannon began for Joseph F. Smith when his friend was called as the president of the British and European missions on May 14, 1862, succeeding Elders Amasa M. Lyman and Charles C. Rich, who had been called home to Utah. By that time, Elder Smith had been in England for almost two years and had played a key role in the leadership of the British mission as a "pastor." In that position, he reported directly to the mission president and was often in counsel with him about the affairs of the conferences he supervised. The mutual confidence these powerful men had in each other was doubtless strengthened by their common ties to the Polynesian culture and language.

Perhaps sensing a need for the young "pastor" to expand the scope of his knowledge and experience, the apostle invited Joseph F. to temporarily leave his duties in the British Mission in the fall of 1862 to accompany him on a tour of Denmark. Crossing the channel, Hyrum's son set foot on continental Europe for the first time, seeing a culture and way of life he hardly would have thought existed in the days when he had herded his mother's animals in the primitive environment of Winter Quarters. Now in company with an apostle of the Lord, he was exposed to an ancient and highly developed civilization whose libraries, museums, and art galleries held the learning and attainments of the past and pointed the way toward even higher intellectual achievements in the future. But while these and other aspects of continental Europe intrigued Elder Smith, he was more absorbed in the cause that had taken him there, the cause of bringing scattered Israel into the fold of the Church and perfecting them. As he and his senior companion visited numerous small branches in Denmark, branches composed of enthusiastic and dedicated Latter-day Saints, Joseph F. could not have failed to be impressed by the extraordinary growth that had occurred in the twelve short years since the apostle Erastus Snow and his two companions, George P. Dykes and John E. Forsgren, had docked at Copenhagen on June 14, 1850, and were met by the convert Peter O. Hansen who had preceded them there. Less than two months later, on August 12, 1850, these diligent missionaries reaped the firstfruits of their proselyting efforts when fifteen converts were baptized in the clear waters of the Oresund near Copenhagen. That first trickle of conversions had grown in magnitude over the years, fueling a sizeable migration of newly won Latter-day Saints who, on arriving in Utah, often were sent to settle in Sanpete County, which now and then was referred to as "Little Denmark" with its liberal complement of Jensens, Hansens, Petersens, Christensens, and other stalwart Danes. It would be difficult to assess the effect on the impressionable young prophet-to-be of this continental visit, opening up to him, as it did, a view of the rapid and powerful impact of the gospel message on a highly civilized population speaking a language other than his native English. And to connect such a proselyting effort with the population of vast valleys in his mountain homeland would surely have given him a new concept of "building the kingdom."

Elder Smith was to have another exposure to the continent before returning home, this time in company with Brigham Young, Jr. This pair traveled through Belgium and France together, observing the rich heritage of these ancient countries, their fertile lands, hardy people, and teeming cities. Of the latter, Paris was by far the most exciting and provocative. It is a fair assumption that these two young men, who had spent most of their lives in rural, sheltered Utah, were wide-eyed at the carefree, Bohemian life-style of some Parisians, at the daring entertainments advertised in the local papers, and at the frenetic pace at which the businessmen and workers seemed to conduct their lives. Along with these perceptions would surely have come an appreciation for the intellectual and artistic advantages this city offered. But to missionaries of the caliber of these companions, the condition of the Church and its members was of first importance. Here they saw the fruits of the labors of Elder John Taylor (who had opened the work in France) and those associated with him or who had followed him.

Only two years separated Elders Smith and Young. Brigham, the elder one, was born in Kirtland in 1836. Both of them bore in their names the heavy weight of ancestral distinction, a weight that drags down many able men. But, as later events were to prove, Joseph F. and Brigham seemed to be goaded and buoyed up by it. Indeed, both of them were to be elevated to the Quorum of the Twelve within a few years and ultimately would gravitate to the highest seats of power in the Church. Had the Parisian saints been blessed with clear spiritual perceptions, they would have seen that in less than forty years Joseph would occupy the prophetic office while Brigham would stand as the president of the Quorum of the Twelve Apostles.

Joseph F. received an honorable release from his British labors on April 25, 1863. Cousin Samuel and several others were released at the same time. However, the released missionaries, who did some traveling in the meantime, did not leave England until June 24, when they embarked on the steamship *City of Washington* from the River Mersey pierhead in Liverpool. Among the travelers was Elizabeth H. Cannon, wife of the mission president. George Q. and members of his staff at 42 Islington stood on the pierhead and waved their good-byes as the *City of Washington* maneuvered slowly into the center of the river and steamed westward toward the Irish Sea.

After a customarily rough though otherwise uneventful Atlantic crossing, the *City of Washington* docked in New York harbor in early July, discharging its passengers into a scene of chaos. The Civil War, which had erupted after Joseph F. went to England, was then being waged with increasing ferocity. The New York papers were filled with news of the bloody battle at Gettysburg and of a tough Union general with the classic name of Ulysses who on July 4 had sealed the fate of Vicksburg with the crushing defeat of General Pemberton's army. However, of greater concern than the shifting fortunes of war was the terror that ruled Manhattan's streets, a terror unleashed by violent riots that rocked the city. The thorny issues of conscription and slavery, dissatisfaction with living and working conditions, grousing about the alleged ineptness of President Lincoln's administration, and the stifling heat created a highly volatile situation that could be ignited by the most innocent, innocuous occurrence. So Joseph F. found everything and everyone on edge when he arrived in Manhattan. The tension, the suspicions, and the ominous sense of unease that pervaded the city doubtless reminded the returning missionary of the dark days in Nauvoo between the martyrdom and the exodus. Such conditions and the memories they evoked would surely have prompted the missionary to leave New York City as soon as possible. However, a lack of money prevented him from leaving. He therefore worked at various odd jobs. By the time the next immigrant party docked, he had accumulated enough savings to enable him to return home. After bidding farewell to the New York Saints, who had shown great hospitality, and some of whom had made small though much-appreciated contributions, Joseph F. and his friends left Manhattan bound for Utah. Traveling by train, boat, and carriage, they made their way safely to Florence, Nebraska, where a typical Mormon wagon train was formed. It had the customarily tight organization, resembling a military unit. Joseph F. was appointed as the chaplain-physician of the company, a role in which he was to provide counsel in matters of physical, emotional, and spiritual need. Nothing in Elder Smith's background qualified him to serve as a doctor, so his appointment to this position suggests that his extensive travels, his experience in counseling, and his inherent abilities made him as well qualified as any other member of the company to fill this role.

Ironically, on arriving in Salt Lake City, he found there was more need for his healing skills among his family than among the members of the wagon train. The principal object of his care was his wife, Levira, whom he found in a highly agitated mental state. The concerned husband tenderly ministered to his ailing wife for six weeks, being with her almost constantly both day and night. At length her health was restored and she was able to take up her domestic duties again, although the illness had taken a heavy toll and presumably helped to plant or to nurture seeds that would grow into serious marital discord in the future, producing one of Joseph's most trying experiences.

His family was uppermost in Joseph F.'s mind when he returned to Salt Lake City in September 1863. By now he was within two months of being twenty-six years of age. It is somewhat incredible that for a period of almost nine years this diligent young man had been either preaching the gospel or had been in military service helping to defend the Mormon colonies in Utah. In appreciative recognition of this service, and wanting to help his young protégé lay the foundation of his family life, President Brigham Young publicly announced his intention to give Joseph F. a thousand dollars from Church funds to help him get started. The president made a similar announcement as to Samuel H. B. Smith. This act of generosity for the benefit of one who had given so unselfishly of his time for so long without monetary compensation would seem to have been unanimously approved. It was not. Indeed, so many vigorously opposed it as smacking of a paid ministry and as giving preferential treatment to a member of the Church's most prominent family that the proposal died before it reached fruition. In the aftermath, Joseph did receive several minor gifts, including some molasses, a parlor stove, a pony, and some miscellaneous money gifts from family and friends, the total value of which was less than a hundred dollars. However, these were insufficient to increase his standard of living appreciably and did little to advance his financial goals.

Faced with an almost total lack of resources and having no job, no special money-making skills, and practically no formal education, Joseph F.'s first priority was to obtain the competence and the means to establish his family on a solid foundation. Toward that end, he began to work at whatever jobs were available and to cast around for better financial opportunities. He had been engaged in this manner for about five months when one day he received a summons from President Brigham Young. Having learned to expect the unexpected from this unorthodox leader, Joseph put on his best suit and went quizzically to the impressive compound on East South Temple Street from which the Lion of the Lord governed the vast, rapidly expanding Mormon empire. In the state of poverty he then occupied, and with the unpromising financial future that then lay ahead, it was doubtless the furthest thing from Joseph's mind at the time that he would one day occupy these impressive premises and would wield the authority that then lay within the grasp of the man who had summoned him there. With apparently little thought other than the reason why Brigham wanted to see him, Joseph F. passed through the gate in the massive wall that surrounded the President's estate and, entering the presidential suite between the Beehive House and Lion House, he presented himself at the desk of the clerk who guarded the entry to Brigham's sanctuary. This private office, with a front, south window that admitted the cheerful rays of the winter sun this February day, was located just across a hallway from the great man's bedroom in the Beehive House. Thus, he was seldom "off duty." The Lion of the Lord, ruddy and well-barbered, greeted his young friend with a fatherly embrace and motioned him to a nearby chair. Knowing that the Mormon prophet seldom, if ever, invited anyone to his study merely to pass the time of day, Elder Smith waited expectantly for the bombshell that he seemed to know would soon explode. It was not long in coming. After a decent interval filled with the usual pleasantries and inquiry into the health and well-being of Joseph and his bride, President Young got to the point. He wanted the Patriarch's son to fill yet another mission! This one, however, was to be rather short and entailed an objective entirely different from the one that had inspired his two previous missions. Here the purpose would be to chastise and perhaps excommunicate rather than to teach and baptize. As the president of the Church briefed him, Joseph learned that after the withdrawal of the missionaries from the Hawaiian Islands at the outset of the threatened invasion by Johnston's army, a fortune hunter named Walter Murray Gibson had usurped priesthood authority and had set himself up as literally a king over the Saints in the islands. As a means of straightening out these bizarre affairs, President Young had appointed two members of the Twelve to go there, Elders Ezra T. Benson and Lorenzo Snow. Since neither of these brethren spoke the native tongue, it had been decided to send along with them three returned Hawaiian missionaries who were skilled in the language. Joseph F.'s unusual linguistic ability placed him at the top of this list. The other two on it were Alma L. Smith and William W. Cluff. As expected, Joseph accepted the call promptly and without qualification and immediately commenced his preparations to leave. As was true with his call to England, Joseph's preparations were minimal, as he had no property that required management during his absence. There was, of course, the need to make arrangements for Levira's care, but they had spent such little time together that there were no personal family effects to speak of, and consequently Joseph's departure merely signaled Levira's return to her relatives. To leave her in this way doubtless caused Joseph moments of regret, particularly in view of the serious illness she had suffered upon his return from the British Isles.

But whatever feelings of reticence or reluctance Joseph may have felt at again leaving her to venture abroad were concealed behind a cloak of quiet optimism. Although he was still several years away from his call to the Twelve, Elder Smith seemed already to have the driving sense of dedication and commitment usually associated with the apostleship, a sense that all personal wants and desires must yield to the demands of the ministry.

Chapter Eight

The Third Mission—
Return to the Pacific

T he five brethren assigned by President Young to quell the insubordination of Walter Murray Gibson left Salt Lake City by stage on March 1, 1864. On this trip, however, instead of traveling the southern route to San Bernardino as Joseph's party had done a decade before, the brethren headed due west on a course that took them across the barren salt flats and through the seemingly endless valleys that undulate westward from the Great Salt Lake to the Sierras. The slow pace of travel and the confining condition in the coach enabled Joseph to become well acquainted with his traveling companions. He already knew elders Cluff and Smith quite well, sharing with them the mystical bond of having served in the same mission. And he had met elders Benson and Snow on many occasions and was well acquainted with their background and achievements. While Joseph held these apostles in high regard and revered the positions they occupied in the Quorum of the Twelve, he felt no sense of inferiority or abasement in their presence. From the days of his earliest conscious recollections, he had been intimately acquainted with many high leaders of the Church. And his relationship to the Prophet and the Patriarch, and the significant name he bore, had elevated him to a high status, both in the estimation of others and in his own eyes, and had placed

him in an exclusive circle of prestige and privilege. So Joseph
F. was able to converse and associate with general authorities
of the Church with an ease and composure that would have
been difficult for one lacking these advantages. These circumstances, along with his characteristic self-confidence and
forthrightness, enabled him a few weeks later to speak to
Elder Lorenzo Snow with a straightforward bluntness that
likely surprised both of them. In the meantime, these qualities
enabled him to travel with elders Benson and Snow in complete ease and to enjoy and to absorb the insights they provided through their conversations about the history, doctrines, and procedures of the Church.

In addition to the intellectual and spiritual stimulation
this lengthy overland stage trip gave to Joseph F., it opened
up to him an understanding of a vast new section of western
country that, in the future, would play an increasingly important role in the affairs of both the nation and the Church. The
ride also provided insights into the foibles of human nature
and into some of the realities and brutalities of life outside
the sheltered Mormon communities in which he had been
reared. Early one Sunday morning, for instance, he witnessed a cold-blooded killing in a remote Nevada mining
camp when a shirt-sleeved white man stepped out of a saloon
and killed a black man, shooting him in the back as he ran
away in terror. What startled Elder Smith and his companions
almost as much as the killing was the indifference of their
driver, who insisted that they hitch up and leave immediately
without tendering any aid or seeing that the killer was arrested and charged. And their annoyance at this driver was
supplanted by a genuine fear of the driver who took his place.
The second driver was at the reins when the stage commenced a long, steep descent over a rough, narrow road.
Seemingly jovial and competent when he took over, driver
number two turned surly and reckless as the trip progressed,
the apparent result of sobering up. While he was in this
mood, a wheel of the stage struck a rock, causing the vehicle
to bounce and swerve sharply. This seemed to trigger a form
of insanity in the driver, who began to whip the team brutally
while shouting and cursing at it as if the animals were respon-

sible for what had happened. When Elder Benson shouted, telling him to slow down, the driver responded by whipping the team harder than before. "Our coach swayed fearfully," wrote Elder Snow of the incident, "the wheels . . . striking fire as they whirled over the rocks, with a double span of horses upon a keen run, tossing us up and down, giving us a few hard strokes of the head against the cover of the coach." (BFRLS, p. 274.)

Joseph and his companions felt more secure when a third driver took charge to guide the team over the steep, narrow, and rocky trails of the Sierras. While this one drove with caution and judgment, he seemed to take perverse delight in calling attention to the places along the way where vehicles had fallen off the trail into the deep chasm below. "These nerve-stirring recitals," wrote Lorenzo, "caused us more seriously to realize the gravity of our situation and our dependence on God for the preservation of our lives." (Ibid., p. 275.) Upon reaching the western base of the Sierras, the apostle presumably expressed the feelings of all five passengers: "We . . . felt our pulses restored to their normal state as we dismounted." (Ibid.)

At San Francisco, Joseph F. introduced his companions to Dwight Eveleth, an old friend who had practically made a career of entertaining Mormon missionaries going to or returning from the Pacific. During the few days the travelers enjoyed Brother Eveleth's hospitality, Joseph F. and elders Cluff and Alma Smith took pleasure in showing the two apostles the cosmopolitan sights of San Francisco, whose oriental population had ballooned in recent years as thousands of Chinese workers had been imported to provide inexpensive labor for the mammoth railroad construction projects then underway.

Booking passage on a Pacific line ship, the Utah party traveled to Hawaii without incident, docking at Honolulu on March 27. Two days later, they sailed for Lahaina on Maui in a schooner, the *Nettie Merrill*. On the morning of March 31, the *Nettie Merrill* anchored a mile from the harbor, there being no docking facilities. A stiff wind was up, and the sea was running high, which warned Joseph F., who was well-acquainted with these waters, that there would be danger in trying to maneuver the ship's small freight boat through the narrow, reef-guarded channel that led to the harbor. He therefore urged a delay in landing until conditions were more favorable. However, the apostles, who were anxious to get on with their assignment and who were misled by the captain, who raised no question about possible danger, directed that their party's gear be placed on the freight boat. This action was met by a strong dissent from young Joseph F. Smith, who insisted it would be too risky to try to land until the weather had improved. Dismissing his argument as being founded on needless fear, everyone else in the party went forward with preparations to land. At this point, the assertive qualities in Joseph's character surfaced but were moderated by his respect for the apostles and by his lifelong training to be subservient to priesthood authority. Addressing Elder Snow, Hyrum's son is reported to have said, "If you by the authority of the Priesthood of God, which you hold, tell me to get into that boat and attempt to land, I will do so, but unless you command me in the authority of the Priesthood, I will not do so, because it is not safe to attempt to land." (IE 22:848.)

Apparently not wanting to impose his will on the young man, Elder Snow did not order him to join the others in the freight boat but allowed him to remain aboard the *Nettie Merrill*. Watching from that vantage point with great apprehension, Joseph's worst fears were realized when he saw an enormous wave throw the boat like a matchstick into the roiling sea, which frothed and foamed over the treacherous reefs. Being too far away for voice communication, even had voices been able to rise above the din of the roaring surf, Joseph could only watch helplessly as the drama unfolded before him. Soon after the boat capsized, he saw heads begin to bob to the surface only to disappear behind successive waves that rolled in upon the hapless swimmers. Then he saw activity on the beach, where oarsmen, alerted by watchers on shore who had seen the accident, manned two rescue boats, which soon reached the swimmers and pulled them aboard to safety. Only later did Joseph learn that the last one to be plucked from the sea was Lorenzo Snow, who had been submerged for some time before being rescued and who was presumed by some to be dead. That judgment was affirmed by several people on shore who had witnessed many drownings and who told elders Cluff and Alma Smith that their efforts to revive the victim were useless. Ignoring these dire predictions, the elders, whose missionary experiences in the islands had taught them special skills, continued to work over the unconscious apostle, rolling him on a barrel to remove the water from his lungs, pumping his lungs while he lay on his face, and finally resorting to mouth-to-mouth resuscitation. This last procedure proved effective. "A slight wink of the eye," Elder Cluff reported, "which, until then, had been open and death-like, and a very faint rattle in the throat, were the first symptoms of returning vitality. These grew more and more distinct, until consciousness was fully restored." (BFRLS, p. 279.)

Joseph F.'s refusal to board the freight boat, and the near-tragic accident that followed, would have been fuel for serious discord and recriminations among lesser men. But we see not the slightest hint of a self-righteous, I-told-you-so attitude on Joseph's part. Nor did Elder Snow show any sign afterward of irritation or pique at the failure of the young elder to follow his direction. On the contrary, he reported later that at the moment of Joseph F.'s obstinacy, it was made known to him by spiritual means that this outspoken, volatile young man would one day be the president of the Church. (IE 22:848.) As far as Elder Smith was concerned, any sense of vindication he may have felt in seeing that the judgment he had expressed was correct was swallowed up in his joy in learning that no one was drowned or permanently injured.

It required several days for Lorenzo to recover fully from his brush with death. During his convalescence, the party remained at Lahaina on Maui, planning for the expected confrontation with Walter Murray Gibson, which would take place soon on nearby Lanai, where the apostate ruled with regal power. It was not difficult for Joseph and the other Hawaiian missionaries to understand how an able, aggressive, and unprincipled man could have ingratiated himself into the confidence of the Polynesians as this man apparently had done. The natives, who had had little opportunity for education and who for generations had been dominated by tyrannical monarchs who played on their ignorance and superstition, were gullible, childlike, and easily led. Finding himself among such people at a time when the regular missionaries had been called home, and having a semblance of authority to act for the Church, Elder Gibson stepped into the vacuum created by the missionaries' departure and, step by step, had proceeded to carve out an island empire. The ostensible authority to do what he ultimately did was in the form of a written commission signed by Brigham Young, empowering him to proclaim the gospel "to all nations upon the earth." This paper, which was valid and was given to Mr. Gibson with the understanding that he was to fulfill a proselyting mission in the Orient, was identical to thousands of other missionary certificates given to the elders called to preach the gospel. Stopping in the Sandwich Islands en route to Japan and finding there what seemed to him to be a fertile field for his proselyting skills, Elder Gibson decided to stay, since his commission did not designate a specific country in which to labor. Soon detecting the superstitious nature of the natives and their penchant for pageantry and ceremony, he began to adjust his demeanor and objectives to capitalize on their weaknesses for his own benefit. To mislead those who had been converted to the Church and who owed allegiance to the leaders in Salt Lake City, he produced his misisonary call signed by President Young. However, to remove it from the realm of the ordinary and to impart a special significance and authority to his call, he adorned his certificate with an elaborate array of ribbons and seals to make it appear more "official" and important. Once he had convinced the member natives that he came with authority and the blessing of the Church leaders, Mr. Gibson slowly began to mold them and their worship practices into a form that bore little if any resemblance to the one established by Joseph F. and his fellow missionaries. He had, for instance, begun to sell priesthood offices to both men and women. To keep them in subjection, he insisted that they approach him on their hands and knees in the same way their ancestors had approached the ancient

Polynesian kings. He had inducted all male members into a militia he had organized; had designed a new flag that floated over every chapel in the islands; had assumed private owner-ship of all real and personal property possessed by the mem-bers; and had decreed an end to family and personal prayers and scripture reading because, he said, spiritual matters had been overemphasized and a greater emphasis on temporal affairs was long overdue. Finally, he had designated a certain rock as a "holy place" in which a Book of Mormon and other objects had been placed. Trading again on the superstition of the people, he had given this place an aura of mystery, warn-ing that anyone who so much as touched the rock without au-thorization would instantly die.

These and other innovations introduced by Walter Gibson finally caused someone to report his conduct to the Church in Salt Lake City. This in turn had brought about the appoint-ment of the party that now counseled on Maui awaiting Elder Snow's recovery. From all the reports they had received, it seemed unlikely that Elder Gibson would repent and mend his ways, so a direct and unpleasant confrontation seemed in-evitable.

Faced with this prospect, the two apostles and their three young interpreters and aides left Maui a few days after the ac-cident and crossed to Lanai, where the apostate had estab-lished his headquarters and had accelerated the gathering that had started during Joseph F.'s first mission. During their trip inland by horseback the day after landing on Lanai, Joseph F. and the other two former Polynesian missionaries were impressed by the many physical improvements that had been made under Elder Gibson's leadership. The cultivated lands were orderly and well-tilled, and the sheds and other outbuildings were neat and attractive. On reaching the vil-lage, the travelers were treated to another evidence of the managerial skill of the man they had come to discipline. The residences of the natives were clean and comfortable as were the public buildings where council meetings and worship ser-vices were held. There was an air of industry and purpose about the thriving community that belied some of the nega-tive reports about Mr. Gibson's conduct. This, added to the fact that the alleged apostate had promptly furnished horses at the request of the visitors to carry them and their gear to the inland village, likely caused a temporary reappraisal of the character and intentions of this self-anointed king. However, during two days of intense and wearing meetings with him, the apostles concluded that Walter Murray Gibson, though able and diligent, was thoroughly apostate in his doctrinal views and moral perceptions and that unless a radical change occurred in his attitudes before they departed, it would be necessary to excommunicate him.

While these meetings were in progress, Joseph and his two young companions inspected the island more closely, since their interpreting skills were not needed in conversing with Mr. Gibson, who spoke English. Their guide was Elder Gibson's young daughter, Talulua, who took great pride in calling attention to the many improvements her father had directed since taking charge. Obviously convinced that her father possessed supernatural powers, Talulua took special pains to warn the three elders against touching the "holy rock" where the Book of Mormon and other special objects lay concealed, lest they suffer the fate of Uzziah who fell dead after touching the Ark of the Covenant. Oblivious to this warning, Joseph F. and Alma Smith dismounted to inspect the repository in the rock while Elder Cluff removed brush that had been piled around the rock to conceal it. Whether the young guide was more surprised by the "sacrilege" of the Mormon elders or by their immunity from retribution was never made clear. It is a safe assumption, however, that some seeds of doubt may have been planted in her mind as the result of the events of that day. But any weakening in the confidence she had in her father does not appear to have been shared by his native followers, as the events of the next few days were to prove.

As Elders Benson and Snow counseled with Walter Gibson, they learned he had already scheduled a meeting for April 6. Not wanting to cancel that meeting, the apostles decided to defer any action against Mr. Gibson until the meeting had been held. Correctly judging that his standing in the Church was in jeopardy, and unwilling to mend his ways,

Elder Gibson did all in his power to structure the meeting and to conduct it in such a way as to strengthen his position and to put the visitors at a disadvantage. His maneuvering began shortly before the 10:00 A.M. meeting on April 6 when he excused himself as he was entering the bowery with the visitors, explaining that he had some chore to finish. His purpose soon became clear when he entered the bowery alone after the visitors had all taken their seats. At his appearance, the entire congregation rose to their feet (except the Salt Lakers) and remained standing until he had taken his seat. Promptly following up on this psychological advantage, Elder Gibson rose and walked to the pulpit as soon as the audience had settled down. Without consulting the apostles, who presided, he announced the opening hymn and prayer, implying that he was in charge. Immediately following the prayer, Elder Gibson announced the second song, again without consulting the apostles, and then went to the pulpit to deliver a lengthy and impassioned speech in an attempt to nullify what he knew would be forthcoming from the visiting brethren. His first task was to seek the allegiance of the audience, not on the basis of any authority he had to lead them emanating from Salt Lake City, but on the basis of what he had done for them. "Did I not come here and find you without a father, poor and discouraged?" he asked. "Did I not gather you together here, and make all these improvements that you today enjoy?" By way of contrast, he said accusingly of the visitors, "These strangers may say they are your friends; but let me remind you, when they lived here, years ago, they lived upon your scanty substance. Did they make any such improvements as you see I have made?" (JFS, p. 219.)

As soon as Mr. Gibson had finished his harangue, Elder Benson called on Joseph to respond. In summarizing Joseph's speech, delivered under the most stressful circumstances, Elder Lorenzo Snow wrote, "It seemed impossible for any man to speak with greater power and demonstration of the Spirit. He referred the Saints to the labors of Brother George Q. Cannon and the Elders who brought them the Gospel. He reminded them of facts with which the older members were well acquainted—the great disadvantage the Elders labored under, and the privations they suffered in first preaching the Gospel on the islands. How they slept in their miserable huts and lived as they lived; how they traveled on foot in storms and in bad weather, from village to village, and from house to house, exposing health and life. How they went destitute of clothing, and what they had been in the habit of considering the necessaries of life, to bring to them the blessings of the Gospel, without money and without price." (JFS, p. 220.) Having reminded the native Saints of things they apparently had forgotten, Elder Smith then challenged the soundness and fairness of the serious charges made by Mr. Gibson. "The Spirit and power that accompanied Brother Smith's remarks astonished the Saints and opened their eyes," wrote Lorenzo Snow. "They began to see how they had been imposed upon. Every word he spoke found a response in their hearts, as was plainly manifest by the eager looks and animated countenances." (Ibid.)

In an afternoon session that day, which Elder Benson conducted, the two apostles followed up on the advantage gained by the eloquent sermon Joseph F. had delivered in the morning. Using the young elders as their interpreters, the two special witnesses contrasted the teachings of the Gospel with the unauthorized innovations Mr. Gibson had introduced, pointing out the eternal blessings to be gained by adhering to the simple teachings of the Church and the sorrow and disappointment to be reaped by following the apostate course defined by Walter Murray Gibson. A similar meeting was held the next morning, following which Elders Benson and Snow felt the time was ripe to bring this unpleasant matter to a head. They therefore scheduled a special priesthood meeting for that evening in which the insubordinate conduct of Mr. Gibson was to be considered.

A tense air of expectancy pervaded the bowery that evening as the native priesthood brethren quietly entered and took their seats. On the stand before them were the two members of the Twelve who had spent most of the day in quiet, meditative counsel and prayer. Near them were the three young elders who were prepared to interpret or perform other duties at the direction of their leaders. Also on the stand was the brilliant, wily apostate, although he did not occupy the position of prominence he enjoyed the day before, nor was he on this occasion given the regal welcome that greeted his first appearance on April 6. Judging from the surprising results of the meeting, it is also inferred that Mr. Gibson had been very busy during the day trying to neutralize the powerful impact of Joseph F.'s sermon and to reassert his dominance over the native Saints by an appeal to their ignorance, superstition, and understandable yearning for loaves and fishes.

After the usual preliminaries, the formal charges of apostasy against Walter Gibson were read in the hearing of all the assembled priesthood. Called upon to answer them, the accused, who showed no signs of submission or contrition, repeated essentially the harangue he had delivered the day before, appealing to the selfish interests of the audience. In addition, however, he defended against the charge of lack of authority by holding up his beribboned missionary certificate, gaudy with its seals and emblems, while declaring, "Here is my authority, which I received direct from President Brigham Young. I don't hold myself accountable to these men." (Ibid., p. 221.)

Elder Benson followed with a detailed catalog of Mr. Gibson's faults and his doctrinal and procedural deviations. High on the list, and the most grievous as far as the apostles were concerned, was the way in which he had sold priesthood authority and privileges and had exercised kingly control over the people.

But the eloquence of the apostles and young Elder Joseph F. Smith, the soundness of their counsel, and the weight of the evidence condemning Walter Murray Gibson were unavailing against his flamboyant impudence. When a vote of censure was taken, only one person of the vast audience stood with the visiting brethren. Whether moved by superstition, fear of reprisal, or honest mistake, the native brethren assembled that night on Lanai stood with the apostate except for one lone man.

As their final act on Lanai, the apostles designated Joseph F. Smith as the president of the mission and instructed the members present from other islands to go back to their homes.

Returning to Lahaina on Maui, the apostles rendered final judgment against Walter Murray Gibson based on the charges and the evidence given in the priesthood meeting on Lanai. They also instructed Joseph F. in his duties as mission president and eight days later departed for San Francisco, leaving Elders Cluff and Alma Smith to assist and counsel Joseph F. Soon after, these three young men were joined by John R. Young and Benjamin Cluff, who had been sent to the islands by President Brigham Young to help salvage whatever possible from the wreck created by the apostate. Many of the Saints heeded the counsel given by the visiting brethren to return to their home islands. Others who could not be weaned away from Mr. Gibson remained and thereby lost their standing in the Church. But enough departed that the hypnotic spell cast by Mr. Gibson was broken, and his power and influence among the Church members in the islands waned from that time until it completely disappeared. In this is seen the fulfillment of a remarkable prophecy made by Lorenzo Snow at one of the meetings on Lanai when he predicted that very result.

But though Mr. Gibson's influence was broken by his excommunication, that did not untangle the legal snarl as to the properties on Lanai, the title to which had become vested in his name by devious means. Because of political ties he had skillfully cemented (evidenced by the fact that later he was appointed as King Kalakaua's prime minister), the Church was unable to recover the title to the lands on Lanai. On this account, Joseph F. and his associates strongly recommended to Church leaders that the Church purchase additional lands on another island to provide a focal point for the building up of the Church in that area. That recommendation was followed, and when Joseph and his companions returned from Hawaii near the end of 1864, they met Francis A. Hammond and George Nebeker, who were en route to the islands with authorization and funds to purchase a plantation. Adopting Joseph F. Smith's recommendation, these agents of the Church purchased a large tract of land on Oahu at Laie, which was later developed into a thriving agricultural enterprise and which is still owned by the Church.

Arriving home in December 1864, Joseph F. could look back on one of the most unusual and inconclusive experiences of his career. The near-drowning of Lorenzo Snow and the dramatic confrontation with Walter Murray Gibson imparted a theatrical and almost unreal aspect to the whole affair. And the inconclusive results that were achieved seemed to cast a shadow of dissatisfaction over Elder Smith and the other participants. While Mr. Gibson was excommunicated, his authority and influence over the members in the islands were not immediately broken. And the powerful sway this man held over the Saints through his oratory, his creative skills, and his vast ability as an organizer and entrepreneur could scarcely have failed both to annoy and to evoke the grudging admiration of these men who were known for their ability to lead and motivate. There seemed to be a curious ambivalence in the feelings Joseph F. and the others had toward this strange man. On the one hand, they abhorred and denounced his unorthodox teachings and practices. At the same time, he had likable qualities that surfaced years later when, as a power in the government of the Hawaiian king, he rendered assistance to the Church. And on several occasions in later years when Joseph F. met Mr. Gibson, he betrayed none of the spirit of bitterness and animosity so evident among some other apostates. Once this man saw he had lost the contest for the loyalties of the Saints, he turned his full attention to other matters and seemed to derive as much satisfaction and self-esteem from exerting influence in King Kalakaua's administration as he had in occupying leadership positions in the Church. Viewed in this light, Walter Murray Gibson seemed to be nothing less than a benign, likable fraud and con man who had no apparent intention to hurt others but only to feed his enormous ego through the exercise of power and authority.

Chapter Nine

Laying the Foundations of Church Authority and Family Influence

lthough Joseph F. did not know it at the time, his return from his second mission to Hawaii opened nine years of continuous residence in Utah, free from the obligations of foreign missionary service. This enabled him to establish his finances on a firm foundation for the first time and to begin to develop a consistent pattern of family life (which was to undergo some unusual and cataclysmic changes and upheavals during this period).

Joseph immediately obtained employment in the Church Historian's Office, where he worked under the direction of his cousin George A. Smith, who was then a member of the Twelve and who was later to become a member of the First Presidency upon the death of President Heber C. Kimball. When Joseph F. commenced this employment, Elder George A. Smith had served as the Church Historian for ten years. The knowledge he had gained in that position, added to the personal acquaintance he had had with the Prophet Joseph Smith and other early leaders of the Church, made him a veritable walking encyclopedia of Church facts, doctrine, and procedure. And the paternal attitude the experienced apostle had toward his young cousin, who had been orphaned so young and who had had such little opportunity for formal education, caused the older man to use the relationship both as a means of performing the heavy and ever-growing duties of the Historian's Office and of tutoring Joseph in the arts of study and composition. Because Joseph also served intermittently during this period as secretary both to the First Presidency and to the Quorum of the Twelve Apostles, he was exposed almost daily to the high leaders of the Church, which of itself provided him with a broad education in Church doctrine, procedure, and leadership. Also during this period he served as a recorder in the Endowment House under the direction of presidents Brigham Young and Heber C. Kimball, both of whom were instructed personally by the Prophet Joseph Smith in the details of the sacred ordinances performed there. Moreover, Joseph continued to serve as a member of the high council of the Salt Lake Stake during this period and fulfilled occasional proselyting assignments in different parts of the territory.

Such a regimen guaranteed that this future prophet would be trained and disciplined in every aspect of the work he would later be called to direct. And a significant event on May 5, 1866, set Joseph on a new path of family life and seemed to foreshadow his call to the apostleship, which would occur less than two months later. On that day he was sealed to his second wife, Julina Lambson, in the Salt Lake Endowment House. This ceremony took place with the knowledge and consent of Levira, Joseph's first wife, who stood as one of the witnesses to the marriage. The new bride, seventeen years old, was the daughter of Alfred B. and Melissa Jane Bigler Lambson. She was also a niece of George A. Smith, whose wife was the sister of Julina's mother. The newlyweds became acquainted while Julina lived with her aunt and uncle, in whose home the Historical Department was then housed. When President Young asked Joseph to enter plural marriage, Joseph selected this exemplary young woman with whom Levira had been "intimately acquainted from her childhood." (JFS, p. 226, 231.)

This act of willing obedience on the part of twenty-seven-year-old Joseph F. Smith, singling him out as one prepared to follow the direction of the prophet regardless of how difficult or personally traumatic it might be to do so, seemed to be the last test qualifying him to receive the extraordinary call extended to him on July 1, 1866. On that date President Young ordained Joseph an apostle and set him apart as one of his counselors. This action, which was unsought by the young man, and as to which he seemed not to have had even a vague premonition, came as a distinct surprise to him, as it did to Brigham Young and the others who witnessed it. It occurred following a prayer circle held by President Young with several of the apostles. Joseph was present as the secretary to the council to take the minutes of the business meeting that was to follow. After the prayer and as the brethren were leaving the room, President Young called them back, saying, "Hold on, shall I do as I feel led? I always feel well to do as the Spirit constrains me. It is my mind to ordain Brother Joseph F. Smith to the Apostleship, and to be one of my counselors." Before acting on this impression, President Young asked for the comments of the other brethren as to the propriety of this action. When each of them expressed "hearty approval," they joined President Young in laying hands on the head of the surprised secretary. The Prophet then acted as voice in pronouncing the blessing: "Brother Joseph F. Smith, we lay our hands upon your head in the name of Jesus Christ, and by virtue of the Holy Priesthood we ordain you to be an Apostle in the Church of Jesus Christ of Latter-day Saints, and to be a special witness to the nations of the earth. We seal upon your head all the authority, power and keys of this holy Apostleship; and we ordain you to be a counselor to the First Presidency of the Church and Kingdom of God upon the earth. These blessings we seal upon you in the name of Jesus Christ and by the authority of the Holy Priesthood. Amen." (JFS, p. 227.)

This ordination, and his induction into the Twelve, which followed fifteen months later, gave Joseph F. Smith all the authority necessary to lead the Church. However, until such time as he became the senior apostle by succession and had been called and set apart by the united action of the Twelve, that authority was to remain in suspension. In the meantime, however, he was empowered to exercise apostolic authority in building up the Church around the world to the extent authorized and directed by the Church president, who held the keys.

In the absence of personal records describing them, one can only speculate on Joseph's feelings about this extraordinary event. He had been close to the source of power and authority in the Church from the time of his earliest recollections and knew, therefore, the burden of responsibility the apostleship entailed. And the tragic martyrdom of his father and uncle would have demonstrated clearly the extreme price that might be exacted by his Messianic discipleship. Faced with such a prospect and with a knowledge of the discipline and self-denial the apostleship would impose upon him and his family, it is safe to assume that any momentary feeling of elation or self-congratulation would soon have yielded to sobering thoughts of duty, responsibility, and sacrifice.

While President Young directed that a record be made of what had taken place, he swore those present to secrecy for the time being. So, when Joseph Young, Sr., a president of the Seventy, entered the council room shortly afterward, not a word was spoken about the significant event that had just taken place. And Joseph could not have failed to be impressed by the tight-lipped security among the apostles when a few days later, Heber C. Kimball, President Young's first counselor, who was not present at the prayer circle, confided to Joseph an impression he had had that Joseph would be called to the apostleship!

The Joseph F. Smith who awakened July 2, 1866, was the same man who had awakened twenty-four hours before. But vast changes had taken place in the status he occupied in relation to others. Beforehand, he occupied only a subordinate staff position in which he was amenable to the direction of the Twelve, whom he served intermittently as their secretary. Afterward, the Twelve, which included men of wide experience and great ability like John Taylor, Wilford Woodruff, and Lorenzo Snow, were subordinate to him. To grasp the significance of that and to adjust to such a radical change in relationship entailed a major revision in thought and action by all concerned, and especially by young Joseph F. Smith. That he met this challenge well, and that he grew in the position rather than swelled in it, is attested by the uniform way in which he was accepted by the older, more experienced brethren who, in the years ahead, were to honor him by calls to serve as a counselor to them when they assumed the prophetic mantle.

Elder Joseph F. Smith served as a counselor to the First Presidency for fifteen months. Then, at the October general conference in 1867, he was sustained as a member of the Quorum of the Twelve. The luster and excitement of this call were dimmed for the new apostle by the fact that he filled the vacancy in the quorum created by the apostasy of Amasa Lyman, who had served as his presiding officer during the first part of his mission to Great Britain. And the sorrow created by Amasa's fall was aggravated for Elder Smith by his close relationship with Francis M. Lyman, the apostate's son, who was one of his fellow missionaries in England and who would later share the apostleship with him.

Not long after his induction into the Twelve, Joseph F. accompanied President Young and a group of the brethren to northern Utah, where a series of meetings was held in Cache Valley. Among them was a meeting in Wellsville, where the audience included eighteen-year-old Charles W. Nibley, who, forty years later, would be called as the presiding bishop of the Church by President Joseph F. Smith and who later still would be called as a counselor to President Heber J. Grant. Bishop Nibley left us this insight into the impression the newest member of the Twelve made on the Latter-day Saints in Cache Valley during this 1867 trip: "I heard him preach in the old meetinghouse at Wellsville, and I remarked at the time what a fine specimen of young manhood he was—strong, powerful, with a beautiful voice, so full of sympathy and affection, so appealing in its tone, that he impressed me, although I was a youth of but eighteen. He was a handsome man." (JFS, p. 228.)

The personal appeal and magnetism of President Smith here commented on by Bishop Nibley was to increase as he grew older. One need only look at the famous painting of

President Smith that hangs in the Salt Lake Temple to see how the admirable qualities of his intellect and spirit shone forth in his handsome features. Much of this can be attributed to heredity. Joseph's father, his uncles, and his grandfather, Joseph Smith, Sr., were all tall, handsome, and powerfully built. Hyrum, who in his maturity was taller than his son, stood about six feet four inches, while his brother, the Prophet, was two or three inches shorter. All the Smiths had a certain look of distinction that caused them to stand out in a crowd. Lorenzo Snow, for example, said of Joseph Smith, Sr., that he "had never seen age so prepossessing." He added, "Father Joseph Smith, the Patriarch, was indeed a noble specimen of aged manhood." (BFRLS, p. 10.)

In a sense, then, what the young Charles W. Nibley saw in the new apostle was a reflection of Joseph's ancestry. But the temple portrait of the mature Joseph F. Smith, with his full head of hair, flowing white beard, and steady, piercing brown eyes, reveals the spiritual increments added to his personality and character by several decades of faithful, apostolic service.

Charles W. Nibley's reminiscences of Joseph F.'s 1867 visit to Cache Valley also contain an interesting anecdote about the apostle that sheds additional light on the incident that ended his formal education. "At that time," wrote Brother Nibley, "I was clerking in a little store owned by Father Ira Ames, one of the old Kirtland veterans of the Church. Apostle George A. Smith was one of the company and he was entertained at Brother Ames' home, where I also lived. I recall that at the dinner table, Father Ames asked George A. who of the Smiths this young man Joseph F. was. George A. replied that he was Hyrum's son; his mother, Mary Fielding Smith. Brother Ames remarked that he looked like a likely young fellow, and George A. replied in about these words: 'Yes, I think he will be all right. His father and mother left him when he was a child, and we have been looking after him to try and help him along. We first sent him to school, but it was not long before he licked the schoolmaster, and could not go to school. Then we sent him on a mission, and he did pretty well at that. I think he will make good as an Apostle.'" (JFS, p. 228-29.)

Joseph F. Smith's Salt Lake City residence. (Utah State Historical Society.)

Two months before his call to the Twelve, Joseph became a father for the first time when Julina gave birth to a daughter, Mercy Josephine. Destined to live for only three years, this baby girl was the first of eleven children Julina was to bear. An adopted son, Edward Arthur, and an adopted daughter, Marjorie Virginia, were to give her and Joseph a baker's dozen. All except Mercy were to live to maturity and to marry. Four other wives, Sarah Ellen Richards, whom Joseph married March 1, 1868; Edna Lambson, whom he married January 1, 1871; Alice Ann Kimball, whom he married December 6, 1883; and Mary Taylor Schwartz, whom he married January 13, 1884, bore him thirty-two other children, and he adopted three children fathered by Alice Ann's first husband, giving him a total of forty-eight. The extent to which Hyrum and Mary's son treasured and loved each of these children is suggested by a diary entry of November 13, 1874: "Children, the greatest of all earthly joys."

Beginning with Mercy Josephine and continuing through the long line of children to be born in the years that followed,

Joseph F. Smith, the orphan who had lost his father as a boy and his mother as a young teenager, lavished upon his children all the love and affection of which he was capable. His feelings were shown not only by his words but by his looks and actions. The members of his family were customarily greeted by a warm smile and a fatherly hug or kiss, and within the limits of his modest means, he usually remembered anniversaries and special events with a gift of some kind. An observer can hardly escape the feeling that President Smith's overflowing love for his family emanated not only from his tender nature but also from an attempt to prevent some of the deprivations he had suffered because of the premature loss of his own parents.

This special quality in Joseph F. Smith, this patriarchal love for family, intensified the feelings of remorse and upset he experienced about this time because of a serious problem in his family. It involved his first wife, Levira, to whom he had been married for almost a decade. During that period, this faithful woman had been unable to conceive. The feelings of frustration and unhappiness her barrenness had produced apparently were magnified when Julina, the second wife, conceived within a few months after being sealed to Joseph. And this, added to the ill health she had suffered periodically during most of the marriage, ultimately caused her to seek a legal separation from her husband and to go to California where she hoped her health would mend. Some time later she returned to Utah where she remained for a short while before moving to St. Louis, Missouri, where she lived out her remaining years, passing away there on December 18, 1888. (JFS, pp. 231, 487.)

The personal resiliency that had enabled Joseph F. Smith to withstand the harsh blows that had taken his parents to their graves and to meet the challenges of pioneering and the privations of foreign proselyting also enabled him to withstand this tragic experience. Putting it aside, insofar as he was able to do so, Joseph immersed himself in his family, Church, and civic responsibilities.

About this time he was sealed to eighteen-year-old Sarah Ellen Richards, who was one of the daughters of Willard

Richards, a secretary and confidant of the Prophet Joseph Smith and later a counselor to President Brigham Young. Also about this time, Joseph F., Wilford Woodruff, and Abraham O. Smoot were called by President Young to move to Provo to help counteract a lawless element that had gained a foothold there. After these leading brethren had lived in Provo long enough to satisfy the residency requirements, they were elected to the city council, where, through political authority and personal and Church influence, they were able to control the criminals whose thefts, trespasses, and assaults had created much public unrest and uncertainty.

The stay of Elders Woodruff and Smith in Provo was short, lasting only long enough to set public affairs in order. However, Abraham O. Smoot stayed on to become the patriarch of one of the largest and most influential families in Utah Valley. This exemplary man was destined to serve as the president of the Utah Stake for almost thirty years, as Provo's mayor, as the leading financier and businessman in the area, and as the first president of the board of trustees of the Church academy in Provo, which later grew into the mammoth Brigham Young University, whose sprawling campus dominates the east bench of the city. And Abraham's son, Reed Smoot, who was a mere boy of six when his family moved to Provo in 1868, was to join Joseph F. Smith in the apostleship thirty-two years later; and a few years after that, these two men were to be spotlighted in a drama played on a national stage in the nation's capitol as bitter enemies of the Church attempted unsuccessfully to deprive Reed Smoot of a seat in the United States Senate.

Joseph F. Smith was not a novice in political affairs when he moved to Provo. Three years previously, in 1865, he had been elected to the territorial House of Representatives, where his intelligence, aggressiveness, and eloquence soon made him a force to be reckoned with. He was re-elected for seven consecutive terms and then stepped down only when he was called to fill his second mission to Great Britain in 1874. In the early 1880s, following his return from England, he served two terms in the territorial Senate, and during the last term he also served as the president of a committee called to draft a constitution for the proposed state of Utah. He also served several terms on the Salt Lake City Council, during which he was one of the moving forces in the development of the Liberty and Pioneer parks.

The decline in Elder Smith's active participation in politics coincided with the passage of the Edmunds Act in 1882 and the vigorous enforcement of it that followed. This act and the more stringent Edmunds-Tucker Act passed in 1887 defined polygamy as a crime and imposed criminal sanctions on offenders. Because of the prominent role he played in Church affairs and his awareness of the desire of federal officials to prosecute the most visible leaders as a warning to others, Joseph withdrew from the active political arena and thereafter limited his political involvement to behind-the-scenes activities.

In 1869, Elder Smith returned to Salt Lake City, where he took up his employment in the Church Historian's Office. This was pleasant and congenial work, well-suited to Joseph's interests and talents and to his role as a member of the Twelve. And, presumably, it relieved him of some stress and anxiety he had experienced in his employment at Provo, where he had worked in a cabinet shop for two dollars a day and had received part of his compensation in produce.

During the October 1869 general conference, Julina gave birth to her second child, a girl, who they named Mary Sophronia in honor of Joseph's mother and aunt. This daughter was to grow to maturity and to become the wife of Alfred William Peterson. And two months later, on New Year's Day, 1870, the apostle's family was further enlarged when he married Edna Lambson, Julina's younger sister.

For a period of almost four years after returning from Provo to Salt Lake City, Joseph F., his three wives, and their children lived a comparatively normal and quiet life. The husband-father was busily engaged in his work at the Historian's Office, in counseling with his brethren of the Twelve and the First Presidency, and in filling the customary assignments to visit stake conferences and to attend special meetings.

During this period Joseph and the other high leaders of

the Church wrestled with the difficult problems created by the rapid influx of nonmembers. This had been greatly accelerated by the completion of the transcontinental railroad in the spring of 1869. And as the ratio of Latter-day Saints to nonmembers decreased, the competition between the two groups increased correspondingly.

That competition was waged chiefly on three levels— economic, religious, and political. To counteract the growing economic strength of the gentile community in Utah and to unify the Saints in their temporal affairs, Joseph F. and the other leaders gave renewed emphasis to the cooperative movement. One manifestation of this was the creation of Zion's Cooperative Mercantile Institution in 1869. And on the part of the nonmember community, the most dramatic thrust in the battle to wrest economic power from the Mormons was the founding of Corinne, the Burgh on the Bear, which, it was hoped, would shift the balance of temporal and presumably political power from Salt Lake City to the new community to the north.

In the midst of these temporal struggles, the Church was confronted with an ecclesiastical challenge when, in the summer of 1869, two missionaries of the Reorganized Church appeared in Salt Lake City in an attempt to convert the "Utah Mormons." This pair more directly involved Elder Joseph F. Smith than any of the other leading brethren as they happened to be his first cousins, Alexander H. and David Hyrum Smith, sons of the Prophet Joseph Smith. These companions reserved Independence Hall, the largest building in the city controlled by the gentiles, and held a series of meetings. The Latter-day Saints turned out in large numbers, chiefly as a matter of curiosity—curiosity about the message but mostly curiosity about the appearance, style, and effectiveness of these offspring of the Prophet.

Although the Saints in Salt Lake City rejected the contentions of those who had brought the Reorganized Church into being and therefore rejected the contentions of Alexander and David Smith, they nevertheless honored the visitors as the offspring of the man whom they revered above all other Latter-day Saints, living or dead. They held great love and goodwill toward the Prophet and his family, which doctrinal differences could not alter or diminish. And the Smith brothers were the beneficiaries of those feelings, so that when they stood in Independence Hall to deliver their message, they were faced with as friendly an audience as could have been found anyplace outside their own sect. But the message they delivered fell on deaf ears and was of such a controversial and provocative nature as to require an answer. The one selected to respond was the eloquent cousin of the visitors, Joseph F. Smith, who, at age thirty-one, was a seasoned platform speaker, having learned the rudiments of his craft in the rough-and-tumble of exposition and debate in Great Britain and the isles of the Pacific. Public debates were held, therefore, where the listeners could judge for themselves the merits of the conflicting views as well as the character and capacity of the speakers.

A non-Mormon writer rendered this judgment of the outcome of this historic debate between the sons of the martyrs: "But the mantle of the prophet had not fallen on his [Joseph Smith's] offspring; they were men almost without force of character, of lamb-like placidity, and of hopelessly mediocre ability; not shrewd enough to contend with their opponents, and not violent enough to arouse the populace. They accomplished little for the cause of the reorganized church." (Hubert Howe Bancroft, *History of Utah*, p. 646.)

Chapter Ten

President of the European Mission

J oseph F. Smith received the call to preside over the European mission at the October 1873 general conference. As he stood at the pulpit in the "new tabernacle," whose balcony had only recently been installed, he presented a picture of youthful vigor and power. Now in the prime of life as he approached his thirty-fifth birthday, Hyrum's son faced his first position of principal executive responsibility. While he had served in important positions both in Hawaii and England, he had never before had the ultimate authority for directing a large segment of the work as he would have in directing the proselyting as well as the administrative work in all of Great Britain, Europe, and Scandinavia. Faced with such vast responsibility, the usual tendency would have been to make some allusion to the coming event as he addressed the Saints on October 7. The fact that no mention was made of it shows again a facet of Joseph F.'s character that was so evident in his correspondence from Hawaii as a teenager—a complete devotion to the work and an apparent selflessness. So in what might be termed his farewell address, there will be found no reference to himself (except to emphasize a point), to his family, to what he had done, or to what he proposed to do. Instead will be found solid teaching and counsel to the Saints. "I do believe," he told them, "that I have no claim

93

upon God or upon my brethren for blessing, favor, confidence or love, unless, by my works, I prove that I am worthy thereof, and I never expect to receive blessings that I do not merit." As to the quality of one's work or service, he had this to say: "The Lord does not accept obedience from men except that which they render cheerfully and gladly in their hearts, and that is all that is desired by his servants. That is the obedience we ought to render, and if we do not we are under condemnation." And later he reverted to a theme to which every Prophet of God gives important emphasis: "Let us keep the commandments and counsels that have been given to us," he admonished his listeners. "Let us not be hearers of the word only, but let us be doers of it as well as hearers. Let us put away the foolish fashions of the world, live up to the truth, and seek to find out God, whom to know is life eternal. The road to this knowledge is obedience to his laws and to the whisperings of the still small voice in our own hearts. That will lead us into truth if we will hearken, and do not blunt the monitor that is within us. Let us do our duty, and be for God and his kingdom. Let our motto be—'The kingdom of God or nothing.' Because in the kingdom there is everything, and outside of it nothing at all." (JD 16:246, 248, 249.)

It took almost five months for Elder Smith to wind up his affairs before leaving for England. His life now was quite different than it had been in the early years when he had only himself and later a childless bride to be concerned about. Now he had three wives and five children: Julina with Mary Sophronia and Donette, ages four and one; Sarah Ellen with Leonora and Joseph Richards, ages two years and eight months; and Edna with nineteen-month-old Hyrum Mack. By the time Joseph F. left for England, Edna had conceived again and would give birth to a second son, Alvin Fielding, before her husband's return.

With provision having been made for the care of his young family, Joseph F. left Salt Lake City on February 28, 1874. The transcontinental railroad having been completed five years before, this trip across the United States was made with speed and comfort, covering in a few days a distance that only a few years before would have required weeks of laborious effort to traverse. In Washington, D.C., Joseph spent some time counseling with his old friend and fellow apostle George Q. Cannon, who was in the nation's capital serving as a representative from Utah Territory. It may have occurred to one or both of these well-traveled friends that in the two decades of their acquaintance, they had been engaged in a kind of charade in which they were constantly saying hello or good-bye to each other.

After bidding good-bye to Elder Cannon still another time, Joseph traveled by train to New York City, where he embarked on the steamship *Idaho* which docked in Liverpool at the now familiar Mersey River pierhead on March 21, 1874. There to meet him were members of the mission staff, who took him to 42 Islington, which would be his headquarters for a year and a half.

Elder Smith's previous acquaintance with his new home had been cursory, based upon brief, intermittent visits as he came and went on assignment. Now, however, he looked at the place through the eyes of a semipermanent resident who was interested not only in the details of the home but also in its environment. He found that the building was ample enough in size to accommodate staff offices, printing facilities for the *Millennial Star*, comfortable though not lavish living quarters, and spare rooms to house itinerant missionaries, visitors from Zion and, occasionally, Saints preparing to immigrate to the United States. A canvass of the neighborhood showed it to be middle class with neat though old buildings and orderly streets. A facet of his surroundings that intrigued Elder Smith and that was typical of English cities of the day was the uncommonly large number of pubs, which he referred to as "Gin Palaces." So intrigued was he by this phenomenon that on one stroll through the neighborhood with his assistant, L. John Nuttall, he counted forty gin palaces within a mile radius of 42 Islington. Suggesting the preponderant emphasis the English placed on drinking over religion, he also reported that the same area included only five churches. This condition prompted Joseph to confide to his diary that "liquor in some form has become an indispensable necessary to the English people." (Diary, Jan. 5, 1875.)

Joseph F. Smith. Photograph taken on May 25, 1874, in Far West, Missouri. (Church Archives.)

This aspect of the English culture, added to its addiction to tea as the national beverage, presented significant proselyting challenges to Elder Smith and his abstemious brethren. Notwithstanding, the missionaries regularly harvested a substantial crop of English converts, most of whom, heedful of the admonition to gather, immigrated to the United States. On October 14, 1874, for instance, Joseph supervised an operation that was routine for his office when he saw 150 "souls" off on the steamship *Wyoming*, headed for America. Adopting a procedure that had been followed for several decades, Joseph appointed a presidency to supervise the Mormon passengers until they arrived at their destination. W. N. Fife was called as president of this company, with James Bywater and V. King as counselors. These brethren would act as shepherds to the flock, directing worship services, helping the sick, and providing spiritual counsel as needed. Elder Smith noted in his journal that the Saints who departed on the *Wyoming* comprised the sixth immigration company to leave Liverpool in 1874, aggregating a total of "1996 souls."

To wave good-bye to a departing company as President Smith did on this brisk October day was symbolically akin to a farmer garnering a season's crop. It did not mean that the work was completed but only that one cycle had ended to be followed by another almost identical. That cycle consisted of organizing the missionaries into an effective work force through appointments and transfers. Joseph devoted much time and prayer in making missionary assignments, being fully aware of the spiritual nature of the work and of the need to look beyond the physical externals in making organizational changes. Once the organization was in place, it was necessary to move it toward its objective, to inspire and motivate it. This President Smith did through personal counseling, through sermons and instruction given at formal meetings, and through the pages of the *Millennial Star*, which he edited during the period of his presidency. He traveled regularly into the districts in Great Britain, where he not only instructed and motivated the missionaries but also set in order the affairs of the local branches. These of necessity were comparatively weak and struggling organizations that suffered from regular losses of some of their strongest members through emigration. President Smith also periodically visited the other areas under his jurisdiction: Scandinavia, the low countries, Germany, Switzerland, and France, although not with the regularity that he visited the districts in Great Britain.

But while the proper administration of his mission was the object that claimed most of his attention, the duties, trials, and trauma of daily living occupied a substantial portion of each day. Like most missionaries, Joseph had to care for his personal needs. A cryptic diary entry on October 2, 1874, that he had mended his own clothing speaks volumes about the myriad daily tasks that had to be sandwiched in between the weightier matters of the kingdom. And several entries about attacks of rheumatism that afflicted his left shoulder indicate the physical discomfort that burdened him from time to time.

This condition was aggravated by the fog and rain of a dreary Liverpool autumn. Giving vent to his feelings about the weather, Joseph F. recorded this bit of doggerel on October 8, 1874, a day he described as "another wet disagreeable day":

> *Dirty days hath September*
> *April June and November*
> *From January up to May*
> *The rain—it raineth every day*
> *All the rest have thirty one*
> *Without a blessed gleam of sun*

The sable tinge the foul weather and Joseph's rheumatism cast upon his spirits is best shown by the diary entry of November 13, which commemorated his thirty-sixth birthday: "The day was cold, bleak and dreary, a fit and proper anniversary of the dark and trying day of my birth; When my father and his brother were confined in a dungeon for the gospel's sake and the saints were being driven from their homes in Missouri by a merciless mob. The bright sunshine of my soul has never thoroughly dispelled the darkening shadows cast upon it by the lowering gloom of that eventful period." Typically, however, after having expressed this deep sense of melancholy, he went on to record feelings of joy bordering on exultation that had grown out of these tragic circumstances: "Yet the merciful hand of God and his kindliest providences have ever been extended visibly toward me, even from my childhood, and my days grow better and better thru humility and the pursuit of wisdom and happiness in the kingdom of God; The objects of my life becoming more apparent as time advances and experience grows. Those objects being the proclamation of the gospel, or the establishment of the kingdom of God on the earth; The salvation of souls, and most important of which to me—that of myself and family. The richest of all my earthly joys is in my precious children. Thank God."

As tokens of the love expressed for them in his diary, Joseph sent occasional gifts to his wives and children to the extent allowed by his meager resources. To make sure of their safe delivery, these were usually sent along with missionaries returning to the United States. One such courier was an Elder Fenton, whom President Smith loaded up with gifts for his family. "I let bro. T. Fenton have a tin or sheet iron trunk," he recorded on February 24, 1875, "to put his things in and to take to my family, with the two satchels (for the girls), the three pair of clogs (for the little boys) the four handkerchiefs (for the wives) three little leathern pockets for the children and a woolen blanket."

In this same entry, Joseph meticulously listed the cost of each item and the total, ending with the notation, "Private means and matters," so that no one could ever wrongfully infer that he had used the Lord's money for personal benefit. This reflects the exactness that characterized all of his dealings and throws light on the image of precision and rectitude he always projected to the Church. Joseph F. Smith expected the Latter-day Saints to measure up to the high standards of the gospel. But he never asked of others what he had not already given or was prepared to give in obedience and dedication.

Notwithstanding the puritanical dedication to work and duty this aspect of Joseph's character suggests, he was not a drudge. He interspersed his heavy work schedule with recreational and cultural activities. He was fond of skating, and during the cold winter months occasionally indulged in this sport. His favorite exercise, however, was walking, and he frequently took long walks that not only were physically invigorating but also had a mentally soothing effect. Walking also enabled him to appraise a neighborhood and to better understand its character. President Smith also enjoyed visiting the museums and fairs, which were educational and stimulating and provided a better insight into the British people, their history, and their culture. Indeed, these provided a better insight into his own character and motivations, since his ancestry was predominantly English. On his mother's side, of course, he was only one generation away from English soil.

While it does not appear that Joseph found the place of his mother's birth while in England, he was in the general area on several occasions. Mary had been reared on a farm in the beautiful Bedford Valley some fifty miles north of London. (Corbett, *Mary Fielding Smith, Daughter of Britain*, p. 4.) There can be little doubt that the rural scenes Joseph saw in that area were essentially the same as those his mother carried in memory from her childhood.

In the spring of 1875, Joseph left Liverpool for a tour of the continent. On Sunday May 16, he recorded his impression of the English countryside through which he had passed the day before en route to London. "Bright, beautiful morning as yesterday was a beautiful day," he wrote approvingly. "The fields and all nature are just in their bloom of freshness and verdure. England looks like a garden well tilled." It is not dfficult to read into this glowing description a sense of pride in his English roots and in the land that had nourished his forebears for generations.

While for the most part Elder Smith's service as president of the European mission was a joyful, uplifting experience, it had its dark moments. To one so devoted to family, the separation from loved ones was the heaviest cross to bear. On a cold December day, a few months after arriving in Liverpool, he opened a letter from home to find several family pictures. "I had peculiar feelings," he confided to his diary, "went into my room and wept and prayed and wept again and felt relieved."

But this was an anguish that would heal with time and would loom up in the years ahead, after reunion with his family, as an experience adding depth and a pleasing hue to the past. There were other experiences, however, of such a melancholy nature as would always arouse feelings of sadness, despite the lapse of time. Invariably these related to the misconduct or misfortune of his missionaries or Church members. One such incident occurred when one of his missionaries had to be sent home for transgression. "I came as a missionary," the repentant elder told President Smith, "and now I go back like a dog. I would rather have died on the way honorably as my brother did." Not only were the president's sympathies aroused for this young man, but the spectacle of his disgrace and the years of regret and self-recrimination that lay ahead of him moved Joseph to deep reflection. "Thus a man may almost fill a mission," he wrote of the incident, "or live a lifetime honorably and faithfully, and at the last moment, as it were, by a single act of crime or folly or error, overturn and destroy it all in a moment, turning all the sweetness in the cup of life into gall and bitterness." Conscious as he perhaps had never been before of the tenuous nature of one's reputation and standing before the Lord and the Church, and aware of his own weaknesses and of the special protection he had enjoyed in the past, President Smith was led to record this beautiful prayer of contrition, thanksgiving, and praise: "O! how I thank my God for his protecting, watchful care which has been over me thus far through life; Preserving me from the deadly sins of the world, and many thousand times from my own weaknesses and proneness to err: Snatching me several times in my life from the very brink of moral ruin, which to me would have been more intolerable than lingering death. That man who can look his fellows in the face, and with a clear conscience before God, stand erect in honest pride of truth, morally and sexually pure from his youth up, is in the world unlooked for, and would be disbelieved. But such an one tho considered a moral anomaly alone can feel how glorious a thing it is, to look back upon a clean, unspotted record of the past. O! my God, such an one help me to be for ever—not that I arrogate to myself, but that I acknowledge from the depths of heartfelt gratitude that I owe all to God, whose ever present, unseen hand has held me and saved me thus far. I live in the pure unsullied love of my darling children. My wives can trust me. I would not abuse their love and confidence for all I have or am, so long as I can retain my reason and the light of God's Spirit. O! My Father preserve me in thy holy keeping from the power of temptation I could not resist, and forgive my past foolish inclinations and desires and be thou my master, my head, by thy spirit control me ever." (Diary, April 28, 1875.)

The writings and sermons of President Joseph F. Smith

will be searched in vain for a more moving and eloquent statement than this one showing at once his humility, his strength of character, his integrity, and his purity. It reveals a man who had been tried by but who had resisted the temptations of the world. It also reveals a man who, though strong and able, placed his ultimate trust in God, not in himself. And it reveals a man in whom his associates could place absolute confidence. It is not difficult to trace these qualities into the later conduct of this unusual man who, as he neared the end of his service as European mission president, could count important new credentials qualifying him for longer service in the First Presidency of the Church than any other man.

Joseph wound up his labors in Liverpool and returned to Salt Lake City in time to participate in the October general conference. He stood on Sunday morning, October 10, 1875, to address the Saints in the new tabernacle. It was his homecoming sermon. Having been away from the city for twenty months engaged in exciting, important labors in Europe, one reasonably might have expected some kind of report of his labors and the condition of the work there. But, following the precedent of his farewell address, Elder Smith remained silent about his experiences abroad and instead preached a solid doctrinal sermon, emphasizing the duties resting upon the Saints. He again touched on the quality of one's service and provided a hint as to the reason he seemed loathe to talk about himself or his work. "The rich man may enter into the kingdom of heaven as freely as the poor," he told the Saints, "if he will bring his heart and affections into subjection to the law of God and to the principle of truth; if he will place his affections upon God, his heart upon the truth, and his soul upon the accomplishment of God's purposes, and not fix his affections and his hopes upon the things of the world." After having defined what the goal of the Latter-day Saints should be, he prescribed a blueprint for attaining it: "Then let the Saints unite; let them hearken to the voices of the servants of God that are sounded in their ears; let them hearken to their counsels and give heed to the truth; let them seek their own salvation, for, so far as I am concerned, I am so selfish that I am seeking after my salvation, and I know that I can find it only in obedience to the laws of God, in keeping the commandments, in performing works of righteousness, following in the footsteps of our file leader, Jesus, the exemplar and the head of all. He is the way of life, he is the light of the world, he is the door by which we must enter in order that we may have a place with him in the celestial kingdom of God." (JD 18:134, 135.)

Chapter Eleven

Other Missions at Home and Abroad

The joy President Smith felt in being reunited with his wives and children was tempered by the death of George A. Smith, who passed away September 1, 1875, in Salt Lake City. This powerful man, whose giant physique (over three hundred pounds draped on a massive form) was overshadowed by his spiritual stature, had been a surrogate father to Joseph F. since Hyrum's martyrdom. And the bond of blood relationship between the two had been immeasurably strengthened by their association in the exclusive apostolic brotherhood. Whenever the younger man had a problem, he always found a sympathetic ear and a helping hand in the person of George A., whose position as the first counselor to President Brigham Young added weight and influence to his words. And it is suspected that a vague, perhaps unexpressed, mutual admiration had grown up between the two that had its roots in the combative nature of their personalities. We have already seen the manifestations of this quality in Joseph F.: in his vow of retaliation against the wagonmaster who had offended his mother; in the physical whipping administered to the teacher who had disciplined his sister; and, to a lesser degree, in the outspoken way in which he had opposed the decision of his leaders on the *Nettie Merrill* off Lahaina. And the same quality shone forth in the older Smith, revealed in numerous incidents but none as dramatic or illustrative as one that occurred in his adolescence. The beginning of what happened was the surprising speed with which George A. grew as a young teenager. He sprang up almost overnight, soon towering high above his classmates. But he was clumsy and uncoordinated, and this, added to the thoughtlessness of his peers, soon made George A. an object of abuse and ridicule. However, unlike many who wilt under pressure and accept humiliation and defeat without resistance, George A. quietly and deliberately prepared to retaliate, and at the only level his tormentors would understand—physically. So when George A. was ready to act, he methodically, one by one, challenged and whipped every one of the boys who had taunted and insulted him. From that time forward, his classmates ceased to annoy and intimidate him.

In later years, this combative quality in George A.'s and Joseph F.'s makeup was masked and concealed or overshadowed by other dominant characteristics. Notwithstanding, it was there, lying just below the surface, but it was manifested in other ways than physical or verbal response. But these cousins doubtless were aware of the quality in each other and recognized in it a common bond, tracing it in large part to an inheritance from forebears who were positive, forceful, and self-reliant.

With the passing of George A., Joseph assumed a dominant position in the leadership of the extended Smith family in Utah, a leadership that would continue and grow throughout his life. More and more every branch of the family would turn to him, recognizing in his character and ecclesiastical prominence the prospect of his attaining the highest status in Mormondom, a status even above that of his illustrious father.

In the meantime, Joseph F. still had many lessons to learn through subordination to his presiding officers and service to those under him. The next step was an assignment from the First Presidency to direct the affairs of the Church in Davis County, just north of Salt Lake City. This area, which had not yet been organized into a stake, was growing rapidly as communities sprang up amidst the rich farmland the Saints tilled with customary vigor and thoroughness. Their new leader, who was now a seasoned veteran of over twenty years of constant service in the priesthood, was admirably prepared to lay the groundwork for the creation of a stake in that area. That event would take place not long after he assumed the direction of affairs there. What Elder Smith found was similar to the situation in the European Mission, although there were significant differences.

The similarities revolved around the process by which members of the Church are taught and inspired in matters of doctrine, procedure, and conduct. Here Joseph was able to bring to bear his vast experience from four foreign missions and his intimate association with the general authorities from the earliest days of the Church. As important as these, however, was the spiritual insight he brought to the work, made manifest through his eloquence, virility, and regal bearing. And overshadowing all was the impression of honesty and rectitude the new leader's reputation, appearance, and demeanor conveyed. Those over whom he presided seemed to know instinctively that this man was genuine and wholehearted and could be relied upon.

Insofar as the application of these principles and qualities was concerned, little difference could be found between presiding in Davis County and in Europe. The differences were to be found in the environment and stability of the subordinate leaders. In Farmington and its environs, the population was overwhelmingly Mormon, so the customs and standards of the Church dominated the culture. The gin palaces that proliferated in Liverpool were unknown to Davis County residents. Nor were almshouses, bordellos, or prisons to be found there. It was a young, progressive, self-confident society filled with a millennial vision. And unlike the struggling branches in Europe, whose leadership ranks were periodically decimated by emigration, the local units in Joseph's new pastorate were led by men and women who were there to stay—at least as long as Brother Brigham wanted them to.

Given these materials to work with and using the strengths developed by his predecessors, Elder Smith moved forward promptly and confidently to prepare the area for stakehood, which came in June 1877, less than two years after he was placed in charge.

The short period during which he presided in Davis County was a welcome and comparatively relaxing interlude for Elder Smith. He was able to enjoy the companionship of his family, involve himself again in the interesting work in the Historian's Office, counsel with his brethren at headquarters, and direct Church affairs in the area where he presided. In addition, there were intermittent assignments to attend stake conferences and other special meetings outside the Salt Lake area, where he functioned in his preeminent role as a member of the Council of the Twelve Apostles. One such occasion was the dedication of the St. George Temple, in the spring of 1877. Since the dedication was scheduled near the time of the April general conference, these two events were combined.

Spring, which had only begun to free itself from the grip of winter in Salt Lake City, was in full bloom when Joseph arrived in balmy, pleasant St. George. The little Mormon community had an air of excitement and expectancy and had put on its best face to receive Church members from throughout the territory, especially the general authorities and members of their families from the north. The main focus of attention, of course, gleaming white in the Dixie sun, was the holy temple, which the Saints had labored so diligently to complete. Because it was the first temple to be completed since the expulsion from Nauvoo, the minds of the Saints were led to reflect not only upon the sacred purposes for which the beautiful edifice had been built, but also upon the travails through which they had passed before and since the exodus. This sense of nostalgia even descended upon Elder Smith who, as we have seen, customarily refrained from personal references in his public addresses. But on this occasion, apparently caught up in the excitement, he deigned to talk about his background in public. But as we shall see, this deviation from his fixed habit was allowed only as a basis for developing important gospel themes. After tracing his early experiences, he said in a sermon delivered April 2, 1877, in the St. George Tabernacle, "In this way I have learned the Gospel which I was first taught to believe, which belief is now superseded by knowledge. For now I know that God lives, and that Jesus Christ was sent into the world to atone for the original sin, and also for the actual transgressions of mankind, inasmuch as they themselves will repent of their sins and humble themselves before Him in their pursuit of the gift and blessing of eternal life."

Having borne this beautiful testimony and commented favorably on the testimony of others, he posed the question of whether a hearsay or secondhand testimony is sufficient. The answer was a resounding no. "It will not suffice me to believe that *you* know the true and living God," he told the Saints. "I must receive this knowledge for myself as you have received it." Elder Smith went on to explain why it is necessary for every person to have a personal knowledge and testimony of the truth: "The possession of this heavenly knowledge is absolutely necessary to keep us in the paths of life and truth, for without it we cannot distinguish the voice of the true shepherd, which is spiritually discerned; and although we may be in fellowship with the Church, fully believing the counsels of our brethren to be dictated by wisdom, yet without something more than mere belief or supposition we cannot stand." (JD 19:22, 23.)

Five days after delivering this sermon, Joseph was treated to another of the "surprises" that President Young seemed so fond of arranging. At that time it was announced during one of the general conference sessions that Elder Joseph F. Smith would be leaving the territory soon to take charge of the European mission with headquarters in Liverpool!

Any surprise Joseph may have had at being called to preside again in Europe so soon after having returned from there was not reflected in either his words or his actions. Like the good soldier he was, he returned home from St. George and commenced planning for his fifth foreign mission without fuss or fanfare. Having been authorized to take one of his wives with him this time, it was decided that Sarah would go. The fact that Julina had a nine-month-old baby, Joseph Fielding (a future Church president), doubtless explains why she was not selected to accompany her husband. Also, Sarah had buried an infant, Heber John, in March 1877, and the trip abroad may have been thought desirable to help lift the burden of such a heavy loss.

One of Sarah's children, Joseph Richards, a lively four-year-old, accompanied his parents while his sister, Leonora, who had reached school age, remained at home in the care of the other two wives, Julina and Edna. Undoubtedly, the presence of her two sisters, Mary Sophronia and Donette, Julina's daughters, who were, respectively, two years older and one year younger than she, served as a powerful magnet to keep Leonora in Salt Lake City.

The three Smiths, accompanied by Elders Alma L. Smith and Charles W. Nibley, left Salt Lake City in early May and arrived at Liverpool on May 27. Alma was the cousin who had been with Joseph and the others during the second mission to Hawaii in 1864, and Elder Nibley was the young Cache Valley merchant who had been so impressed by Joseph F. ten years before when he was first called to the Twelve.

During this, Joseph's third mission to England, short though it was, the foundation of his friendship with Elder Nibley was established, a friendship that was to burn with undiminished brightness during the rest of Joseph's life. Indeed, that friendship was to be the most intimate and lasting one President Smith would ever form outside his family. The depth and quality of it is indicated by a letter Joseph wrote to his friend on November 16, 1907, acknowledging receipt of a birthday remembrance. Addressed to "My Beloved Brother Charlie," it contained these expressions of appreciation, made by a man who was careful with words and not given to overstatement: "I thank you my best earthly friend, for your purest friendship for me, as expressed in your letter, and as demonstrated in so many tangible ways all through our acquaintance. My soul overflows with gratitude for such a brother and such a friend. . . . I cherish your fervent words of love and friendship above all the treasure of the world. May nothing ever come to change the current of this life-giving flood. Nothing can come to change it within the compass of God's precious gifts of truth and honor. O, that we may ever keep well within that charmed circle." (JFS, p. 235-36.)

It was the original intention in assigning Elder Smith to England for a third time that he would remain there for several years. With that in mind, Sarah immediately busied herself trying to create a new atmosphere at 42 Islington, converting it from a barracks-like stopping place for itinerant missionaries into a home-like refuge. She was well into that project when, three months after arriving in Liverpool, an event occurred that shattered all her plans and, indeed, sent shock waves throughout the entire Church. This was the death of President Brigham Young, the Lion of the Lord, who died in Salt Lake City on August 29, 1877. The passing of this valorous man, who had exerted such a profound influence on the Saints for over three decades, presented the leadership of the Church—especially the Council of the Twelve—with a challenge of immense proportions. The precedent set following the death of Joseph Smith, Brigham's predecessor, suggested that a period of uncertain length would intervene before a new president of the Church would be designated. During that interval, the worldwide affairs of the Church would be administered by the Twelve; facility in administration demanded that all the members of that body be clustered in or near Salt Lake City. So, within days of President Young's death, John Taylor, president of the Twelve, sent word summoning all the apostles home.

Accustomed by now to precipitate, unscheduled calls, Joseph, assisted by and in some instances directed by Sarah's calm efficiency, began systematically to pack the belongings that had only so recently been unpacked. Everything was ready within a few days, and on September 12, 1877, the Smiths boarded a packet ship in company with Elder Orson Pratt of the Twelve, who had arrived in England less than a month before to supervise the publication of a new edition of the Book of Mormon and Doctrine and Covenants. Also with the party was Franklin S. Richards, Sarah's cousin, who had been proselyting in England.

It is a fair assumption that Sarah was both sad and pleased at this unexpected turn of events—sad because she would be unable to research her English ancestral lines or to visit the places in England where her British forebears had originated, but happy because she would soon be reunited with Leonora and other relatives. And the prospect of such a reunion would have gladdened Joseph's heart, given his love for family. Yet he, too, doubtless had some regrets, sorrows, and apprehensions as his ship made its way toward New York, regret that his mission had been cut short, sorrow at the loss of his friend and mentor Brigham Young, and apprehension about the heavy burden resting upon the Twelve and the grave decisions they faced. Preeminent among these was the ever-increasing pressure being exerted by the federal government against polygamists, the legal complications involved in the transfer of authority from the former administration to the new one, and the ecclesiastical question arising from the action taken by President Young in June 1875 to reorder the seniority of two members of the Twelve.

At that time, in connection with meetings held in San Pete, President Young had announced that John Taylor was the senior member of the Twelve instead of Orson Hyde, despite the fact that Brother Hyde had served as president of the Twelve for many years. Also at that time he announced that Elder Orson Pratt, who for years had sat next to Elder Hyde in the circle, was out of order in terms of seniority. These changes were based upon the temporary estrangement of these two brethren during the trying days in Missouri and Illinois.

Arriving home on September 27, Joseph F. plunged immediately into his work as a member of the governing body of the Church. Since in the interval between President Young's death and Joseph's return the other members of the Twelve had formally declared John Taylor to be the president of the Twelve and the Twelve to be the presiding quorum of the Church, President Taylor and Elder Orson Pratt joined in a statement published in the *Deseret News* the first of October concurring in that decision. Then followed lengthy discussions about the order of sustaining the members of the Twelve at the October general conference, the upshot of which was that Joseph's traveling companion, Orson Pratt, was sustained as number seven in seniority and Elder Hyde was sustained as junior to John Taylor and Wilford Woodruff.

While this was a most sensitive issue that, given different personalities, could have threatened the unity of the Twelve, it was resolved amicably so that when the names of the Twelve were read for sustaining vote at the general conference in the revised order, there was no dissension or upset.

Once this question was laid to rest and the general conference had sustained the Twelve as the presiding quorum, the Twelve began to administer Church affairs as a committee of the whole. Joseph participated in the deliberations of this body as it decided a wide range of questions dealing with the construction of the Salt Lake, Manti, and Logan temples, with colonization in Utah and neighboring territories, and with emigration from abroad. The Twelve also decided to reopen the Endowment House, which had been closed for some time, and placed Joseph F. and Daniel H. Wells in charge. Interspersed with major undertakings and issues of this kind were a myriad of details like the call and release of missionaries, changes in boundaries of ecclesiastical units, the call and release of stake presidents and bishops, and the handling of statistical and financial reports. The sheer burden of this detail ultimately resulted in broad delegations of authority to President Taylor and to committees of the Twelve assigned to handle specific items.

By far the most complex and stressful issue Joseph F. and his brethren of the Twelve faced was the settlement of the estate of President Brigham Young. Because of the provisions of the 1862 Morrill Act, which severely limited the amount of property that could be held by a church in the territories, there had been much intermingling by President Young of private property with property beneficially owned by the Church. So at Brigham Young's death, there was much uncertainty as to the actual ownership of property held in his name. To unravel this complication, an audit committee was appointed from the Twelve comprised of Wilford Woodruff, Erastus Snow, Franklin D. Richards, and Joseph F. Smith. This committee scrutinized all of President Young's accounts and holdings in conjunction with three other members of the Twelve, George Q. Cannon, Brigham Young, Jr., and Albert Carrington, who were the executors of the estate.

Due to apparent misunderstanding about the meaning and effect of the Morrill Act and about President Young's records, Elder Smith seemed critical of the deceased president in the early phases of the audit. However, as the work progressed and the full picture came into focus, his views moderated. By April 1878, Joseph F. and his brethren of the audit committee had reached an accord with the executors that resulted in the transfer to the Church of real and personal property held in the name of Brother Brigham at his death valued at approximately $700,000. This resolved the thorny issue as far as Church leaders were concerned, although later certain heirs of the departed president brought legal action questioning the correctness of the settlement.

With this unpleasantness out of the way, Joseph was ready for a more constructive assignment. It came in the form of an appointment from President Taylor to him and Elder Orson Pratt to undertake a mission to the east to gather or confirm important data pertaining to early Church history.

Joseph F. left the Salt Lake City depot on Tuesday, September 3, 1878, in a heavy, late summer rain. He had been accompanied to the station by Edna and her two boys, Hyrum Mack, age six, and Alvin Fielding, age four. Edna had suffered a great loss a few months before in the death of her sixteen-month-old baby, Alfred Jason. After seeing her husband off on still another mission, she took her sons to Lake Point for an outing to help ease the pain of her loss.

At Ogden, Elders Smith and Pratt and a traveling companion, W. C. Staines, took berths in the sleeper *Palmyra* destined for Omaha. From there the two apostles traveled to Kansas City and thence across the river to Independence, where they registered at the Merchants Hotel. Taking time only to freshen up and eat breakfast, the pair walked to the temple site, which they examined with nostalgic interest. On making inquiry, they learned that about seventy families living in or near Independence were members of the Reorganized Church and were ready to "redeem Zion and go to work at the temple." (Diary.) Among these were Mrs. William Eaton, the remarried widow of John E. Page, and William E. McLellin, whom the visitors wanted to interview .

The reception given to the Utahns at the Eaton residence was hardly cordial. Mrs. Eaton, particularly, was frosty and aloof. "She had great difficulty to restrain the expression of her bitterness toward polygamy," Joseph recorded, adding tongue-in-cheek, "but we chatted so cordially she succeeded." Thawed out somewhat by the geniality of the visitors, she treated them to some grapes which, she hastened to point out, were raised "in Zion." (Ibid.)

Leaving the Eatons, the pair went to the home of William E. McLellin, one of the original members of the Quorum of the Twelve, who had been excommunicated in Independence more than forty years before. He welcomed the apostles "heartily" and was described by Elder Smith in these words: "He is a very tall, strong man, quite grey, but well preserved. He says when younger he measured 6 feet 3 inches in his stockings." (Ibid.)

This rangy, outspoken man, who was fond of being addressed as Doctor, spent several hours with the visitors expounding his unorthodox views and showing them around town. While asserting the truthfulness of the Book of Mormon, he denounced the Doctrine and Covenants as being the product of a fallen prophet. Like Mrs. Eaton, he also denounced polygamy, alluding to it as the foulest "blotch" on the Bible. He also disavowed any belief in the offices of either the Aaronic or Melchizedek priesthoods, except the apostleship. In an attempt to explain this anomaly, he said that while he believed in the apostleship, he did not believe that any man could confer it.

During a walking tour of Independence, Dr. McLellin pointed out the site where the Church's printing office had stood before it was burned by the mob. He also seemed to take delight in calling attention to the home of a blacksmith, Richard B. Humphreys, who was one of the few members of The Church of Jesus Christ of Latter-day Saints in the area and whom he derisively referred to as a "Twelvite" or "Brighamite."

Finally the apostles' talkative guide told them about David Whitmer, who then lived in Richmond, north of Independence. The doctor said one of David's grandsons, George

Schweich, held himself out as a "seer" and was destined, according to David, to translate certain hidden plates which the grandson was reported to have seen through a certain "peepstone." Mr. McLellin told the visitors that it was George Schweich's pretensions of seership that had caused a rupture between him and David Whitmer. "Dr. McLellin believes this is a species of superstition," Joseph reported in his diary, "and denounces it as from the devil."

Significantly in this account, as in all others recorded by Elder Smith during his historical tour with Orson Pratt, he did not question, argue with, or reject any contention made by William E. McLellin. He merely put the questions and recorded the substance or the exact wording of the answers, leaving the reader to draw his own conclusions.

Following up on William McLellin's comments about David Whitmer, Elder Smith and his companion next traveled to Richmond, where they found great devastation from a recent cyclone. They checked in at the Shaw Hotel, Richmond's best, which was under repair. While seated in the reception room of the hotel not long after their arrival, the object of their visit, David Whitmer, stopped by. To the seventy-three-year-old who greeted the historians, Joseph F. Smith was merely a handsome young man with a distinguished name, but his elder companion evoked vivid memories of the past. "He seemed somewhat surprised and delighted at seeing his old acquaintance, Orson Pratt," Joseph recorded. (JFS, p. 241.) After exchanging the pleasantries customary at such a chance meeting, the trio made arrangements to meet later at the office of "Whitmer and Co's" livery stables, where the two travelers hoped to interrogate David about his role as one of the witnesses to the Book of Mormon. Finding that conditions at the company office were not conducive to the discussion of such a sacred theme, the three, accompanied by several of David's relatives and friends, went to the apostles' hotel room, where, after all were comfortably seated, this dialogue took place:

Orson Pratt: "Can you tell the date of the restoration of the Apostleship by Peter, James and John?"

David Whitmer: "I do not know. Joseph never told me. I can

115

only tell you what I know: I will not testify to anything I do not know."

Joseph F. Smith: "Did Oliver Cowdery die here in Richmond?"

David Whitmer: "Yes, he lived here about a year, I think, before his death; he died in my father's house, right here."

Orson Pratt: "Do you remember what time you saw the plates?"

David Whitmer: "It was in June, 1829, the very last part of the month, and the eight witnesses, I think, the next day. Joseph showed them the plates himself. We (the Three Witnesses) not only saw the plates of the Book of Mormon, but the Brass Plates, the plates containing the record of the wickedness of the people of the world, and many other plates. The fact is, it was just as though Joseph, Oliver and I were sitting right here on a log, when we were overshadowed by a light. It was not like the light of the sun, nor like that of fire, but more glorious and beautiful. It extended away round us, I cannot tell how far, but in the midst of this light, immediately before us, about as far as he sits (pointing to John C. Whitmer who was sitting 2 or 3 feet from him) there appeared, as it were, a table, with many records on it, besides the plates of the Book of Mormon; also the sword of Laban, the Directors (i.e. the ball which Lehi had) and the Interpreters. I saw them just as plain as I see this bed (striking his hand upon the bed beside him), and I heard the voice of the Lord as distinctly as I ever heard anything in my life declaring that they (the plates) were translated by the gift and power of God."

Orson Pratt: "Did you see the Angel at this time?"

David Whitmer: "Yes, he stood before us. Martin Harris was not with us at this time. I don't think he saw all that we did, but our testimony as recorded in the Book of Mormon is strictly and absolutely true just as it is there written. Before I knew anything about Joseph I had heard about him and the plates from persons who declared they knew he had them and swore they would get them from him, and that he had promised them an interest in them when he should get them. The fact is he could not, for they were not to be made merchandise of, nor to be a matter of profit to anyone—they were strictly for sacred purposes, and when Oliver Cowdery went to Pennsylvania he promised to write me what he should learn about the matter, which he did. He told me Joseph had told him his secret thoughts and all he had meditated about going to see him, which no man on earth knew, as he supposed, but himself. So he stopped to write for Joseph. Soon after this Joseph sent for me to come to Harmony, to get him and Oliver and bring them to my father's house. I did not know what to do. I was pressed with my work. I had some 20 acres to plow and so I concluded I would finish plowing, and then go. One morning I got up as usual to go to work. On going to the field I found between 5 and 7 acres of my ground had been plowed during the night. I don't know who did it, but it was done, just as I would have done it myself, and the plow was left standing in the furrow. This enabled me to start sooner. When I arrived at Harmony, Joseph and Oliver were coming toward me, and met me some little distance from the house. Oliver told me that Joseph had told him when I started from home, where I had stopped the first night, how I read the sign at the tavern, where I stopped the next night and that I would be there that day before dinner, and this was why they had come out to meet me, all of which was exactly as Joseph had told Oliver, at which I was greatly astonished. When I was returning to Fayette with Joseph and Oliver, all of us riding in the wagon, Oliver and I on an old fashioned wooden spring seat and Joseph behind us, we were suddenly approached by a very pleasant, nice looking old man in a clear open place, who saluted us with 'Good morning, it is very warm,' at the same instant wiping his face or forehead with his hand. We returned the salutation and by a sign from Joseph I invited him to ride if he was going our way, but he said very pleasantly, 'No, I am going to Cumorah.' This was something new to me, I did not know what Cumorah meant, and as I looked enquiringly at Joseph, the old man instantly disappeared so that I did not see him again."

Joseph F. Smith: "Did you notice his appearance?"

David Whitmer: "I should think I did. He was, I should think, about 5 feet 9 or 10 inches and heavy set, about such a man as James Vancleave, there, but heavier. His face was as large. He was dressed in a suit of brown, woolen clothes; his hair and beard were white, about like Brother Pratt's, but his beard was not so heavy. I also remember that he had a sort of knapsack on his back, and something was in it which was shaped like a book. It was the messenger who had the plates."

Orson Pratt: "Have you any idea when the records will be brought forth?"

David Whitmer: "When we see things in the Spirit and by the power of God they seem to be right here present. The signs of the times indicate the near approach of the coming forth of the other plates, but when it will be, I cannot tell. The Three Nephites are at work among the lost tribes and elsewhere. John the Revelator is at work, and I believe the time will come suddenly, before we are prepared for it."

Orson Pratt: "Have you got the original manuscript of the Book of Mormon?"

David Whitmer: "I have. It is in Oliver Cowdery's handwriting. He placed it in my care at his death, and charged me to preserve it as long as I lived. It is safe, and well preserved."

Joseph F. Smith: "What will you do with it at your death?"

David Whitmer: "I will leave it with my nephew, David Whitmer, son of my brother Jacob and my namesake."

Orson Pratt: "Would you not part with it?"

David Whitmer: "No. Oliver charged me to keep it and Joseph said my father's house should keep the records. I consider these things sacred and would not barter them for money."

Joseph F. Smith: "We would not offer you money in the light of bartering for the manuscript, but we would like to see them preserved in some manner where they would be safe from casualties and from the caprice of men, in some institution that will not die as a man does." (JFS, pp. 242-45.)

No amount of persuasion or cajoling by the two apostles could induce David Whitmer to part with the manuscript. He seemed to ascribe some spiritual quality to it that he felt would be lost were he to relinquish control of it. Moreover, it was learned he had organized a church with about thirty members, which he had named the Church of Christ and whose sole purpose was to preach "the Bible and the Book of Mormon, and nothing else." (Ibid., p. 246.) The Book of Mormon manuscript was, therefore, looked upon as a sort of sacred artifact that the possessors felt added an element of strength and authority to the teaching of his sect and that would be lost were he to dispose of it.

Although he refused to relinquish the manuscript, David Whitmer did show it to the visitors, who called his attention to the fact that the manuscript in his possession was not the original but was the copy made by Oliver Cowdery for the use of the printer. This was clearly demonstrated by the signatures of the witnesses appearing on it, all of which were in Oliver Cowdery's handwriting.

In answer to questions put by the travelers, David affirmed that each of the witnesses had affixed his own signature to the original manuscript, which the Prophet Joseph Smith later placed in the cornerstone of the Nauvoo House. (When the cornerstone was opened afterward, this manuscript was found to have deteriorated badly, although some pages were retrieved and preserved. About twenty-two of these were later delivered to Joseph F. Smith by Sarah Ann Kimball.)

Aside from David Whitmer's affirmation of his testimony, the traveling apostles gleaned little in the way of historical fact from their visit to Richmond. However, the visit was rich in historical insight, especially for Joseph F. Smith. To visit the last home of Peter Whitmer, Sr., who had hosted the Church's organizational meeting in his Fayette, New York, home on April 6, 1830; to realize that Oliver Cowdery, Peter's son-in-law and one of the three witnesses, had died in that Richmond home; to see the only survivor of the three witnesses occupying the same home; and to hear him bear witness of the truth of the miraculous origin of the Church doubtless gave Joseph a sense of relationship and identity with the roots of Mormonism he perhaps had never had before. Moreover, such a feeling would have been intensified by the realization that his traveling companion, Orson Pratt, was ordained an apostle under the hands of the three witnesses forty-three years before when Orson was a young man of only twenty-three. Now his friend, whose shock of white hair and luxuriant white beard betokened his approach to the magical three score and ten, had grown old under the weight and discipline of the apostolic mandate. But despite his age, the testimony he bore of the truthfulness of the restored Church and the divinity of its head, Jesus Christ, was doubtless as young, fresh, and convincing as in the days of long ago when Orson and David and the group of young men with whom they were associated had helped to lay the foundation of the Church.

The historical insight Joseph received from his visits with David Whitmer in Richmond is perhaps best stated in this journal entry: "I always knew that David Whitmer's testimony was true, since I received the witness myself, but now I know that David Whitmer is as conscious of the truth of that testimony as he is of his own existence. No man can hear him tell his experience in these matters but he can see and sense that he is conscientiously telling the truth of his own knowledge. Some might say he was deceived, but I know that he was not. What is strange to me is that he should live only in the past, and that he seemingly cannot comprehend the present. He is alive, he possesses as much light perhaps as he did 42 years ago, and nothing more—there he stands the one lone monument of the first miraculous manifestation of over 49 years ago at the rise of the church, but the church has gone on towards its grand and glorious destiny fulfilling the purposes of God as revealed through his servant the Prophet. David remarked 'Many things have been revealed which were designed only for the church, and which the world cannot comprehend, but the Book of Mormon and those testimonies were to go to all the world.' I responded, 'Yes, and we have sent it to the Danes, the Swedes, the Spanish, the Italians, the French, the Germans, and to the islands of the sea, in fulfillment of that great design. So we have not been idle, and it is also translated into the language of the East Indies.' In parting, David said to Brother Pratt, 'I may never meet you again in the flesh, so farewell.'"

Leaving Richmond, the two apostles traveled northward

to Far West. This stop at Joseph's birthplace was intended to serve the cause of nostalgia more than the cause of historical research. Excited at making the first visit to the place of his birth, Joseph sought out Jacob Whitmer, the son of John Whitmer, who, he had been told, lived there. Since the father, John, was once the Church historian, Elder Smith apparently assumed the son would be willing if not anxious to assist him and Elder Pratt in their historical mission by showing them the important sites in the area. Any such assumption proved to be false. The visitors found Jacob to be a morose, unfriendly, tobacco-chewing, uncommunicative man who showed his disdain for them and their mission by punctuating his remarks with spurts of tobacco juice and by deliberately referring to the Prophet as "Joe Smith." When asked whether courtesy would dictate that the Prophet at least be referred to as "Joseph Smith," Jacob answered bluntly, "Joe Smith is all he is called around here."

Unable to obtain information from Jacob Whitmer or any other local resident, Joseph F. had to be content with Elder Pratt's vague reconstruction of the places connected with Far West's early history. The focal point of the visit was the temple site, where they found the cornerstones dedicated by the Twelve prior to their mission abroad. Elder Pratt reminded Joseph that it was on this occasion that his cousin, George A. Smith, and Wilford Woodruff were ordained apostles and set apart as members of the Twelve. And across the street from the temple site formerly stood the Hyrum Smith home where Joseph F. was born forty years before. After visiting that spot, and presumably after the younger man had had the opportunity to reflect upon the bridge of time that connected his birth with the present and to marvel at the miraculous way in which he had been led and protected, the pair traveled to nearby Cameron, where they spent the night before catching the train the next day to Quincy, Illinois.

From Quincy the apostles traveled to nearby Colchester, where they were warmly received by Joseph's Aunt Lucy Millikan, whose reminiscences brought back memories of Elder Smith's childhood and his happy-sad days at Nauvoo. Learning that Joseph Smith III, the head of the Reorganized Church, had taken up residence at Plano, Illinois, the pair traveled there, hoping to interview the Prophet's son. Finding him away attending a conference, they wired him saying they would await his return; but receiving no answer, the Utahns went on to Kirtland.

Their reception there was hardly more cordial than the frigid one given to them by Jacob Whitmer at Far West. A notable exception was the warm greeting extended by two aged members, Electra Stratton and Rebecca Dayton, both of whom were well acquainted with the Prophet and Hyrum and their wives. Indeed, Mrs. Dayton was present when Hyrum's first wife, Jerusha, died, and willingly led the visitors to her grave.

After paying his silent respects to this beloved "aunt" whom he had never met but whose memory he had always honored as his father's first wife, Joseph was enthralled as Elder Pratt conducted him on a tour of the town, which, until then, had existed for him only in imagination. The streets, which were strange to him, suddenly became familiar when he learned their names—Joseph Street, Hyrum Street, Cowdery Street, and so on—given in honor of the early leaders of the Church, who, during seven short years of residence there, had left an indelible imprint that time could not erase. The most enduring mark these early apostles had left was the imposing temple, where had occurred some of the most astonishing spiritual manifestations since Pentecost—the appearance of the Savior, of Moses, and of Elijah, among others. To one imbued with a historical sense as Joseph F. Smith was, and being there on assignment to gather historical data, Kirtland became an object of special interest and study.

It was here that Joseph F.'s father had commenced his role as a Church administrator, serving in the bishopric, and then on the general level as a counselor and assistant to his younger brother, the Prophet. Also it was to this place his beloved mother had come after her conversion in Canada. And it was here that his parents had become man and wife and had commenced their short, turbulent life together. In a real sense, then, the young apostle's earthly roots extended back to this sleepy Ohio town, once so vibrant and bustling as it pulsated with the unleashed energy of men and women bent on changing the world; and now languishing in a backwash of apostate bitterness and hatred. The two apostles felt that animosity almost the moment they entered Kirtland, a feeling that was to remain with them until they departed for Palmyra, New York.

At Palmyra, the cradle of the Church, the traveling historians felt a sense of peace and spirituality lacking in Kirtland, a feeling that was greatly intensified when they visited the Hill Cumorah. There they cut branches from a grove of trees, intending to have canes carved from them, and feeling a compulsion to do so, knelt in prayer. "We prayed long and fervently for all Israel and for all the interests of Zion," wrote Elder Smith, "earnestly thanking, praising and beseeching God." (Diary, Sept. 16, 1878.) Then, moved upon by a prophetic impulse, Elder Pratt laid his hands upon Joseph's head and gave him an apostolic blessing, following which Elder Smith reciprocated and blessed his companion. Although Orson Pratt had been a member of the Twelve for three years when Joseph Fielding Smith was born, there was no generation gap between this pair, whose lives were wrapped up in testifying of the Savior's divinity and redemptive mission and in helping to prepare a people for his second coming.

Traveling on to New York City, where they transacted business pertaining to missionary work and immigration, the elders started home on September 21, 1878, using railroad passes obtained for them by Church agents John Sharp and William C. Staines. This gratuity came just in time, as the brethren, whose traveling budget was exceedingly tight, were almost out of money.

As the train carrying the two apostles slowly left the Grand Central Station on Manhattan Island, Joseph wrestled with a problem whose complexity baffled him. It involved his cousin, Joseph Smith III, whose snub at Plano had annoyed the brethren and had given them cause to ignore him thereafter. But they were unable to do this because President John Taylor had asked them specifically to try to examine the original transcript of Joseph Smith's revision of the scriptures, which was then in the possession of the president of the Reorganized Church. President Taylor's mandate had caused Joseph F. to wire his cousin at Plano from New York City, requesting permission to see the manuscript on the way home. The curt answer, sent collect, was unsettling to say the least: "Cannot tell till I see you."

With his funds running low, and knowing that a side trip to Plano would be costly and time-consuming and its outcome uncertain, Joseph F. toyed, if only momentarily, with the idea of abandoning the attempt to see the manuscript. However, convinced at last he could not explain to President Taylor his failure to make a final attempt, he parted with Elder Pratt at Chicago and spent most of his remaining funds to purchase a round-trip ticket to and from Plano.

The results were disappointing but not unexpected. Unlike the visit of these sons of the martyrs in Nauvoo in 1860, when Joseph F. was en route to England, the Plano interview was marked by a pronounced coolness and aloofness on the part of the Prophet's son. He flatly refused Joseph F.'s request to see the original manuscript. He did, however, present him with a printed copy the Reorganized Church had published in 1867. However, this was of little help to the Utah visitor, since the Church already had a copy of the manuscript that had been made by Dr. John M. Bernhisel while Joseph Smith was still alive.

The reasons for the radical change in attitude of Joseph Smith III toward his cousin between 1860 and 1878 are nebulous. It is inferred that part of the difficulty lay in Joseph F.'s elevation to the Twelve in the interim. The problem here would not have been that Joseph F. had advanced, but rather that he had advanced to the body upon which Emma and her children laid the blame for what they regarded as serious doctrinal deviations—chiefly polygamy. And it may be that the president of the Reorganized Church still smarted from the embarrassing failure of the proselyting mission his brothers, Frederick and David, undertook to Utah several years before. Whatever the reason, the abrupt and unfriendly treatment Joseph F. received from his cousin in Plano the latter part of

September 1878 was to color the relationship between this pair during the remainder of their long lives and, to an extent, was to infect their families with resentments that only now are beginning to dissipate.

It was a sad and disappointed Joseph F. Smith who returned to Chicago, where he boarded a train headed west. The evening of September 28, 1878, he arrived at the Salt Lake City depot, where he was greeted lovingly by his family.

Upon his return, Elder Smith again took up his duties in the Historian's Office and assumed the direction of the Endowment House. He also continued to fill stake conference and other speaking assignments and unfailingly gave good counsel and admonished the people to obedience and diligence. A talk delivered at the April 1879 general conference typifies the selflessness of his service and provides insight into the special challenges and problems that faced Elder Smith and the Twelve at that time: "We should all be willing to labor for the welfare and salvation of the people—to sacrifice our own desires and feelings for the good of the whole, being perfectly willing to do the bidding of the Almighty, with no will of our own but to serve the purposes of the Lord. . . . When we possess the spirit of the Gospel and faith in God, as we should, we will have no burdens that will be difficult to bear; on the contrary, we will find our 'yokes easy and our burdens light,' and it will be a pleasure to do our duty, whatever that may be." Having spoken about the principles of sacrifice, faith, and diligence, Elder Smith went on to catalog some of the special challenges that faced the Church: "The sending of Elders from year to year, and thousands of dollars annually to gather the poor is not all we have to do. We have home industries to look after. We must provide employment for our people, that when they are gathered home they may not be idle for want of remunerative labor. We should establish branches of industry from which we could at least provide for our own necessities and as soon as possible be able to export our home productions, and thus give employment to every faithful Latter-day Saint who is gathered to Zion, that individuals may not only become self sustaining but contribute their proportion to the general good. Our manufactories should be fostered, patronised and protected, and their staple wares sought after and preferred by the people, even though they were more costly at first. It needs no argument to prove to the sagacious and far seeing that this policy will pay the best in the end." (JD 20:343, 346.) Elder Smith then went on to sound a theme that had dominated the thinking of the leading brethren since before the completion of the transcontinental railroad and that would be in the forefront of their planning for many years in the future. "Every Latter-day Saint should be proud to wear *home made* clothes, from head to foot," he admonished, "and when we begin to study our *best* interests, and the interest of Zion we will do so though it costs us more now than to wear the stuffed, starched, glossed and glittering shoddy of the world, or even the best the world affords." The philosophy behind this policy was not hard to enunciate or understand: "Money spent in home manufactures is money saved to the community, it is money laid up for future use and benefit at home, while money sent abroad builds up New York, Boston, Philadelphia, Lowell, and the world generally all of whom are opposed to the people and the work of God and will only return evil to us for the patronage we bestow upon them." (Ibid., p. 347.)

This talk, perhaps as much as any other he ever delivered, shows the metamorphosis of Joseph F. Smith from the preacher-proselyter he had been for almost a quarter of a century to the ecclesiastical statesman he was to be for almost forty years.

Chapter Twelve

Service in the First Presidency Begins

T he economic issues facing the Saints, referred to by Elder Smith in his general conference address in April 1879, were far overshadowed by an issue that had assumed ominous proportions three months before the conference. On January 6, 1879, the United States Supreme Court had affirmed the criminal conviction of George Reynolds, secretary to the First Presidency, who had been charged with unlawful cohabitation under the 1862 antibigamy law. And, necessarily, that decision affirmed the constitutionality of the 1862 law, a fact that threatened serious consequences to the Saints and confronted them with an agonizing dilemma—whether to follow the prophetic mandate to live the doctrine of plural marriage or to observe the conflicting law of the land, whose constitutionality had now been affirmed. And the problem was further complicated by a tenet of the Saints that obligated them to honor, obey, and sustain civil law.

Until the Reynolds decision, Church leaders had been able to reconcile this conflict by an honest assertion that the 1862 law was unconstitutional. But the Reynolds decision completely destroyed that premise, leaving the stark alternatives of abandoning plural marriage or entering on a course of deliberate civil disobedience. That the Saints embraced the second alternative only hints at the depth and sincerity of their religious convictions, for there could have been little doubt that they clearly foresaw the fearful consequences that would result from that course. President John Taylor voiced his views on the subject at a July 24 celebration held in 1880 during the Church's Jubilee year, views also held by Joseph F. Smith and the other members of the Twelve: "There are events in the future," President Taylor told his listeners, "and not very far ahead, that will require all our faith, all our energy, all our confidence, all our trust in God, to enable us to withstand the influences that will be brought to bear against us. . . . We cannot trust in our intelligence; we cannot trust in our wealth; we cannot trust to any surrounding circumstances with which we are enveloped; we must trust alone in the living God to guide us, to direct us, to teach us and instruct us. And there never was a time when we needed to be more humble and more prayerful; there never was a time when we needed more fidelity, self-denial, and adherence to the principles of truth, than we do this day." (JFS, p. 253.)

Less than three months after uttering these prophetic words, John Taylor was sustained as the third president of the Church. And selected to stand with him as the Church faced one of its greatest challenges were two able young apostles, George Q. Cannon and Joseph F. Smith, who had proven their loyalty and demonstrated their faith and abilities during long years of service at home and abroad.

In assuming the heavy responsibilities of the presidency, John Taylor, speaking for himself and his counselors, said this about the Quorum of the Twelve Apostles, out of whose ranks the new First Presidency had been drawn: "And now let me refer with pride to my brethren of the Twelve here, which I do by saying that while they as a quorum held the right by the vote of the people to act in the capacity of the First Presidency, yet when they found, as Brother Pratt expressed it this morning, that they had performed their work, they were willing to withdraw from that Presidency, and put it in the position that God had directed, and fall back into the place that they have always held, as the Twelve Apostles of the

Church of Jesus Christ of Latter-day Saints. I say it is with pride that I refer to this action and the feeling that prompted it. I very much question whether you could find the same personal exhibition of disinterested motives and self-abnegation, and the like readiness to renounce place and position in deference to principle, among the same number of men in any other place." (JD 22:40.)

It was with a sense of regret, then, that President Taylor and his counselors left the quorum they had learned to love and launched into the deep waters of the First Presidency, where they were to experience alternating exhiliration and apprehension as they piloted the Church through some of its darkest days.

The new president had chosen his counselors well, selecting young, vigorous men who not only were effective expounders of the faith but who were efficient and knowledgeable administrators with experience in public affairs. George Q. Cannon, whose literary interests and attainments paralleled those of his president, had had wide experience on a national level through his membership in the U.S. Congress, and Joseph F., as already noted, had been active in the Utah Territorial Legislature and on the city councils of Salt Lake City and Provo.

While the new First Presidency immediately became involved in a wide variety of affairs covering the whole spectrum of Church administration—proselyting, immigration, colonization, and the regulation of Church affairs at home and abroad—the issue that most absorbed their attention was the one spotlighted so dramatically by the Reynolds decision—plural marriage. As soon as that decision was handed down, enemies of the Church intensified their attacks upon the Latter-day Saints, agitating for more repressive legislation intended to stamp out the practice. Given their commitment to the revelation upon which the doctrine of plural marriage was based, the reaction of the First Presidency was predictable. They began to resist the enforcement of what they considered to be unjust laws with every reasonable device available to them. President John Taylor set the tone of the Church's stand in these tough words: "While we are God-fearing and law-abiding, and respect all honorable men and officers, we are no craven serfs, and have not learned to lick the feet of oppressors, nor to bow in base submission to unreasonable clamor. We will contend, inch by inch, legally and constitutionally, for our rights as American citizens." (Smith, *Essentials in Church History*, p. 486.)

In the meantime, President Taylor's counselors were politically active at the federal and territorial levels in an effort to shape policies more congenial to the Saints. President Cannon continued to serve in the U.S. Congress (although he was later illegally deprived of his seat) and Joseph F. Smith served in the territorial legislature and presided over the constitutional convention called in 1882.

But the brethren were fighting against a powerful tide of anti-Mormon sentiment that crested in March 1882, with the passage of the Edmunds Act. This harsh bill effectively deprived the Mormon leaders of the right to vote and hold political office and imposed criminal sanctions upon those cohabiting with more than one wife. Soon after the enactment of this law, the federal government commenced an intensive campaign of enforcement made more ominous by the adoption by the courts of what was called the segregation ruling. The effect of this extraordinary device, which was later held unconstitutional, was to constitute each day during which one lived in plural marriage as a separate offense, punishable to the full extent allowed by the statute. This creative legal doctrine carried the potential threat of lifetime imprisonment for Mormon polygamists and is credited with being the chief reason for the flight of Church leaders to the underground.

As if to underscore his resolve to adhere to the revelation on plural marriage, President Taylor directed many leaders to take additional wives during the early 1880s. Among those was President Joseph F. Smith, who, in obedience to his leader, was sealed to Alice Ann Kimball on December 6, 1883. And on January 13, 1884, he was sealed to his last wife, Mary Taylor Schwartz.

It is doubtful that President Smith ever experienced a more stressful period than during 1884 following his marriage to Mary Schwartz. He was then responsible for the sustenance of five wives and seventeen children; and later in the year, Julina give birth to her namesake, Julina Clarissa, and Sarah gave birth to another son, Willard Richards Smith.

Even under the most favorable circumstances, it would have been difficult to support and direct a family of this size. But to add to the task of clothing, feeding, and housing such a clan, the trauma of helping to direct an international church and of contending with the harassment of a zealous corps of federal sleuths and prosecutors imposed a crushing, almost unbearable burden. And because of his position in the First Presidency, his connection with the Church Historical Department, and his supervision of the Endowment House, Joseph F. was a special target of the federal establishment.

To avoid arrest and prosecution, President Smith had been living on the underground for some time prior to 1884. During the early phase of this interlude, he had several places of retirement, called "Solitude Gloria," "Serene Plentiful," "Camp Affinity," and "Camp Tempora Mutata." These code words enabled correspondents to know his whereabouts without divulging the location to enemies who might intercept the mail. These places of refuge were located in Davis, Weber, and Box Elder counties north of Salt Lake City.

To give Joseph a respite from the constant pressure of remaining concealed in a "safe place," President Taylor sent him on a tour of Latter-day Saint communities in Utah, Colorado, New Mexico, and Arizona the latter part of August 1884. Using a disguise, as he often did during these days, he boarded a train on August 29. Joining him later was his wife Edna and their ten-month-old son, Robert. Also accompanying him was Elder Erastus Snow of the Twelve and his wife, Elizabeth, and Andrew Jensen of the Historian's Office, who went only as far as Price, Utah. There the travelers were joined by Elder John Morgan, a promising young leader who would be sustained as a member of the First Council of Seventy at the following October general conference.

Going by rail, stage, and wagon, President Smith's party traveled over thirty-seven hundred miles during a thirty-three-day trip, in the course of which they held dozens of meetings with Church members in such remote places as

Mancos, Colorado; Bluff, Utah; Tera Maria, New Mexico; and St. Johns, Arizona. In all these communities and many others like them resided Latter-day Saints who had been called or assigned to settle in particular localities as part of the Church's vast colonization plan. Often these colonists were hand-picked to fill specific roles in designated communities. Many others settled of their own accord or were assigned on an impromptu basis. President Smith made an assignment of the latter kind on September 24 when he encountered a Brother Barney while traveling in an isolated part of Arizona. "We were met at noon by Bro. Barney," President Smith recorded, "whom we directed to Erastus to settle." Assuming that Brother Barney was a typical Latter-day Saint of that time and place, he would have gone on his way rejoicing that he had been assigned by a member of the First Presidency to settle in a community bearing the first name of the apostle who was with him. It would have made little difference that Erastus was one of the least promising communities in the entire area and that the chances of making an abundant living for his family were practically nil. The important thing was that he had been directed by one he sustained as a prophet and that following the direction of one of God's emissaries carried its own reward.

On September 29, at La Junta, on the way home, President Smith received this cryptic telegram: "Am advised to say do not the Saints need your instruction? You are not needed here at present. Snow and Morgan can return." The diarist then furnished us with this interpretation of what might otherwise have been viewed as a garbled message: "This means a 'packed grand jury' and their intention to indict polygamists."

Forewarned about the dangers at Salt Lake City, Joseph F. immediately went into seclusion on arriving home on October 3. The following day he was visited by George Q. Cannon, who advised that he "continue quiet a season." His friend and fellow counselor also told him that President Taylor would have come "but did not want to know anything, was uncertain whether he might not be subpoenaed soon or at any time as a witness."

Following the counsel of his brethren, President Smith remained in the seclusion of his Salt Lake home and did not attend any of the sessions of the general conference. A few days later, having been informed by John R. Winder that marshals had been appointed especially to subpoena him and Daniel H. Wells, the second counselor prepared to leave the comfort of his home and to begin an odyssey among the several places of refuge that would hospitably open their doors to him.

During the days on the underground that followed, Joseph F. endeavored to occupy himself with reading, handling a voluminous correspondence, keeping his diary, and counseling with his hosts and those who came periodically from headquarters. But this was hardly enough to occupy a man who had been accustomed to carrying a heavy load of family and Church responsibilities that had filled his waking hours to overflowing. Now, time often was an excess and unwanted commodity. So during this period—perhaps for the only time in his life—President Smith devoted considerable time to games. Checkers was a favorite. "Bro. W. W. Burton bantered me for a game of checkers," he recorded on October 24, "so we got to work and during the day we played some 38 games out of which he got 2 games and 2 drawn games which left me 25 straight games, 7 'skunks' and 2 drawn." As if to make it plain that even champions have their off days, he added, "Last Saturday evening I played two games with him and he beat me straight."

News that came on November 29 was received with mixed emotions. A message from George Q. Cannon advised that President Taylor had called Joseph on another mission to Hawaii as a means of preventing him from being subpoenaed. This prospect of returning to the islands he had come to love was exciting. But the thought of being so far away from his family for an indefinite period was distressing. Packing his valise and donning a disguise, he left the place of refuge and returned home, where he received an enthusiastic welcome. "I found my family all well and overjoyed to see me," he recorded on December 1. "I think my little son Willard Richards, born Nov. 20th at 12:40 a.m. standard time, who was blessed on Nov. 28th by Pres. Geo. Q. Cannon, is a very fine bright boy. This is the first time I have seen him."

At home, Joseph remained in concealment while preparing to leave on his mission. When neighbors or friends came without invitation, he withdrew from sight to avoid detection. The awkwardness of this situation in a home teeming with children is suggested by this December 7 entry: "I am getting quite an experience. It is rather funny to try to conceal oneself at home with so many little prattlers, so happy to see their papa."

Among Joseph's preparations to leave was a visit to his dentist, A. B. Dunford, who, reflecting the accumulated dental wisdom of the day, decreed that all his patient's teeth be extracted! This also required that a plate be made for him. Joseph had hardly become accustomed to his new dentures when on December 18 he blessed all his wives and children, except Julina and her ten-month-old baby, Julina Clarissa, who were to accompany him on his mission. The next day the travelers crossed the Jordan to "Camp Solitude," the home of Bishop Albert W. Davis, President Smith's brother-in-law. At his request, Joseph also blessed all of Bishop Davis's children before departing for Ogden the following day.

The original plan was that the Smiths would travel to Portland, Oregon, there to embark on a ship bound for Hawaii. En route there, however, they received word that heavy snow had blocked the mountain passes and that it was uncertain how long the track would be impassable. Communicating this news to Salt Lake City by telegraph, President Smith was directed to return. Arriving in Salt Lake City, he was advised that his Hawaiian mission would be deferred for the time being. In the meantime, he was invited to accompany a party led by President John Taylor on a three-week trip into Arizona and Old Mexico to counsel and instruct the Saints and to examine the prospects for expanding the Church's colonization effort. The party left Salt Lake City on January 3, 1885, in a private car obtained by Bishop John Sharp, who was a railroad official.

Where necessary, the private car was left on sidings in railroad depots while the party traveled by stage or wagon to remote communities without rail connections. In this manner the brethren traveled through Arizona and into Old Mexico, preaching and counseling as they went. At Hermosillo, the capital of Sonora, Mexico, the Mormon leaders called on Governor Luis E. Torres, who treated them cordially but made no commitments about establishing Latter-day Saint colonies there.

It was a novelty for the travelers, who were accustomed to the harsh winters of the Rocky Mountains, to find citrus groves thriving at Hermosillo in mid-January. Joseph's amazement at this phenomenon can best be measured by the frequency and vividness of his journal entries alluding to it. There was a sense of disbelief in one entry describing a cluster of lemons taken from a grove near Hermosillo which included one specimen with a sixteen-and-a-half-inch circumference.

But Joseph and his brethren were not misled into thinking that they had entered another Eden. They knew from experience the toil, skill, and prayers necessary to coax fruits, grains, and vegetables from an arid soil. And based on counsel they received along the way, they also learned that even were they to obtain the right to establish colonies in this part of Mexico or to acquire new townsites in Southern Arizona, the tribulations of farming would not be the greatest of their difficulties. Here, as in Utah, the practice of polygamy would arouse powerful enmities and suspicions; and in Arizona, as they knew from experience in other communities, they could expect to bear the full weight of federal wrath in the vigorous enforcement of the Morrill and Edmunds Acts.

Reflections of this kind were not calculated to produce feelings of joy or optimism as the party wound its way homeward via California. Traveling in a leisurely fashion through San Bernardino to Los Angeles, the party headed north to San Francisco, passing through some of the most fertile and scenic country to be found anywhere. At the City by the Golden Gate, Joseph F. joined President Taylor and several others in paying a courtesy call on California Governor Leland Stanford, thereby renewing an old acquaintance that stretched beyond the transcontinental railroad linkup at Promontory Point in 1869.

While in the Bay area, the brethren received a cryptic wire

from President George Q. Cannon suggesting that they not leave for Salt Lake City until they received a message from a courier he was sending, a message whose contents he felt could not be entrusted to unknown telegraph operators. The courier, Samuel Hill, brought the disturbing though not wholly unexpected news that arrest warrants and subpoenas awaited the leading brethren on their return, the object of which was to obtain evidence under oath against polygamists. Because the Church historical and Endowment House records were under his charge, and because of his detailed knowledge of their contents, Joseph F. Smith was more sought after by the government investigators than any of the other leading brethren. After weighing the dangers and alternatives, President Taylor at first decided that all would return to Utah as planned. However, during the trip from San Francisco to Sacramento, the President had second thoughts and felt impressed to send Joseph F. immediately on his once-aborted mission to Hawaii. President Taylor put the proposition to a vote. It carried unanimously. So, with little advance notice, President Smith hurriedly prepared to leave the train at Sacramento, which he did during a thirty-minute stop there.

As the train carrying his brethren hissed and puffed its way out of the Sacramento depot, Hyrum's and Mary's son, left alone again, faced an uncertain future fraught with potential dangers and privations. But we detect no sense of self-pity or fear as he turned his face toward the west, toward the warm-hearted and loving people who had nurtured and cared for him more than thirty years before when he was hardly out of boyhood.

Chapter Thirteen

In Exile

Registering at the Silver Palace, a reputable Sacramento hotel that traced its name to the feverish rush for mineral wealth that had agitated that part of California for decades, President Smith spent a restful night January 25, 1885. The following day was a busy one, beginning with the kind of down-to-earth duties he had performed for himself intermittently during much of his adult life: "This morning I mended my clothes, sewed on buttons, etc.," he recorded. After taking a brisk constitutional, Joseph sent two telegrams, both of which he signed "J. Field" for security reasons. The first was to W. W. Burton in Ogden, Utah, asking that he have "Julina accompany Farr to San Francisco." The second was to John W. Young in San Francisco, requesting that he "meet J. F. Speight at foot of Market St. tomorrow." (J. F. Speight was the pseudonym by which President Smith would be known during his exile in Hawaii.) He then wrote letters to Edna, Sarah, Alice, and Mary, took another constitutional, and retired early.

The following morning at breakfast, President Smith was pleased to see his friend George Romney, who had just arrived on the westbound train and who was also destined for Hawaii. These two friends, whose paths would cross many times in the years ahead, joined as companions to travel to San Francisco, where they registered in adjoining rooms at the Truesdell, a quiet hotel on Market Street.

John W. Young, Joseph F.'s host in San Francisco, was President Brigham Young's son and for a while served as one of his father's counselors. Urbane and well connected with the railroad barons in San Francisco, John W. showed President Smith and George Romney the sights, hosting them at some of the fine theaters and restaurants. This unusual diversion for one so habituated to disciplined work was indulged in because President Smith was traveling incognito, and he had a few days to kill until Julina and the baby arrived.

Not content merely to lounge around charming San Francisco while he waited, Joseph decided on two outings that proved to be highly interesting and educational. The first was a trip across the Bay to visit the library and art gallery of the State University at Berkeley. At that time the now-famous University of California boasted a student body of 236 and a potential enrollment of 500. Joseph pronounced the campus and facilities to be "very fine."

On the return trip to the city, President Smith and his companion, Brother Romney, stopped in Oakland, where they called on Ina Coolbrith, President Smith's first cousin, the daughter of Don Carlos Smith. This talented woman, who was later designated the Poet Laureate of California, had rejected the Church and her family heritage. Unwilling to divulge her true identity, she had concealed herself under her mother's maiden name. With no apparent attempt at either humor or irony, President Smith noted that Miss Coolbrith received the visitors "cooly but kindly," making them wait for some time before she received them. In later years, he was able to break down his cousin's prejudice in part by carrying on a friendly correspondence with her and by giving her money in times of need.

The second outing was to San Quentin, the state penitentiary, where the visitors were shown through the entire facility by a guide. In contrast with the turmoil that has recently beset many of today's prisons, Joseph noted, "Everybody was busy and orderly," a fact presumably the result of the numerous industries carried on within the prison. "They had machinery and steam power for manufacturing doors, sash, shutters and furniture of various descriptions," he recorded, "a tannery, saddle & boot & shoe manufacturies; jute sack manufactury; iron foundry and numerous other means of industry."

Julina and her baby arrived on Friday, January 30, 1885, and three days later the party boarded the *Mariposa*, a three-thousand-ton steamship bound for Hawaii. The extraordinary pressure on President Smith at the time, occasioned by the threats to arrest him and to seize the important records under his control, is suggested by the manner in which he boarded the *Mariposa:* "Bros. Romney, Davis, Farr and Young took the women and children to the boat," Joseph noted in his journal. "Bro Geo Crismon and I sauntered over to the adjoining pier and there he left me to reconnoiter. Meanwhile Bros. J. W. Young, O. P. Arnold, L. Farr, Geo. Romney, & A. W. Davis were on the lookout on and around the vessel. The way seemed to be clear and at about 20 minutes to 3 I came on board and at exactly 3 p.m. we cut loose from the pier and were soon underway."

After a week at sea, the travelers reached Honolulu, where they were met by Elder Enoch Farr, who drove them across Oahu to the Church plantation at Laie. The presiding officer in the islands at the time was Edward Partridge, whom President Smith had known during his first mission to Hawaii thirty years before. Elder Farr approached the mission president alone upon arriving at Laie and informed him that several "strangers" would soon arrive to see him. The mission president said this news almost made his wife Sarah sick, because there was nothing in the house to feed guests. Two of the strangers were identified as Mr. and Mrs. J. F. Speight from San Francisco. The annoyance and anxiety of President Partridge and his wife turned to elation when the Speights turned out to be Joseph F. and Julina, with whom the Partridges were well acquainted and with whom they felt at ease.

During the short time they were together at Laie, President Smith and Edward spent many happy hours reminiscing about their boyhood missionary experiences in the islands and about the vast changes time had wrought. Joseph treasured the friendship of old and trusted associates, a quality clearly evident in a farewell he extended to Elder Partridge, who left the islands for home shortly after Joseph arrived. Following the presentation of a gift to the departing leader by the missionaries and Saints, President Smith said to him, "My Dear Brother Edward: Had this means of brotherly confidence and affection been tendered to you some thirty years ago, when we were boys together on these beautiful isles of the Sea, I would have claimed a position in the first rank in rendering my mahalo, amekou aloha, and even now while others and newer friends endeared by more recent association may claim the pleasure and the honor of presenting you with this souvenir of their love, I doubt not that my confidence, esteem and brotherly regard, for a friend so worthy, would favorably measure in height and depth and width with any man's. In this regard I do not yield the first place, but with pleasure I accept the privilege of feebly asserting the strength of my weakness for you. I am happy that our motto now, as thirty years ago, is, never shrink from duty nor fear to meet the consequences of an honest, righteous act." (JFS, pp. 264-65.)

This eloquent tribute to an old friend befitted the dramatic ritual during which the Hawaiian Saints bid farewell to the departing mission president and his wife. Dressed in their best clothing, clean and brightly colored, and decked with wreaths and leis of fragrant tropical flowers, and carrying flags and banners, the members at Laie, both old and young, paraded in front of the mission home before the scheduled departure of the Partridges. A band leading the procession set a tone of enthusiasm and gaiety that was echoed in all the proceedings that day.

Forming a square opposite the porch of the home, leaders and friends read prepared tributes to the departing couple, including the one given by President Smith. After the tributes and the formal presentation of gifts, the well-wishers followed the band in a holiday mood to the schoolhouse, the entire floor of which had been covered with clean mats. Three "settings," or tables, arranged to form an open-ended square, groaned with the bounties of Polynesian cuisine—poi, yams, beef, fowls, fish, pork, bananas, coconuts, and a variety of other foods. Accompanying the meal were songs and hymns, some composed for the occasion, as well as mystic chants that traced the ancient legends and customs of Polynesia. Following the banquet and entertainment, which occupied most of the afternoon, the party returned to the mission home, where the Hawaiian Saints offered their manao alohas and shook hands with the honored pair until late hours. In the course of these farewells, many asked for and received special blessings from both Joseph F. Smith and President Partridge. "I suppose," President Smith said of the festive event, "this exhibition of love and respect for a returning Elder was never excelled."

It was the warmth and overflowing love shown in this farewell that so endeared the Hawaiian Saints to President Smith. And these feelings were reciprocated in kind by a people who seemed to adopt a proprietary attitude toward this mature, powerful man who now occupied a position of high authority in the Church but who to them—at least to the older Hawaiian Saints—would always be their Iosepa, the orphan missionary.

President Smith's stay in Hawaii on this his third mission there was to be a time of unsettled joy. What prevented it from being one of the most delightful and idyllic periods of his life was the separation from most of his family and from his associates in the leadership of the Church. Moreover, uncertainty about the length of his stay, and a vague sense of unease about being unable to fulfill his worldwide responsibilities while pinned down to a few small islands in the Pacific added to his feelings of impatience and unrest.

But Joseph F. had a philosophical bent that enabled him to minimize unpleasant or negative thoughts and experiences and to live for the day. It was in this spirit, then, that he began to take advantage of the opportunities exile afforded. While he continued to exercise priesthood authority, counseling with the young mission president who succeeded Elder Partridge, holding conferences, instructing missionaries and the Saints, and supervising aspects of the work at the plantation, this did not occupy all his time, and he was left free to pursue personal interests in a way he had never before been able to do. This sudden change in his way of life is graphically reflected in his writings, which, until this epoch, had been essentially factual and almost clinically precise and brief. An entry made on March 16, 1885, suggests the vast change in outlook and literary style six weeks in exile had wrought: "Took a short walk with Julina & baby on the hill overlooking the rice lois and valley of Laie. The picture was beautiful. The mountains rising high up in the west and south bathed in fleecy clouds, and in the falling shadows of the early evening formed a dark background studded here and there by the star-like glimmering of the lighted cottages of the natives, which sparkled like golden spangles on a robe of velvet; and in the north and east the sea, illumined by the reflections of the mellow rays of twilight, appeared like a vast mirror, limited only by the distant horizon, set in a flame of floss-like clouds and standing on the base of coral reefs along the shoreline ruffled in the gausey frills of the foaming surf."

The obvious care with which this was written implies that the author had the time to select his words carefully and to craft them so as to convey a clear picture of the scene he described. And the elevation and beauty of the language also suggests an innate poetic gift that, given time and motivation, could have brought the author significant literary success.

Another offering, among the many Joseph composed during his exile, is this excerpt from his description of Haleahala, the mammoth crater on Maui, which towers to a height of ten thousand feet: "Frequently during the day, over its desert plains, strewed with cinders and ashes, and its black and frowning chimneys, soft, white clouds would float in through the fissure in the northern wall, far below us, completely covering its ugly face with a beautiful vapor; which seemed like a rare-wrought veil of exquisite gauze and floss, as if to conceal from view its scarred and blackened features. But the scene all round was scarcely less magnificent. We seemed suspended in mid-air at a dizzy height above the clouds, which lay far below our feet and stretched out in all directions, as far as the sight could reach, in snow white banks piled mountain high. It seemed like a new ethereal world, or as though we had started on an aerial flight to some distant sphere, and could behold our own terrestrial globe far below, wrapped in fleecy robes; and reflecting from its watery surface, through the rifts in the clouds, their beautiful and ever-changing light and shade. Away to the southeast, loomed up the towering summits of Maunas Kea and Loa on the island of Hawaii, far above the mystic, cloudy drapery, shrouding their base. To the west and north, lay the Islands Kahoolawe, Lanai, Molokai, and West Maui, in full view, and in the distance, Oahu, all crowned with ponderous banks of glistening snow-white clouds; which, together with the shadows of their lower surface, reflected back from the ocean mirror, the vastness and ethereal grandeur of the view; presenting a panorama of unbroken splendor, profoundly calculated to fill the mind with awe, and inspire the heart with love and the soul with adoration and humble submission to Him who made the world." (JFS, p. 275.)

One who reads these sentences without knowing their author would be inclined to classify them as the product of one with an advanced education. And it would stretch the credulity of one who did not know their origin to learn that they came from the pen of a man whose formal training had ended in his mid-teens, and that the minimal schooling he did receive was in frontier classrooms that lacked highly trained teachers and adequate equipment and library facilities.

That Joseph F. Smith developed a classic literary style of the kind these excerpts suggest is as much a tribute to his innate mentality as to the discipline and training his home life and ecclesiastical callings imposed. During the few years he had the benefit of parental instruction, Joseph became convinced that the status he would attain on earth or in the hereafter depended largely upon his own exertions. This understanding brought with it a goad for self-improvement and a constant thirst for knowledge. Added to this was the discipline and motivation that grew from the many Church callings he received, beginning in his boyhood. These factors, strengthened by the influence of the Holy Ghost, propelled Joseph F. Smith to a level of accomplishment attained by few. We should not be surprised, therefore, to find a level of intellectual and scholastic achievement in this man that one normally associates with the alumni of our finest universities.

It is easy, however, in appraising Joseph F.'s successful life to assume erroneously that all aspects of it were positive. Joseph F. Smith's life had both peaks and valleys; he had good days and bad days. "I have felt gloomy," he noted on March 18, 1885; and a few days later, on April 3, he recorded, "I have felt humble and solemn today. I trust it bodes good and not ill."

It is apparent that the main source of his uneasiness was concern about his family and Church affairs at home. "O' that I knew my family were all well and comfortable tonight," he confided to his diary on April 1. "There is a strong east wind blowing which, in a colder clime, would be wintery and harsh. Is it blowing gently or unkindly upon my loved ones? Are they warm or cold? Are they wandering and houseless or cozily nestled in their own homes? Are they hungry or fed?; in the midst of friends or foes, fretted or peaceful? Peace be still!"

Isolated as he was from the great drama being enacted at home, and powerless to play any role in it other than as an interested spectator, he avidly read all the news about it that came to him in newspapers or letters. The intensity with which he entered vicariously into the battle that raged far across the Pacific is suggested by this entry made on March 19, 1885: "I read the report of the celebration of Grover Cleveland's inauguration and his inaugural address, in which he went out of his way to hit Utah a dab as follows: '. . . and that polygamy in the Territories, destructive of the family and religion, and offensive to the moral sense of the civilized world, shall be repressed.' This seals his doom! for if he falls on this rock he will be broken to pieces." (The antagonism of the Mormons toward President Cleveland, which Joseph F.'s diary entry implies, was moderated in later years when he extended pardons to many Latter-day Saints who had been convicted and imprisoned for polygamy. Indeed, he was memorialized by some Latter-day Saints by naming a street or a child after him in recognition of his acts of compassion toward them.)

A few months after arriving in the islands, President Smith made a discovery that aroused his historical instincts and absorbed him in a sensitive negotiation with L. L. Rice, an eighty-five-year-old Honolulu resident. Mr. Rice, who had been an antislavery editor in Ohio, as well as the state printer, had retired to Hawaii, taking with him many documents accumulated during a long career. In early 1885, James H. Fairchild of Oberlin College in Ohio visited Mr. Rice in Hawaii and urged him to sift through his papers and to donate to Oberlin for safekeeping any valuable antislavery documents he might find. While acting on this suggestion, Mr. Rice found an old, faded manuscript, about one hundred seventy-five pages, at the end of which was a certificate, signed by several individuals, declaring the manuscript to the composition of one Solomon Spaulding. Word of this discovery soon reached the ears of President Smith, who was understandably excited, because for years enemies of the Church had accused Joseph Smith of having plagiarized the Book of Mormon from the Spaulding manuscript.

On May 1, 1885, President Smith called on Mr. Rice in Punahou. His journal entry of that date sheds important light on the origin of the manuscript and explains how it came into Mr. Rice's possession: "Afternoon we hitched up the horses to the buggy and drove to Mr. Whitney's at Punahou, where we had an interesting interview with Mr. L. L. Rice. We learned from him that he published for a number of years at Ravenna, Ashtabula Co. Ohio The Ohio Star, an anti-Masonic paper, and that in 1839, he and Mr. Philander Winchester, bought the Painesville Telegraph, of Mr. Eber D. Howe, taking the establishment off the hands of a brother of Mr. E. D. Howe. Names of parties who had written to Mr. Rice for the Ms. were as follows: Mr. Eber D. Howe of Painesville (who gave in his letter an account of how the Ms. came into his hands, namely, it was brought to his printing office by D. P. Hurlburt and left, etc); Mr. A. B. Denning of Painesville, Ohio (who was moderator in the Kelly-Braden discussion in Kirtland some time ago, and who says he is writing a book entitled, "The Death Blow to Mormonism"; he seemed more than eager to get possession of the Ms, and almost imperatively demanded it be sent to him 'without delay', as he wanted to make some extracts from it); Joseph Smith of Lamoni, Iowa, who wanted it sent to the Chicago Historical Society; and also from Albert D. Hayes, librarian of the above; also from Mrs. Elden E. Dickenson, grand niece of Solomon Spaulding, from whose mother, Mrs. Davison, the Ms. was stolen by D. P. Hurlburt."

In these words, President Smith set the stage for the climax of a drama that had commenced almost half a century before. The main actors in it were the Eber D. Howe and the D. P. Hurlburt he referred to in his journal, the former being the author of *Mormonism Unvailed,* the ancestor of most of the anti-Mormon works that followed, and the latter being the man who had either compiled or composed the spurious affidavits upon which Mr. Howe's book was largely based. The apparent reason for Eber D. Howe's eagerness to regain possession of the Spaulding manuscript is to be found in two related facts. First, the title page of his fanciful book states in reference to the Book of Mormon, that he would provide "full detail of the manner in which the famous Golden Bible was brought forth before the world to which are added inquiries into the probability that . . . the said Bible was written by one Solomon Spaulding, more than twenty years ago, and by him intended to have been published as a romance." Second, James H. Fairchild, the Oberlin College representative, who was a disinterested nonmember, wrote an article that appeared in the February 5, 1885, issue of *The New York Observer,* which stated in part, "The theory of the origin of the Book of Mormon in the traditional manuscript of Solomon Spaulding will probably have to be relinquished." After detailing the circumstances under which the manuscript was found among Mr. L. L. Rice's papers, the article went on to say, "There seems no reason to doubt that this is the long lost story. Mr. Rice, myself and others, compared it with the Book of Mormon and could detect no resemblance between the two, in general or detail. There seems to be no name or incident, common to the two. The solemn style of the Book of Mormon, in imitation of the English Scriptures, does not appear in the manuscript. The only resemblance is in the fact that both profess to set forth the history of the lost tribes. Some other explanation of the origin of the Book of Mormon must be found, if any explanation is required."

From this appraisal by men who had nothing to gain or lose in the outcome, it is inferred that Eber D. Howe was anxious to obtain and suppress the manuscript to prevent further erosion of the credibility of his book, which even beforehand was at low ebb among intelligent, objective observers. Moreover, the contents of the manuscript made it clear that from the beginning Mr. Howe had set on a course of deliberate deception, a fact he would have wanted to conceal. Such considerations would explain the apparent urgency President Smith felt to obtain a copy of the manuscript, since he was told at the May 1 meeting that Mr. Rice intended to send it to the Oberlin College Library by the next steamer, scheduled to leave in two weeks. The risk was too great that the manuscript would become "lost" again, either through accident or through deliberate theft by those who stood to lose the most by its publication. So Joseph F. pleaded with Mr. Rice to allow him to borrow it in order to make a copy. He refused. He seemed to harbor vague suspicions about the petitioner's motives, suspicions carrying overtones of animosity toward the Church. But President Smith had felt such animosity intermittently throughout his life and had become immune to it. Indeed, there are hints that he was stimulated by it. In any event, like the good missionary he was, he did not take no for a final answer. He returned again and again until he had broken down Mr. Rice's prejudice.

At length it was agreed that President Smith could borrow the manuscript to have printed copies made provided that it be printed verbatim with fifty printed copies to go to Mr. Fairchild and twenty-five copies to Mr. Rice, along with the manuscript. On learning about this, Mr. Rice's daughter objected strenuously, insisting that the mansucript should not leave her father's possession without the consent of Mr. Fairchild, to whom it had been promised. This protest temporarily impeded President Smith's effort to obtain and print the manuscript. Later, however, the daughter relented to the extent of agreeing that he borrow it to make a single handwritten copy. This was done during a few days of feverish activity in which Joseph enlisted the aid of Julina and several of the missionaries. Working almost around the clock, this team carefully copied and proofread the manuscript, thereby ensuring against the possibility that it would ever again become lost or that Messrs. Howe and Hurlburt or other enemies of the Church would be able to obtain it to alter or destroy it, to the embarrassment of the Church.

This extraordinary effort by President Smith and his associates was later proven unnecessary. Through further contacts and explanations, he was able to persuade both Mr. Rice and the daughter of his reliability and good intentions. Thereupon he was permitted to take the manuscript under the original conditions. He then sent it to Salt Lake City, where the necessary copies were printed. It was then shipped back to Hawaii, where Joseph turned it over to Mr. Rice.

In addition to the copies delivered to Mr. Fairchild and Mr. Rice, the Church published many other copies, which were promptly put up for sale in Mormon book stores. With such wide publicity being given to the actual contents of the Spaulding manuscript, the enemies and detractors of the Church were deprived of a favorite weapon.

Basking in the afterglow of his success in obtaining this historic instrument, Joseph F. decided to take a trip into nostalgia toward the end of the summer of 1885. Accompanied by several missionaries, he left Oahu in late August for a tour of several of the other islands. As anyone acquainted with the president's first mission could have predicted, Maui headed his list. As his small craft, expertly maneuvered by native oarsmen over the tricky reefs and surf, approached the palm-lined beach, a flood of memories must have surged into his mind, memories of illness and health, joy and sorrow, success and failure.

If he needed the lesson, Elder Smith discovered on this trip to Maui that it is never possible to recapture the past except in memory. Soon after stepping ashore, he saddled up and rode inland to Kekoas, where his surrogate mother, Kuaana, lived. The old house had been abandoned and a new frame structure had been built nearby in which his faithful friend now lived. "We visited the old familiar spot, where stood the house," he wrote nostalgically, "now covered with

maniania, and surrounded by paninis, but still looking familiar to my eyes." Continuing with an inventory of this special
place, he recorded: "We visited the place where we used to
bathe, and water our animals, where stood the large wide
spreading kukui tree on which we wrote our names, the site
of the old meeting house on the brow of the hill to which we
were called by the loud kaniana o ka pu each morning at the
break of day, and other familiar spots." Then, as if to reconcile
in part the mental image he carried of the place with the
realities of the present, he observed, "The wide spreading
kukui tree was gone, not a sign of it remaining. The Luawai is
filled up, and over-grown with cactus, and maniania, so also
with the drinking well above."

In token of his visit and by way of a salute to the past, President Smith "gathered a few leaves of ilima and plucked a few
from a eucalyptus tree" and then went in search of Pake, his
first missionary companion in the islands. Although Pake
was now an old man, the years had dealt kindly with him so
that life continued to be a joy and not a burden. The two
friends, whose paths had gone their divergent ways in the intervening years, found a common ground for conversation in
their commitment to the Church and in their shared experiences of long ago. Pake, with his ready smile and friendly
manner, occupied a place in President Smith's memory that
no one could ever claim or usurp. And to Pake, Iosepa was
the epitome of grace and achievement, an apostle of the Lord,
whom he dearly loved and admired.

While on Maui, Joseph's mind was called up to serious re-
flection about his associate in the First Presidency, George Q.
Cannon, whose Polynesian name was Pukuniahi. He visited
Kapalaalaia, where Pukuniahi first made his home on Maui.
There Joseph F. was shown the Kiawai where his friend baptized the first Hawaiian convert. At this place, President
Smith recorded, he and the other visitors "were shown a large
koa tree, just below the Kiawai, where the natives declare
Pukuniahi was wont to hold forth, and from whence at the
close of his meetings he would repair to the water and bap-
tize." In commemoration of their visit to this place, so rich in

historical lore of the early Church in Polynesia, President Smith and Enoch Farr carved their initials on a nearby koa tree along with the numeral 85.

It was also during this tour of the islands that President Smith visited the crater of Haleakala, the description of which has already been noted.

After a few months, President Smith's life in exile settled into a routine. He interspersed counseling, speaking, and writing assignments with labor on the Church plantation. The hard physical exercise of fencing, cultivating, and harvesting served as a necessary outlet for his pent-up physical energies and also assuaged his mind and spirit of the anxieties that periodically afflicted him. However, no sooner would one source of irritation or distress be laid to rest than another would rise to take its place, or one thought to be dead would be resurrected with all its annoyances alive and well. Usually he could temper his negative feelings about distressing events or circumstances by resorting to the spiritual and philosophical concepts he had spent so long teaching to others. "Trials are necessary to the perfection of mankind," he counseled one of the Hawaiian missionaries, "as friction is necessary to separate the dross of human judgment from the pure gold of divine wisdom." (JFS, p. 280.) Such a philosophy casts a golden hue on all events, whether they be good or bad. Positive and enjoyable happenings are looked upon as just rewards for virtuous conduct, while negative events and adversity are regarded as the honing and burnishing medium by which character is made sharp and bright. But the woes of the human condition often blur or obscure the power and efficacy of philosophical truth. It was so with President Smith, as with all mortals, though not to the extent or the frequency seen in others. So diary entries like this one made on January 6, 1886, show his humanity and his feelings of helplessness as well as his faithful reliance on the power of God: "These are momentous times! My heart feels sick of the world and the awful corruption and abominations that revel it, not only not checked, but upheld and encouraged by the powers that be. O Lord, have mercy on the upright and speedily adjudge and award the wicked according to their works."

150

This anguished plea, recorded January 5, 1886, was prompted by a legal charade enacted in Salt Lake City the previous month. Joseph had spent January 5 reading the December *Deseret News*, whose pages told the titillating story of the arrest of three prominent gentile officials, Samuel H. Lewis, assistant U.S. prosecuting attorney; Oscar C. Vandercook, deputy marshal; and C. E. Pearson, U.S. commissioner, who were chargd with "lewd and lascivious cohabitation." The facts, as they unfolded in court, showed that the three officials had been found and arrested in a house of prostitution. The investigator who gathered the evidence was B. Y. Hampton, a member of the Church. Haled before C. S. Zane, one who stood in the front rank of the gentile judges who rigidly applied the Edmunds Act against Mormon polygamists, the charges, filed against the embarrassed three under a city ordinance, were dismissed because, the judge ruled, their misconduct occurred secretly, and not openly, as he interpreted the ordinance to require.

Undeterred by this setback, the investigator and others obtained a second arrest of the trio, who were then charged before a justice of the peace under a territorial statute; each was convicted and sentenced to pay a fine of $299 and to serve three months in prison. On appeal, the district court dismissed the charges on the motion of Assistant Prosecuting Attorney C. S. Varian, a colleague of the defendant, Samuel H. Lewis, whose scourging prosecution of polygamists had made him anathema to the Mormon community. What seemed to gall President Smith more than anything was that after the charges were dismissed against the three officials, Mr. Varian obtained indictments against B. Y. Hampton and two of the prostitutes with whom the three had consorted on the apparent grounds of entrapment.

Whatever the supposed legal justification for what was done, Joseph F. Smith, who was living in lonely exile because he refused to cast off his polygamous wives whom he loved and honored, was enraged to see a cordon of legal protection thrown around dissolute men who patronized houses of prostitution. His wrath came to a boil when, a month later, he recorded this scathing denunciation on learning that the benign apostle, Lorenzo Snow, had been convicted on three counts of unlawful cohabitation and given the maximum sentence of eighteen months in prison and a fine of $500: "Let lightning strike the infamous, hypocritical bigots who are engaged in this raid," he thundered. And, by way of postscript, he added, "The sooner the better is my prayer." And when, about the same time, he read of the arrest of George Q. Cannon at Corinne when twenty-six armed soldiers took him into custody and guarded him closely until they reached Salt Lake City, he wrote, "It is one of the most outrageous and infamous cowardly proceedings ever perpetrated by this infamous gang of robbers and thieves."

President Smith's understandable anger at the plight of his friends on the mainland, his anxiety over the welfare of his own family, and his feelings of concern about the condition of the Church weighed heavily upon him during this year.

There can be little doubt that all this contributed significantly to the serious illness with which he was afflicted in November. The symptoms began to appear on the sixth of the month, when he recorded that he was "half sick with a cold." Two days later, he characterized his illness as "a severe cold and bronchitis," and by the tenth he noted, "My chest is very sore and my cough is severe." By the sixteenth, he was being troubled with "weakening sweats and chills" at night; and five days later, the President was caught in a heavy rain. "We were all soaked through. My boots were full," he noted.

The height of Joseph's illness was reached on November 24. "My head is very painful and my chest is sore," he recorded on that day. "My cough is terrible and my nightsweats very weakening. I eat less and less food and I am losing flesh rapidly."

This serious illness was aggravated by President Smith's insistence, in the early phases of it, at least, to be up and about his duties. He seemed to be under a constant compulsion to work. Even when he was suffering serious chills and fevers and distressing head and chest pains, he traveled here and there and carried on his varied duties as if he were well. At last, when his weight had dropped to an alarmingly low level and he was devoid of energy, he stayed in bed and allowed

Julina and her daughter Donette (who had arrived in the islands the last of October) to nurse him back to health.

Fourteen-year-old Donette originally had been brought to the islands to help her mother care for a new baby, Elias Wesley, who had been born at Laie on April 21, 1886. Two-year-old Clarissa, an active toddler, also required much attention. This, added to the demands of supervising the household, nursing a new baby, and performing motherly duties for the missionaries, imposed on Julina too heavy a burden, which Donette's assistance was expected to lighten. Her arrival almost coincided with the beginning of President Smith's illness. Fortunately, she was there at the time, otherwise the burden on Julina could have been overwhelming. The role this noble woman and the other wives played in the life of Joseph F. Smith can scarcely be overemphasized. Julina, the first of this group of unusual women, gave birth to eleven children, ten of whom lived to maturity. In addition she raised two adopted children, giving her a baker's dozen. She went about her daily duties with poise, dignity, and complete selflessness, giving love and support to her husband and children and performing endless tasks of charity for those outside the family circle.

In March 1887, Julina and Donette and the two babies returned to the mainland with Albert Davis and his wife. From reading this beautiful and tender excerpt from a journal entry made on March 15, we can gauge the sense of loneliness the exile felt when his family left: "The steamer cut loose at 12 p.m. and at exactly 12:15 she commenced her course out of the harbor; and I took the last look at the receding forms of my loved and loving ones until God in his mercy shall permit us to meet again. When the ship passed the line of sight, I hastened to the Brake with Bro. E. W. Davis, and we drove up past Aaicroaiolimu, where I left Edwin to return the Brake, while I climbed Puuoina to look again at the speeding steamer *Australia* with her precious sacred treasures until lost behind Diamond Head. When once alone, my soul burst forth in tears and I wept their fountains dry and felt all the pangs and grief of parting with my heart's best treasures on earth."

Anyone who has been alone in a foreign land, separated

from loved ones, can understand the anguish that filled President Smith as the steamer carrying his family disappeared from view. And that anguish likely was intensified by the uncertain conditions that existed at home and that had been made worse by the passage a month before of the Edmunds-Tucker Act. This repressive legislation, which sounded the death knell of polygamy, created a federal board to take charge of re-registration and all the election machinery of the territory; abolished women's suffrage; abolished the Emigration Fund Company; dissolved the Church as a corporation; abolished the Nauvoo Legion; escheated most of the Church's property; and established an odious test oath for voters. Because it was confidently expected that this newest tool, fashioned for the destruction of the Church, would lead to a further escalation of the government's vendetta against polygamists, it had been decided that President Smith would remain in the islands for a longer, indefinite period. This decision likely heightened his sadness at the departure of Julina and her children, it being unknown how long they would be separated.

An intervening and unforeseen event abruptly ended Joseph F. Smith's exile in Hawaii and hastened the reunion for which he yearned. This was the illness of President John Taylor. Advised the last of June that the prophet was dangerously ill, Joseph made immediate plans to leave for the mainland. Traveling to Honolulu, he found the city in great turmoil from a widespread revolt against the royal government. On June 30, 1887, President Smith purchased a small trunk, "packed up for off," and then attended a mass meeting at the armory, where about three thousand angry Hawaiians had assembled. Following several vehement and radical speeches, the assembly unanimously adopted resolutions "calling for reform and condemnatory of the constitution, the King and his cabinet." After the meeting, a corps of militia called the Honolulu Rifles "virtually took charge of the City," placing guards over government and other buildings. Ironically, one of the buildings placed under guard was the residence of Joseph's old nemesis, Walter Murray Gibson, who had been one of the king's principal ministers. As if to write a dramatic *finis* to Joseph's exile, Mr. Gibson, the man who had been the cause of the special mission to the islands in 1864, was arrested the next day, not long before the president's departure for the mainland on the steamer *Mariposa*. That arrest signaled the end of the strange, checkered career of one of the most unusual and unorthodox men who ever strode the stage of Mormon history.

Chapter Fourteen

The Storm Intensifies

The fog shrouding San Francisco Bay when the *Mariposa* steamed through the Golden Gate on July 9, 1887, seemed to symbolize and prefigure the three years of trial and uncertainty that faced Joseph F. Smith and the other Church leaders. The most immediate trauma was the serious illness of their leader, President John Taylor. Joseph F. presumably knew that the prophet's condition was grave, or he would not have been asked to leave the security of his exile in Hawaii. It is questionable, however, that he was prepared for the deterioration that had occurred in his leader's health since they were last together. Joseph saw him first on July 18 when he arrived at the president's hideaway in the home of Thomas F. Roueche in Kaysville, several miles north of Salt Lake City. He and George Q. Cannon entered the sickroom together and found the president "sitting in a chair, feet and legs much swollen and in a semi-conscious state." Rousing the patient, Elder Cannon said to him, "This is the first time in two years and seven months since the First Presidency have been together. How do you feel about it?" Answering in a soft, almost inaudible voice, John Taylor uttered the last words Joseph F. was to hear him speak. Said he, "I feel to thank the Lord."

On Monday, July 25, 1887, the prophet, John Taylor, whom Joseph F. Smith called the Great Martyr, breathed his last. The two counselors had spent the day "reading, writing, listening to letters and business" in a room adjoining the prophet's bedroom. Shortly before 8:00 P.M. they were suddenly called to his bedside. "He rallied for a few moments, but precisely at 5 mts to 8 p.m. the Great Martyr breathed his last. Thus what the deadly bullets of the Carthage assassins failed to do 43 years ago the 27th of last June, the malignant persecutions of their successors have accomplished, by driving him into exile to avoid falling into their murderous hands." These bitter sentiments were capsulized into a phrase often heard among the Latter-day Saints: "In Utah was finished what Carthage began." (CHC 6:188.) And later, Joseph F. collaborated with George Q. Cannon to compose this official statement that assessed the blame for President Taylor's death: "President Taylor escaped the death which the assassins of Carthage jail assigned for him. His blood was then mingled with the blood of the martyred Prophet and Patriarch. He has stood since then as a living martyr for the truth. But today he occupies the place of a double martyr. President John Taylor has been killed by the cruelty of officials who have, in this Territory, misrepresented the Government of the United States. There is no room to doubt that if he had been permitted to enjoy the comforts of home, the ministrations of his family, the exercise to which he had been accustomed, but of which he was deprived, he might have lived for many years yet. His blood stains the clothes of men, who with insensate hate have offered rewards for his arrest and have hounded him to the grave. History will yet call their deeds by their right name." (Roberts, *Life of John Taylor*, p. 413-14.)

The anger and outrage these words reflect, which found endorsement in the minds and hearts of all loyal Latter-day Saints, seemed to add fuel to the resolve of their enemies to enforce the repressive antipolygamy laws with increased rigidity. With the battle lines thus drawn, the Latter-day Saints and their enemies moved inexorably toward the climax that would occur three years later.

In the meantime, President Taylor's death brought about significant changes in Church administration. Following the precedents established after the deaths of presidents Joseph Smith and Brigham Young, Joseph F. and George Q. Cannon understood perfectly the subordinate roles they would now play as members of the Twelve, and they were willing to assume those roles immediately. However, following the funeral for President Taylor on July 29, it was found that only five members of the Twelve were present, in addition to the two counselors. Since this did not constitute a majority of the apostles, it was decided unofficially that Elders Smith and Cannon would administer the affairs of the Church until a quorum was present. Acting under this charge, they led out in directing the Church until August 3, by which time three more of the apostles had arrived in Salt Lake City from the underground. At a meeting held on that date, the Twelve, with Wilford Woodruff as their president, formally assumed the leadership of the Church with Joseph F. Smith standing in his place of seniority as the sixth-ranking apostle. This action was ratified two months later at the October general conference when the Quorum of the Twelve Apostles was sustained as the presiding council and authority of the Church.

Aside from the unusual drama of witnessing a change in Church leadership, the conference-goers were treated to an unexpected event when they saw on the stand in the Tabernacle two of the senior apostles who had been on the underground for several years. One of these was Erastus Snow, whose appearance on Saturday, October 8, drew this comment in Joseph F.'s diary: "Bro. Erastus Snow attended and occupied the forenoon. This was his first venture out in public. A rumor was started that a warrant was out for him, so he made himself scarce in the afternoon. It is, however, believed this rumor was a false one."

Once the Twelve began to function as the presiding quorum of the Church, much of the administrative pressure exerted on Joseph F. as a member of the First Presidency was relieved. With the principal governing power now being vested in President Wilford Woodruff, and with policy matters being decided by the Twelve acting as a committee of the whole, Elder Smith, for the first time in many years, found himself in the position of filling ad hoc or committee assignments rather than having defined, continuing duties to perform.

One such assignment came on February 2, 1888, when President Woodruff called him to go to the nation's capital as the Church's representative in the eastern states. A written commission given to him on February 10 defined his authority and responsibility in this highly sensitive position. He was to take charge of all the business affairs of the Church in that region; to preside over the Church branches there and over all the proselyting missionaries; to direct the immigration of new converts; and to act as the Church's political agent. In the last-mentioned capacity, he was to direct and correlate the activities of all Church members in the east who had been or would later be appointed to work toward statehood for Utah.

Armed with this commission, he departed on February 11, 1888, but not before he had been blessed by President Woodruff and Elders Franklin D. Richards and George Q. Cannon, and, in turn, had blessed all his wives and children. His traveling companion was Charles W. Penrose, an able man who sixteen years later would be called to the Twelve by President Joseph F. Smith, and twenty-three years later would be called to the First Presidency, where he would serve as President Smith's second counselor during the last seven years of his administration. It was during this assignment to the eastern states that Elder Smith learned to appreciate the superior qualities of his traveling companion.

Anyone who had checked the passenger list of the train that carried this pair east would not have realized they were aboard, as Elder Smith traveled under the name of Jason Mack, while Elder Penrose was registered as Charles Williams. They would use these pseudonyms during the time they would remain in Washington to conceal their true identities from enemies who might seek to balk them through legal action.

Arriving in Washington on February 17, the travelers were met at the depot by John T. Caine, delegate to Congress from the Territory of Utah, and L. John Nuttall. To see these brethren doubtless evoked memories of long ago for Elder Smith, who had been intimately associated with them over the years under varying circumstances. He had first become acquainted with John T. Caine in 1854 when they traveled together from Salt Lake City to Honolulu as missionaries. At that time, they were not as close as they would be later, as Elder Caine was nine years older than Joseph F. and was then married and had two children. The older man spent most of his Hawaii mission in Honolulu and never learned the native language as Joseph F. did working on the outer islands. Moreover, Elder Caine returned home many months before Elder Smith did. The close relationship between them would not come about until they served together in the constitutional convention that convened in Salt Lake City in April 1882, a convention chaired by Joseph F. Smith and in which John T. Caine served as a delegate from Salt Lake County. The following year Elder Caine, a native of the Isle of Man, who first heard the gospel preached by John Taylor, took his seat in Congress. There he began to use his keen intelligence, his oratory burnished in the fire of missionary service, and his dramatic skills polished on the stages of the Social Hall and the Salt Lake Theatre, to battle the anti-Mormon tide that flowed high in the nation's capital. It was the eloquent voice of John T. Caine that was most often heard in the halls of Congress—indeed it often was the only voice heard—opposing the proposals for ever more repressive legislation against the Mormons. It is no discredit to him that the passage of the Edmunds-Tucker Act in 1887 signaled delegate Caine's defeat in the valiant rear-guard action he had waged.

Once the Edmunds-Tucker Act became law, Elder Caine began immediately to make another effort to obtain statehood for Utah. Toward that end, a constitutional convention was convened in Salt Lake City on June 30, 1887. It was presided over by the Utah delegate to Congress. Convinced that a clause in the proposed constitution prohibiting bigamy and polygamy was the only solution to the so-called "Mormon Problem" and the only thing that would be approved by the United States government, John T. Caine strongly urged its adoption. These sentiments were shared by most of the other convention members and by many Church leaders.

It was less than a month after this constitutional convention that President John Taylor passed away, and but a few months thereafter that Joseph F. Smith received the assignment to go to Washington to act as the Church's political agent.

This was the background against which John T. Caine and his friend L. John Nuttall (who had been President Taylor's personal secretary and who was later to serve President Wilford Woodruff in the same capacity) met the two travelers from Utah at the Washington depot early Friday morning, February 17, 1888.

As the four walked through the station, Delegate Caine called attention to a brass star imbedded in the floor, marking the spot where President James A. Garfield had fallen after being shot by his assassin. Engaging a carriage, the four stopped briefly at Elder Caine's home and then went to the residence of John W. Young, where they also found Latter-day Saint attorney Franklin S. Richards and George F. Gibbs, a secretary to the First Presidency.

That evening a lengthy meeting at the Young residence was attended by those already mentioned and by Senator McDonald and Washington attorney Jeremiah Wilson. The purpose of the meeting was to prepare for a hearing the next day before the Senate Committee on Territories, which was considering another application for statehood from Utah. After making a report about the Washington political scene, Franklin S. Richards and Charles W. Penrose "went to work on an argument to be read before the Senate committee . . . tomorrow." That evening this argument and others prepared by Delegate Caine, Senator McDonald, and Attorney Wilson were read and polished for presentation to the committee. "Our arguments made a marked impression on the committee," Joseph F. recorded the next day. The only negative aspect of the hearing to him was "the vile harangue against Utah" made by Congressman Fred T. Dubois of Idaho. Mr. Dubois had earned the enduring enmity of the Latter-day Saints because of his ruthless enforcement of the anti-polygamy laws while serving as the United States marshal for Idaho. He once boasted in open court that "he had a jury impaneled to try unlawful cohabitation cases that would convict Jesus Christ if he were on trial." (CHC 6:213-14.)

Because of the bitter opposition of men like this, Elder

Smith and his associates felt the need to obtain more documentation to support their position, and for this reason they sought to delay a decision by the Senate committee. "We agreed it was best to work for . . . delay . . . until next session of congress," Joseph recorded after a lengthy meeting on February 20, "as the agitation of our question—the admission of Utah—was bound to excite discussion and prejudice our cause. We also agreed to labor with congressmen to post them on facts, etc."

Having reached a decision about the lobbying strategy to be followed, Elder Smith was able to turn his attention to other matters. One of the most pressing and vexing was the status and attitudes of John W. Young. Prior to the arrival of Elder Smith, Brigham's son had been in charge of the lobbying effort in Washington. And his long association with wealth and power had dictated a style and approach foreign to one having the ascetic background and habits of Joseph F. Smith. Almost the first subject John W. broached after Elder Smith arrived in Washington was his need for $25,000. When it was not forthcoming immediately and when he learned he was to play a subordinate role thereafter in the lobbying effort, Brother Young was "very much worked up." Later Elder Smith understood partially why his friend was in such dire need of money when he saw John W.'s lavish living style. "He is paying $300 per month, for 8 months house rent. He has 4 hired women . . . in the establishment. He keeps two horses and two carriages (and two combination liverymen and butlers). He has Col. Black and family & Col. Smead and family on expenses in Washington; and other heavy drafts upon him."

The differing perceptions of the two men is brought into dramatic focus by the careful, precise way in which Joseph F. Smith recorded every expenditure in his journal. On the day of his arrival in Washington, for instance, he noted, "My expenses today were, porters fees 50¢, cab 50¢ = $1.00." The following day, after noting that he had had an oyster lunch with L. John Nuttall, he recorded, "I took a dozen raw—40¢." And on the first day of a trip to New York, he noted these expenses: "Cab fare 37½¢ [he had shared a cab with Elder Penrose]—provisions 85¢, telegram 25¢, Railway fare $6.50, cash paid to Bro. Penrose, $1, total = $8.97½." And during the time he was in Washington, Elder Smith continued his lifelong habit of mending his own clothes.

A collision was inevitable between men of such diametrically opposed views toward money. The matter came to a head on February 25, 1888, as this diary entry indicates: "Had some talk with John W. Young. He again asked me for $1500.00 but when I desired to know for what purpose, he got mad and vowed he would never ask the church for another dollar. It was quite evident he needs money, and desires this amount to pay up his expenses. . . . I assured him that I could only order the payment of money for legitimate expenses. He railed against the brethren for not sustaining him, for slighting him, ignoring him and much of that sort of thing to which I paid but little attention."

While Elder Young's tirade seemed to have had little if any effect upon Joseph F., it greatly nettled Charles W. Penrose, who was quick to apprise John W. of his feelings: "Bro Penrose did some sharp talking to him," Elder Smith wrote, "and I threw oil upon the troubled waters."

In this incident, we see a mellowing of the combative qualities that were evident in Joseph's demeanor as a boy and young man. Like the disappearance of the acrid flavors of green fruit as it ripens, his personality underwent a gradual change over the years, its prickly aspects being replaced by a loving, indulgent benevolence. Much of this change doubtless came about because of the softening influences of adversity. And the weight of his responsibility added to the self-confidence and feelings of self-worth it produced contributed significantly to his maturation. Also, these sons of the prophets had known each other since boyhood. Joseph F., the eldest by six years, was born in 1838 during the chaos that enveloped Far West before the Missouri expulsion. And John W. was born in Nauvoo in 1844, a few months after the martyrdom of the Prophet and the Patriarch and less than three years before the Illinois expulsion. Therefore, both of them shared a common heritage of persecution and ostracism, of bravery and fortitude. Moreover, they shared the distinction of being the offspring of powerful, influential men in the Mormon hierarchy. At this point, however, their paths diverged sharply, with Joseph F. struggling along the rugged road of orphanhood and poverty and John W. sailing along smoothly under the protection of his influential father.

Joseph F.'s comments about this unpleasant situation reveal a combined sense of pity and irritation. He regretted to see one who had been elevated so high reduced almost to beggary. Yet it was an annoyance to observe in his friend a kind of imperiousness that might be expected only of one occupying a position of dominating authority. But whether moved by pity or irritation, Joseph never questioned John W.'s good intentions and his desires to serve the best interests of the Church. Their views differed only as to procedures, not ends.

In the meantime, other things cried for Elder Smith's attention. One of the most pressing was the regulation of the affairs connected with the emigration of new converts from Europe and the British Isles. Despite the fierce contest in Utah between the Latter-day Saints and the zealous prosecutors who seemed bent on destroying the Church, the proselyting effort flourished abroad. Fervent and aggressive missionaries laboring across the Atlantic, following the traditions set by Joseph F. Smith and others who had preceded them, continued to fuel the Mormon communities in the west with hundreds of new converts. And since the idea of gathering to the United States continued to dominate the thinking of most converts, there were constant problems of transport and logistics that Elder Smith had to oversee.

With matters temporarily in hand at Washington, he traveled to New York City, where on February 23 he conferred with Mr. R. J. Cortis, the general agent for the Huntington Steamship line, deciding the terms on which Mr. Cortis's line would carry Mormon immigrants during the coming year.

In New York City, Elders Smith and Penrose also met Richard K. Thomas, a well-to-do Salt Lake City businessman who made frequent trips east to purchase goods for his store. The merchant hosted his friends at fashionable restaurants and at Broadway plays in the city. Joseph F. was especially pleased with a performance of Shakespeare's "A Midsummer Night's Dream" at the Daly theater, pronouncing it an elegant production with "magnificent" scenery.

In addition to sampling the theaters and cuisine of New York, Joseph did many of the things most travelers do while in this famous city, visiting the Brooklyn Bridge, the Park, the Stock Exchange, and the Produce Exchange, from whose tall tower he had a magnificent view of all the burroughs of Manhattan and the Hudson and East rivers. He also was fitted for a new suit by an exclusive tailor and purchased a new silk hat.

An unpleasant duty he had to perform was to advise the agent for the Guion Steamship Line that the Church was transferring its business to the Huntington Line. The response of the agent, a Mr. Gibson, was predictable and indicates that business negotiations and practices change little from generation to generation. Joseph wrote, "He feels very bad over the prospects of losing our immigration business. We comforted him all we could. He offered a through rate from Liverpool to Kansas City of $32.00. He called the Huntington a 'Tramp Line' and did not think we would be satisfied with the proposed change."

This trip to New York City reveals interesting facets of Joseph F. Smith's character. While he was exceedingly frugal in the management of his own means and those of the Church, he never refrained from spending money on the things he considered important or necessary. So, although he sewed on his own buttons and mended his own garments, he was not reluctant to pay the money necessary to purchase fine and stylish clothing. This same characteristic surfaced often, when, in the latter part of his presidential ministry, he authorized the construction of the Church Administration Building at 47 East South Temple in Salt Lake City, which, in many ways, is palatial in quality and appearance. It also seems significant that he offered no apologies or explanations for having attended the theater three times during his short stay in New York City and for having spent considerable time sightseeing. Meanwhile, he was prompt, thorough, and tough in handling the Church's business affairs and in obtaining the best value for its money, despite the efforts of the disappointed travel agent to belittle and downgrade his decision.

Leaving New York City, Elder Smith and his companion traveled by rail to Philadelphia and thence to Cape Charles, Delaware, where they took a steamer across Chesapeake Bay to Old Point Comfort. From there they traveled by rail to Newport News, Virginia. The reason for this roundabout route from New York City to Washington, D.C., was to enable Elder Smith to inspect the ships of the Huntington Line he had engaged to bring converts from abroad. It was fortuitous that three of the four vessels he had contracted for were in port at the time. So he and Elder Penrose boarded and minutely inspected the *Duke of Buckingham*, the *City of Manchester*, and the *Duke of Westminster*. The last-named ship, which actually made port toward evening of the day of inspection, was pronounced by Elder Smith to be "by far the best emigrant boat." She was "380 ft. long, 41 ft. beam and 8 ft. between decks, with a cabin capacity for 60 persons." The fourth ship, the *Florida*, was a sister ship of the *Manchester*, so, as Elder Smith put it, "we practically saw the whole four, all that have been employed on the line."

The captains of the three vessels, "who were courteous and obliging," doubtless learned early on that while he was an "inlander," he was certainly no stranger to ships. At this point in his career, Elder Smith had made three round-trip voyages of the Atlantic and three round trips to and from the Hawaiian Islands. He had sampled the best and the worst of sea travel, and so it was with a practiced and wary eye that he examined these steamers. Of the *Buckingham* and *Manchester*, he wrote critically, "They are both poorly ventilated, there being but 7 very small port holes on a side—only two of which [on a side] are glass, so that they are almost totally dark."

The Mormon elders were treated to one of those wintry days for which Newport News is noted, featuring a strong northwest wind accompanied by squalls of snow, sleet, and rain. They put up at the Hotel Warwick, where, according to our diarist, everything was first class, "especially prices." At the day's end, Joseph tabulated his expenses, exclusive of the "exhorbitant" hotel bill of $4.00, which he paid the next day:

"Breakfast $1.00 cab 25¢ Bus 10¢ Railway 30¢ Porters fee 37½¢ postage stamps 15¢, total $2.17½¢."

Back in Washington, D.C., Joseph F. launched an aggressive lobbying campaign looking toward statehood for Utah. On March 3, at Elder Smith's direction, Charles Penrose and F. S. Richards counseled with senators Cushman and Davis of Minnesota. Because of Joseph's need to keep a low profile, he also sent this pair two days later to meet with senators David Turpie of Indiana and George Gray of Delaware. In these and other lobbying efforts, the brethren endeavored to present the case for Utah's statehood in the best possible light and to counter any falsehoods the senators may have heard. As to the meeting with senators Turpie and Gray, Joseph F. noted with satisfaction, "These senators were much interested and acknowledged they had heard facts they had not before heard." But not all lobbying produced the same positive results, as witness these acrid remarks about another senator: "Bros. Penrose and Richards had an interview with Senator Henry B. Payne of Ohio; and found him a prejudiced, senseless, soulless old duffer, who, while admitting facts, utterly ignored their force and purpose."

Like a spectator at an athletic contest, Joseph was alternately pleased or dejected as the battle ebbed and flowed. March 10 was a day for rejoicing because of the poor showing of R. N. Baskin, an enemy of the Church from Utah, who once had been a candidate for delegate to Congress and who had been one of the prime movers in the campaign to deprive George Q. Cannon of his congressional seat. Joseph wrote, "R. N. Baskin appeared before the Senate Committee today, but met with a cool reception and fairly subsided or flatted out in the reading of his speech, merely asking for it to be published. Our friends consider it a complete victory for our side, so far as winning the sympathy of the committee, and getting a hearing is concerned. Poor Baskin 'got left'. The brethren were greatly rejoiced."

Despite this temporary "victory," the war for statehood continued unabated. Elder Smith and his brethren did all they could to put the Church's position in the right perspective and to provide legislators with the facts. This was a slow, tortuous process, one that, for the moment, yielded little satisfaction or hope other than this temporary and fleeting success before the committee. So powerful were the forces opposing the brethren and so ingrained were the prejudices against the Latter-day Saints that statehood would be delayed for another eight years.

In June 1888, Elder Smith returned to Salt Lake City, where he remained until December when he returned to Washington, D.C., to continue his lobbying activities. While in Salt Lake City he had to remain anonymous because of the continuing attempts by federal officials to arrest him and subpoena the sensitive records under his control. Therefore, he was unable to participate openly in the October general conference as he would have liked and was forced to do his administrative work behind the scenes.

After spending an enjoyable holiday season in seclusion with his family, Elder Smith departed for the East on December 30, 1888. He left the train just before it reached Ogden and boarded it again after it left the station, thereby avoiding the danger of being recognized and apprehended in the depot. He was joined later by Franklin S. Richards and George F. Gibbs. The other members of the team, Charles W. Penrose and L. John Nuttall, met them later in Washington, where, in cooperation with Delegate Caine and others, they again joined battle to win the elusive goal of statehood.

Because of the danger of being arrested and having the Church's sensitive records subpoenaed, Elder Smith did most of his work behind the scenes. This provided the security he required while enabling him to give overall direction to the lobbying effort. He continued to use the pseudonym Jason Mack and to send and receive all telegraph messages in cipher. He edited and approved the presentations made before the Senate Committee on Territories by F. S. Richards, John T. Caine, and Jeremiah Wilson and afterward arranged to have 15,000 copies of their talks printed. These were then mailed to influential people in Utah and elsewhere, including government officials and secretaries of all bar associations.

In the meantime, Joseph received reports from members of his team about the presentations made at committee meetings and the efforts being made to obtain presidential pardons from Grover Cleveland for convicted or indicted polygamists. Two such cases in which he took a personal interest involved his good friends George Q. Cannon and Charles W. Penrose. These efforts proved successful as to George Q. Cannon on February 21, 1889, when Elder Smith sent his fellow apostle this congratulatory wire: "While deeply regretting the circumstances which have kept you so long confined, I rejoice that today will see you comparatively free once more. I congratulate you and thank God. All here join." And a few days later, this telegram received by Elder Smith, while he was in New York City, signaled a similar conclusion of the efforts to have Charles W. Penrose pardoned: "Report presented yesterday. Williams [Elder Penrose's pseudonym] petition granted. Jon. W. looking after papers. John T. Caine."

At this time, there were no established Mormon congregations in the nation's capital. Therefore, it became necessary for Elder Smith and his associates to arrange for their own worship services, where they bore testimony, instructed each other, and partook of the sacrament. However, given the furtive way in which the apostle had to carry on his activities, it is doubtful he would have attended open meetings of the Saints even had they been held at the time. Occasionally, as a matter of curiosity or to broaden his knowledge of religion generally, he would attend the services of other denominations. Under these circumstances, congregations of Baptists, Quakers, Spiritualists, Jews, and others entertained unawares a modern Christian apostle. Interestingly enough, it was the non-Christian confirmation service of the Washington Hebrew Congregation, held May 16, 1888, that affected him most deeply. "I saw some of the most beautiful children's faces I ever beheld," he said of the fifteen children who were confirmed that day. And as the children embraced their parents, the Mormon patriarch, perhaps reminded of his own beloved children, was overwhelmed with emotion. "I saw through my own tears, Brother Nuttall wiping his eyes, together with many others, as the children embraced their parents and received their blessings. It was too much to resist the sympathetic tear." And then, alluding to the profound affinities between the Mormon and Jewish cultures, he added, "I felt it was a worthy example for my own children, and those of the Saints, who not only should embrace Judaism, but inseparably connected therewith, true Christianity. Christ was a Jew."

As time permitted, the Utah lobbyist also visited the libraries, museums, and art galleries that abounded in the nation's capital. The Smithsonian Institution was a favorite place, where he never tired of inspecting the many exhibits. One day he was looking at an exhibit of mounted marine life when he heard a congressman from Maine ask the curator why he did not get a larger specimen of a certain fish. Bridling, the curator explained condescendingly that this species of fish didn't grow any larger. The congressman disputed the statement, saying he personally had caught larger fish of the kind. Assuring the visitor he was mistaken, the curator said he had made a lifelong study of fish and that he could not be wrong. Seeing he would need facts to convince the man of science, the congressman turned to Elder Smith, saying he intended to write home for a specimen and asking if he would be willing to return when the fish arrived so he could be present when it was presented. Elder Smith agreed, and some time later when the fish had arrived, he returned to the Smithsonian and watched the congressman present a much larger specimen of the fish to an embarrassed curator. "Well, well," said he after measuring the fish with a practiced eye, "a lifetime of scientific study is here destroyed by a demonstration of a simple fact."

Despite the excitement of being in the capital and of being involved in important and challenging work, Joseph had his moments of despondency. "I have felt deep anxiety all day," he wrote on February 2. The reason for his gloomy feelings on this occasion was concern for the welfare of his family. Earlier he had received a wire that said that members of his family might be subpoenaed by the grand jury. He immediately sent instructions as to how the family should be dispersed until the crisis had passed and then offered a fervent prayer for their protection.

By early March 1889, Elder Smith had done all that could be accomplished in Washington, and so he left for home by rail. Following a usual precaution, he left the train in Weber Canyon before it reached Ogden. Having received a prior ciphered message about his arrival, a Brother Doxey met the train in the canyon and, joined later by Joseph's good friend Albert Davis, drove the apostle to his home, where he received a loving welcome from his wives and children.

Chapter Fifteen

The Manifesto

Because of the precedents set following the deaths of Joseph Smith and Brigham Young, and being a keen student of history, Elder Smith was conscious that the First Presidency could be reorganized at any time. But the matter was not discussed in council until shortly before the April general conference. President Woodruff broached the subject at a meeting of the Twelve held in the Gardo House on Friday, April 5. Joseph F. was living in seclusion in the Gardo House at the time, having moved there from his home two weeks before to be near the general Church offices across the street. All of the Twelve except Francis M. Lyman were present at the meeting. Also present was Elder Daniel H. Wells, a counselor to the Twelve.

President Woodruff said he felt it was time to reorganize the First Presidency, and when, after discussion, the proposition was approved and he had been sustained as the President, he nominated George Q. Cannon and Joseph F. Smith as his counselors. In due course, these brethren were sustained unanimously.

There may have been a time when Joseph F. Smith, without actually aspiring to it, had welcomed calls to Church responsibilities. Now, however, at age fifty, after he had been in the harness for many years, had experienced the trials and traumas of leadership, and had gained insight into the demands that would be made upon him and his family, he accepted this call out of a sense of duty, not out of personal choice. "I would rather have taken a mission to Vandeman's land as an elder," he confided to his diary, "than to be called to the responsibilities of a counselor in the First Presidency if my own choice was to be consulted. But inasmuch as the President had expressed his mind upon it—and had given us the 'will of the Lord' on the subject—so far as *I* was concerned, that was the end of the matter with me."

The loyalty and selflessness this entry implies suggest the main qualities that made Joseph F. Smith a superior counselor. He had no sense of self-aggrandizement, and showed complete submission to the wishes of his presiding officer and faith in his spiritual perceptions. In addition, of course, he brought to the task almost thirty-five years of faithful priesthood service in every important aspect of the work—proselyting, temple work, and administration.

The strictures imposed by the judicial crusade prevented Joseph from attending the general conference the next day when he was sustained as a counselor to President Wilford Woodruff. He remained concealed in the Gardo House, where Elder George Teasdale of the Twelve and L. John Nuttall kept him company. Twice during the day both presidents Woodruff and George Q. Cannon stopped by to visit and to report on the conference.

The following day, Joseph and his brethren were heartened by the release of Francis M. Lyman from the penitentiary, the last of the apostles to be incarcerated for polygamy. In mid-May, Elder Lyman paid a courtesy call on President Smith in the Gardo House, presenting him with the gift of a carved oak walking stick that had been made for him in the penetentiary by his longtime friend Bishop William H. Maughan, who presided over the Wellsville Ward in Cache Valley for over forty years and who had been called by Joseph to preside over the Birmingham England Conference in 1875.

Although President Smith was free to move about as he wished, he was essentially a prisoner in the Gardo House during this period. And because of the dangers threatened by federal officers, his families were located at different places—Julina and Sarah at the main home on West First North, Edna at "Camp Solitude," and the others elsewhere along the Wasatch Front. Whenever he ventured forth from the Gardo House, it was usually under cover of night and with a disguise as a double precaution. Shortly after the general conference where he was sustained again as a counselor in the First Presidency, he walked to the First North home to see his family. This entry attests to the effectiveness of his disguises: "After a short visit with my family I returned to the Gardo; meeting only three persons on the trip and they were B. Young, C. O. Card and Geo. W. Thatcher—they did not know me."

Under these less than favorable circumstances Joseph F. began his service as a counselor to a third president of the Church. Each of these three was far different in personality, skills, and achievement. President Young was the consummate organizer and administrator; President Taylor was the intellectual-poet; and President Woodruff's forte was his faith and spirituality. Lacking extensive experience in business, administrative, or government affairs, President Woodruff relied heavily on his counselors in these areas while devoting himself chiefly to spiritual and policy matters. The effect of this was to place on the counselors a much heavier administrative burden than they had previously carried. And the chaotic effect of the Edmunds and the Edmunds-Tucker Acts upon the Church introduced seemingly endless complications and pitfalls. As the First Presidency attempted to pick their way through this perplexing morass, Joseph piled up his books and papers in the seclusion of the Gardo House while the other two members of the First Presidency operated out of the Church offices across the street, then located between the Beehive House and Lion House.

Beyond the Church's administrative affairs, the First Presidency's main concern was polygamy. The overriding importance of that issue was borne in upon President Smith and the other members of the First Presidency each day as they saw the Church struggling and no relief in view. They continued to exert what political influence they could and to contest the court actions brought to implement the Edmunds-Tucker Act. With all this, they continued to implore the Lord for wisdom and guidance as they sought to work their way out of the confusing maze in which they had been trapped. As the tools of politics, diplomacy, and litigation failed to produce the desired results, Joseph F. and his brethren turned even more than previously to prayer and spiritual power for relief from the burdens under which they and the Church tottered. At last deciding to use the vast reservoir of spiritual power in the general membership of the Church, the First Presidency proclaimed December 23, 1889, the eighty-fourth anniversary of the birth of the Prophet Joseph Smith, as a general fast day throughout the Church.

To end this fast, the First Presidency and the Quorum of the Twelve held a prayer circle in the Gardo House. The object of their prayers, which President Smith recorded in his journal, clearly reveals the problems that troubled them most and the specificity they used when invoking divine aid in their solution: "Among the subjects prayed for," wrote President Smith, "were the following: 1. That the plots and schemes which are being framed for the purpose of robbing us of our civil and political rights and obtaining control of our cities, counties and territory, might be confounded. 2. That all who conspire in any manner to injure or destroy the work of God or take from the people their rights and liberties be defeated. 3. That the unfavorable actions of courts and of officials might be overruled in such a manner that no injury will be done to Zion. 4. That the Executive of the nation, the cabinet, the senate, the house of representatives, the judiciary and the people of the nation might be so influenced and controlled that their hearts may be softened towards the people of God, and not inclined to listen to the slanderous reports and falsehoods circulated concerning us, and which may be brought before them; and that all officers of our nation may be inspired with such wisdom, justice and mercy that they may gain the love and esteem of the people and the approbation of the Lord. 5. That the supreme court should be so moved upon and strengthened and filled with courage as to render a righteous decision in our causes before them. 6. That the eyes of the nation might be opened to see us in our true light, and be inclined to treat us with that kindness and consideration due to fellow citizens who are loyal and true to the constitution of our country. 7. For the Lord to come to our help and deliver us from the many snares spread around us for our overthrow and destruction, to make our path plain before us, and to lead us to escape the pits dug for our feet. 8. That the Lord will pour out in great power His Holy Spirit and the gifts thereof upon his servants that they may be filled with qualifications and power necessary to enable them to magnify their offices acceptable to Him, and to fill the hearts of the Saints with comfort and peace, and witness unto them that he has not forgotten and does not neglect Zion. And to pray for such other things as the Saints saw and felt that we needed."

These concentrated prayers, which to a large extent were fulfilled in the years ahead, were symptomatic of the struggling effort the First Presidency was then making to find a permanent solution to the problem of polygamy. Especially was this true of President Woodruff, who held the keys of authority and upon whom the ultimate earthly responsibility for any action taken would rest. This man, faced with the prospect of directing a church without legal form, without assets, and without the freedom its hierarchy required to administer its affairs efficiently, implored the Lord repeatedly for guidance. Throughout the early part of 1890, with the approval of his counselors and members of the Twelve, steps were quietly taken looking toward a suspension of the authority to perform plural marriages. In early September, all three members of the First Presidency traveled to San Francisco, where they stayed for over two weeks as the guests of Colonel Isaac Trumbo. Away from the pressures of day-to-day administrative work at headquarters, this enabled the First Presidency to counsel in a leisurely way. The arrangements were ideal for this, as they had a large suite in the Palace Hotel with separate bedrooms for each and with a large, common parlor. The party returned from San Francisco on September 20. Three days later, the First Presidency received slanderous and distorted reports about the steps that had been taken looking toward the cessation of plural marriage. As a result, President Woodruff recorded this entry in his private journal on September 25: "I have arrived at a point in the history of my life as the president of the Church of Jesus Christ of Latter-day Saints where I am under the necessity of acting for the temporal salvation of the Church. The United States Government has taken a stand and passed laws to destroy the Latter-day Saints on the subject of polygamy or patriarchal marriage, and after praying to the Lord and feeling inspired, I have issued the following proclamation which is sustained by my counselors and the Twelve apostles." He then set out in its entirety what has since been referred to as the Manifesto, by which the teaching and practice of plural marriage was suspended.

While the revelation to take this historic step was recorded in the entry in President Woodruff's journal, the proclamation was a formal document dictated by President Woodruff and, at his direction, later reviewed and edited by John R. Winder, Charles W. Penrose, and George Reynolds; by his counselors; and by members of the Twelve. The final draft was carefully reviewed and approved by President Woodruff and his counselors. On September 24, the proclamation was given to W. B. Dougall, who was in charge of the Deseret Telegraph Office, for telegraphic transmission through the Associated Press. The following day when the AP dispatch arrived from the east, the statement had been edited, much to the annoyance of President Woodruff. At his direction, given to an agent in Chicago, the entire proclamation was then sent out over the AP wire.

The published Manifesto burst like a bombshell, not only on the Church but on the country as a whole. There was disbelief and consternation among many and great feelings of relief and even elation among others. As the reactions poured in from all parts of the country, and as questions were raised about the accuracy and authenticity of the document, the First Presidency and the Twelve considered the steps to be taken at the coming general conference. At a lengthy council meeting on Thursday, October 2, there was a divergence of opinion as to whether the document should be presented for acceptance by the conference. President Smith spoke strongly in favor of it. The matter came to a head three days later when a wire from John T. Caine in Washington, D.C., said national leaders wondered whether President Woodruff's Manifesto "stood alone, unsupported by authority from the Church." This, coupled with conflicting statements issued by the Utah Commission and Governor Thomas, caused the brethren to decide to present the document for action by the conference. This was done on Monday, October 6, 1890, when Bishop Orson F. Whitney read the "Official Declaration" or Manifesto to the general conference assembled in the Tabernacle. Then, on motion of Lorenzo Snow, president of the Twelve, the document was unanimously accepted as "authoritative and binding" on the Church.

Thus ended one of the most stressful and difficult chapters in Church history. But the Manifesto was no panacea for the tribulations that engulfed the Latter-day Saints. It was merely the first step in the long and tortuous process of healing the wounds the controversy had inflicted. Although it would take years to achieve it, this action opened the way for the reincorporation of the Church, for the reacquisition of its properties, and for a return to normalcy in administration. It also unlocked the door of the underground and allowed brethren like President Joseph F. Smith to pick up the threads of their lives in freedom. It heralded an end to the antagonism of men and women of good will whose opposition to the Church had been solely a philosophical rejection of polygamy as a marital institution. And all this foreshadowed the attainment of the long-held political goal of Utah statehood.

But the action did not and would not salve the bitter antagonisms of the sworn enemies of the Church, those who resented or refused to acknowledge the right of its very existence. This class turned immediately from the issue of polygamy to other issues that were pressed with the same relentless zeal and often with the same disregard for facts and lack of reason that had characterized the long contest over polygamy.

As to the effect of the document, the Saints and most federal officials generally understood that it did not operate retroactively so as to interfere with polygamous marriages contracted beforehand. Although this view compromised the letter of the law, whose unforgiving language made no such distinction of time, it was deemed equitable because of the sincerity of the Saints, the special applicability to them of the condemning laws, and the questionable interpretations of the Supreme Court. The case of non-Mormon judge Charles S. Zane, who beforehand was pitiless in his rigid application of the law, reflects the radical change in official attitudes brought about by the Manifesto. He afterward showed an unusual leniency toward polygamists brought before him and went so far as to sign a petition asking that they be given an official pardon. Another judge, James C. Miner, reacted similarly when in one case he dismissed a suit against a polygamist who said he accepted the Manifesto, imposing a fine of only six cents. And federal prosecutors showed a similar leniency by refusing to bring actions, though technical violations of the law were evident. This wise policy of compromise and accommodation received executive confirmation when, in January 1893, President Benjamin Harrison granted amnesty to all Saints who had observed the law since the Manifesto, and when, in September 1894, President Grover Cleveland issued an even broader amnesty.

As to the scope of the proclamation, certain members, including some who occupied positions of high leadership, contended that the instrument applied only to plural marriages performed within the United States and its territories. Those who held this view reasoned that since the Manifesto was written in response to laws enacted by the United States, it should be restricted in its operation to that jurisdiction. Under this view, plural marriages performed outside the United States, for example, in Mexico or Canada, were immune from the proscriptions of the Manifesto. Such reasoning, combined with other relevant circumstances, later resulted in the disaffection and discipline of Elders John W. Taylor and Matthias Cowley of the Quorum of the Twelve Apostles. These men and others who shared their views either were unaware of or had decided to reject the statements President Wilford Woodruff made under oath over a year after the Manifesto was accepted by the Church. In autumn of 1891, a number of leading brethren, including President Woodruff, appeared and testified under oath before a

179

master in chancery in an effort to obtain some of the escheated Church property to be used for the relief of the poor. Answering a question asked by United States Attorney Charles S. Varian, President Woodruff said, "The Manifesto was intended to apply to the Church of Jesus Christ of Latter-day Saints everywhere in every nation and country. We are giving no liberty to enter into polygamous relations anywhere." (*Deseret News Weekly*, Oct. 24, 31, 1891, pp. 563-83; 608-13.)

But some Church members were reluctant to accept the Manifesto under any circumstances. These had dfficulty understanding how or why an eternal principle would be suspended. The First Presidency took pains to respond in detail to inquiries of this kind. Usually the answers were based on both doctrinal and practical grounds. The doctrinal reasons for the Manifesto were elaborated by President George Q. Cannon when it was presented to the general conference for ratification and acceptance. The first reason was founded upon the concept stated in Doctrine and Covenants 124:49-50 that when wrathful enemies prevent the Saints from fulfilling a commandment, the Lord accepts their offering and no longer requires it at their hand. The second was based on the idea that the same prophetic power that authorized the practice in the first place could also order its cessation.

At a meeting in Logan on November 1, 1891, President Wilford Woodruff expounded the practical considerations that drove him to his knees repeatedly in search of the revelatory direction that finally came: "The Lord has told me to ask the Latter-day Saints a question," he said. "The question is this: Which is the wisest course for the Latter-day Saints to pursue—to continue to attempt to practice plural marriage, with the laws of the nation against it and the opposition of sixty millions of people, and at the cost of the confiscation and loss of all the Temples, and the stopping of all ordinances therein, both for the living and the dead, and the imprisonment of the First Presidency and the Twelve and the heads of families in the Church, and the confiscation of personal property of the people . . . or after doing and suffering what we have through our adherence to this principle to cease the practice and submit to the law, and through doing so leave the Prophets, Apostles and fathers at home, so that they can instruct the people and attend to the duties of the Church, and also leave the Temples in the hands of the Saints, so that they can attend to the ordinances of the Gospel, both for the living and the dead?"

Leaving the audience to reflect on this question and to decide how they would have answered it, the Prophet confided how and why he answered it as he did: "The Lord showed me by vision and revelation exactly what would take place if we did not stop this practice. . . . I know there are a good many men, and probably some leading men, in this Church who have been tried and felt as though President Woodruff had lost the Spirit of God and was about to apostatize. Now, I want you to understand that he has not lost the Spirit, nor is he about to apostatize. The Lord is with him and with this people. He has told me exactly what to do and what the result would be if we did not do it. . . . I want to say this: I should have let all of the Temples go out of our hands; I should have gone to prison myself, and let every other man go there, had not the God of Heaven commanded me to do what I did do; and when the hour came that I was commanded to do that, it was all clear to me." (JFS, p. 298.)

With the Manifesto in place, and with the consequent softening of the attitudes of federal officials, the lives of the Latter-day Saints began to assume a different tenor. Joseph F., who had lived under a cloud for almost seven years, and whose duties in the First Presidency required that he have more freedom of movement, decided to take steps toward amnesty for himself. After testing the political waters and finding them favorable, he applied to President Benjamin Harrison for amnesty on July 20, 1891, although the petition was not forwarded to Washington until August 14, the delay being occasioned by the desire to obtain favorable endorsements from prominent gentiles and officials. Among these were territorial governor Arthur L. Thomas and chief justice Charles S. Zane. With support of this kind, Joseph's application received prompt, favorable attention, although at the time, President Harrison was vacationing at Cape May, New Jersey. A press release from that place on September 7, 1891, carried the welcome news: "Amnesty has been granted to Joseph F. Smith." Two weeks later the mails brought the official document of amnesty bearing the signatures of President Harrison and William F. Wharton, acting secretary of state. "I thank God and am grateful to the President of the United States," Joseph recorded in his journal on September 21. These words hardly convey the emotion the document produced, an emotion that showed at last when on the next Sunday President Smith stood at the pulpit in the Tabernacle for the first time in over seven years. "The house was full to the gallery," he wrote. "I spoke briefly, for I was so overcome by my feelings that I could scarcely restrain them. A good spirit was present. . . . This is a memorable day for me, and no words at my command can express my gratitude to God."

The relief and gratitude Joseph felt were shared by his family and associates. His wives and children, who had lived in constant fear of his arrest and imprisonment and who had enjoyed his companionship only intermittently and furtively during those long years, could now look forward to regular and open association. And his brethren of the general authorities, especially the other members of the First Presidency, could now expect Joseph's concentrated attention in helping to administer the complex affairs of the Church as it sought to bind up the wounds inflicted by the bitter and protracted battle and to chart a new course.

Chapter Sixteen

A Return to Normalcy

T he meetings in the Salt Lake Tabernacle in early October 1891 marked the first time in seven and a half years that all members of the First Presidency had been together at a general conference. This symbolic fact signaled a return to some semblance of normalcy for the Latter-day Saints who had endured a long night of stress and uncertainty. All three members of the First Presidency spoke at the Sunday morning session on October 4, following which the Saints thronged the stand to greet their leaders, especially President Smith, who had been absent so many years. "I shook hands with my friends until my hand and arm felt lame," he recorded of the event.

With the cloud of secrecy lifted, Joseph F. turned with enthusiasm to the many tasks connected with his heavy ecclesiastical, business, and family obligations. A chief project at the time was to complete the Salt Lake Temple. President Smith consulted often with architects and builders about various aspects of the work, including the size and quality of the boilers and other equipment and fixtures to be placed in the building. By April 6, 1892, the work had progressed to the point that the capstone was laid, which gave impetus to push toward the dedication a year later.

By now, President Smith had twenty-six living children among his five families. It was no simple task to provide the necessities and the spiritual leadership for such a large clan.

He was constantly involved in improving his homes and holdings, major projects at the time including the installation of steam heat for added comfort and convenience and the construction of a new brick barn. Because of his fairness and desire to preserve unity and harmony, he usually saw to it that a new convenience in one home was soon, if not simultaneously, duplicated in the others. This entailed heavy expense, and because the living allowance provided by the Church was minimal, he had to generate money from other sources. This accounts largely for his involvement in a wide variety of business enterprises, some of which were successful while others failed. But whatever the monetary yield, the thing they had in common was the demands made on Joseph F.'s time. He frequently attended meetings of the boards of directors of the Zions Savings Bank & Trust, the State Bank of Utah, the La Plata Mining Company, and others. And his role in these companies was not an honorary, passive one. His broad experience in Church, business, and government affairs, as well as his astute ability to deal amicably with others, made his counsel valuable and much sought after.

In the meantime, there was much stirring in the Church in addition to work on the temple. Plans were in progress for the creation of the LDS College, for the expansion of the Deseret Hospital, for the acquisition of a large ranch in Nevada, and for the construction of a reservoir in the sink on the Sevier River.

Beyond these activities were the customary and never-ending meetings and worship services, where President Smith was usually called on to give counsel and instruction, and the simple acts of charity and kindness performed for his family or friends. Typical is this incident recorded October 2, 1891: "Immediately after lunch I started with Wm. Calder to visit his mother, now over 90 years of age, at John Mackey's, over Jordan, about 8 or 9 miles from the city. We found the old lady very comfortable, but weak. She told me she wanted to see me before she died, to tell me that more than a year before the gospel came to Scotland it was shown to her that she would be sealed to her husband then dead. . . . After a pleasant visit and administering to Mother Calder, we returned to the city."

By this time, many Hawaiian Saints had been established in Tooele County in a community appropriately named Iosepa in honor of President Smith. He went there occasionally to visit and express love to his old friends and to build up their faith and commitment to the Church. One such visit was made in mid-October 1891, shortly after the general conference. "We had a pleasant drive—found all well at Iosepa," he recorded on October 15. "After looking about the house, barn and yards, we rode about the fields and called on all the Hawaiian families." Preaching services were held that evening, and the next day Joseph and his companions were treated to a traditional Hawaiian feast of "Baked pig & poi-ina-mona, roast chicken, etc."

He seemed pleased to record that on the return trip they "made about 8 miles an hour." As often happened when leading brethren traveled to Tooele during this period, his party stayed overnight with the John Woolley family in Grantsville. President Smith left us this interesting insight into the joys of LDS family life in a small rural community during the last decade of the nineteenth century: "We spent a pleasant social evening with bro. & sister Woolley and family, listening to singing and music, etc. Bro. Noall and I sang some native hymns and Sister Rachel Woolley sang some beautiful songs, bro. F. Gates at the organ & bro. Noall singing bass." The next day, Joseph F. and his traveling companions had an annoying delay from an accident seldom heard of today—a broken "whiffletree" (the pivoting bar of a wagon to which horses are attached).

Interspersed with Joseph's busy schedule was an interested concern about the evolution of political alliances in the territory. During most of the years while the Saints resisted the antipolygamy laws, they generally supported the People's Party, which was regarded as a "shield" against undue political pressure on the Church. After the Manifesto, and as the prospects for statehood brightened, the leaders of the party saw that its continued existence could be an impediment to attaining that goal. The difficulty lay in the image of overwhelming political solidarity among the Mormons. And from the mere existence of the People's Party, opponents inferred that this was the instrument by which Church leaders intended to dominate state government should the efforts toward statehood prove successful. Under these circumstances, party leaders decided that the best course would be to dissolve the People's Party and allow its members to enter the ranks of the national political parties. Because most Church leaders were members of the People's Party, the party leaders felt the need to consult with them as plans for the dissolution were laid. A meeting for this purpose was held in the Gardo House in the forepart of 1891. Out of this meeting grew the extraordinary charge that the First Presidency had "ordered" the dissolution of the People's Party so that Church members could infiltrate and ultimately control the major political parties in the territory. The effect of this, the argument went, would be to give the Church even greater political influence than it had enjoyed before.

To allay the fears of nonmembers on this point, President Smith joined the other members of the First Presidency in answering questions posed by the *Salt Lake Times* on the subject. Among other things, Joseph and his brethren said, "The Church will not assert any right to control the political action of its members. As officers of the Church they disclaim such right. . . . All that is asked for the Church is that it shall have equal rights before the law." (*Salt Lake Times,* June 23, 1891.)

Indicative of the vigor with which bias and suspicion persist is the fact that five years later President Smith found it necessary to again explain that the Church was not involved in dissolving the People's Party. (*Salt Lake Tribune,* May 10, 1896.) And during the Smoot hearings, President Smith testified as follows in answer to a question whether the People's Party was dissolved by direction of the Church: "The People's party was dissolved, as we understand, by the action of its leading members. They have stated to us their conviction that the time had come for a division on national party lines. There has been a growing feeling in this direction for a long time, and the dissolution of the People's party is the result of that sentiment, and not the fiat or instruction of the church. The first intimation we had of dividing on party lines came to us from Ogden. There is, therefore, no foundation for the charge that the church brought about the dissolution of the People's party." (CHC 6:306.)

The repeated charges of Church involvement in political matters resulted from the private political activities of Church leaders and the failure or inability of members and nonmembers alike to differentiate between the two. President Smith, for instance, was an open participant in Republican party affairs after the dissolution of the People's party. "I came to Logan," he noted on October 29, 1892, and "attended the Republican Rallie." From his attendance at this and other such gatherings, many erroneously inferred that the Church officially endorsed the Republican Party and, perhaps, some members affiliated with the Republican Party because of that false inference. An unfortunate incident in Logan several months before President Smith attended this Republican rally prompted an official statement from President Smith and President Woodruff, clarifying the Church's official attitude toward the freedom of Church members to chart their own course in political affairs. The incident began in 1891 when a member of the staff of the First Presidency wrote a letter that was widely circulated in Logan in connection with a municipal election. The letter was interpreted as meaning that the First Presidency had endorsed the Republican Party. To negate that, President Smith and President Woodruff signed and published the following statement: "We emphatically deny that we, or either of us, authorized Mr. George F. Gibbs or any other person or persons to use our names so as to influence citizens to vote the Republican ticket, at Logan or elsewhere. If our names have been used in any such way, it has been entirely without permission from us, and we hereby condemn it as wrong and reprehensible. If we have any desire in this matter it is that the people of this Territory shall study well the principles of both the great national parties, and then choose which they will join, freely, voluntarily and honestly, from personal conviction, and then stand by it in all honor and sincerity. . . . If any man claims that it is the wish of the First Presidency that a Democrat shall vote the Republican ticket, or a Republican the Democratic ticket, let all people know that he is endeavoring to deceive the public and has no authority of that kind from us. We have no disposition to direct in these matters, but proclaim that, as far as we are concerned, the members of this Church are entirely and perfectly free in all political affairs." (*Deseret News Weekly*, Mar. 25, 1892, p. 440.)

While the policy expressed in this statement applied uniformly to the general membership of the Church, a different standard limited the political activity of the General Authorities. While it was permissible for them to attend rallies and give private support to the party of their choice, they were to do little else. As early as the fall of 1892, it was agreed that General Authorities should not give political speeches. "Talked over our political situation," President Woodruff recorded in his journal on October 4, 1892, "and expressed our feelings frankly. The general opinion was for none of the presidency, twelve, or the Presidents of seventy to take the stump to make political speeches." Through an apparent misunderstanding of the effect of that decision, two general authorities, Moses Thatcher and B. H. Roberts, announced their candidacy for federal office in 1895. At a special priesthood meeting held on October 7 of that year, President Joseph F. Smith indirectly referred to the action of these two brethren, implying that it limited their ability to fulfill their overriding ecclesiastical responsibilities, and that having taken it without First Presidency approval, they were insubordinate. (CHC 6:330-31.) These remarks of President Smith set in motion a chain of events that in six months resulted in the adoption of what was later called the "Political Manifesto." Signed by all of the General Authorities except two members of the Twelve (Anthon H. Lund, who was presiding over the European Mission, and Moses Thatcher, who felt it infringed his freedom) this policy further limited their political activity except under certain conditions. By the terms of it they agreed "that before accepting any position, political or otherwise, which would interfere with the proper and complete discharge of his ecclesiastical duties, and before accepting a nomination or entering into engagements to perform new duties, said official should apply to the proper authorities and learn from them whether he can, consistently with the obligations already entered into with the Church upon assuming his office, take upon himself the added duties and labors and responsibilities of the new position." (*Deseret News Weekly*, Apr. 11, 1896, pp. 532-34.)

It was the effect of this Manifesto and Moses Thatcher's refusal to accept it that in a short while resulted in his being dropped from the Twelve and then disciplined. Because President Smith was one of the chief architects of this policy, he was subjected to much criticism years later when, as the president of the Church, he authorized Reed Smoot, a member of the Twelve, to run for the United States Senate. The fact that Elder Smoot sought for and received prior approval of his leaders and Moses Thatcher did not clearly indicates that the need for subordination and unity among the General Authorities is the crux of the policy defined in the "Political Manifesto."

The dedication of the Salt Lake Temple in early April 1893 had both symbolic and practical significance. Symbolically, it marked the end of a forty-year period of great trial and tribulation for the Latter-day Saints. Many mature adults in the territory had lived out much of their lives with the hope and expectation that the building, which they had observed in various stages of its seemingly endless construction, would one day be finished. To see the long-anticipated event finally occur with its pageantry, solemnity, and great spiritual outpourings symbolized that a better day had actually arrived and that the Saints could look forward to directing their energies into the channels that to them held the greatest promise—preaching the gospel to the nations of the earth and performing the sacred work for the living and the dead in the temples.

Practically, the dedication of the temple meant that the vast resources allocated for it in the past could now be used for the many other projects crying for attention. And as far as the First Presidency and the Twelve were concerned, the completion brought about an important shift in administra-

Joseph F. Smith. Photograph taken on April 6, 1893, in Salt Lake City. (Church Archives.)

tive focus. Not long after the dedication, the leading Church quorums began to hold many of their council meetings in rooms provided for that purpose on the fourth floor of the building. The most significant of these was the weekly meeting of the Council of the First Presidency and the Quorum of the Twelve held on Thursdays. For many years, such meetings had been held in the Endowment House before it was razed and later in the First Presidency's office between the Lion House and the Beehive House, in the Historian's Office, or in the Gardo House. With the completion and dedication of the temple, this council, which decides all of the important policies and procedures that govern the Church, had a permanent home.

It would be difficult to assess the powerful spiritual and psychological impact on the Church of these council meetings held in the "upper room" of this sacred building week in and week out for almost ninety years. At the first such meeting held shortly after the dedication, Joseph F. Smith took his place at the head of the circle, seated to the left of President Wilford Woodruff. With few exceptions, he was to return there each week for almost twenty-five years to pray with his brethren, to discuss and decide policy, to hear reports, and to chart the course of the kingdom of God on the earth. He also attended endowment sessions from time to time and often performed temple sealings.

Regardless of the pressures exerted on him by his many commitments, President Smith always found time for his family. He took a personal interest in each child, devoting the time necessary to train and counsel within the limits of his crowded schedule. When, for instance, it was debated whether daughters Donnie and Mamie should receive schooling beyond the curriculum provided by schools in the territory, Joseph decided to send them to New York City. Unwilling to entrust the arrangements to anyone else, he and Edna accompanied them east, where they were enrolled in the Pratt Institute in Brooklyn, which the interested father characterized as "a very elaborate, diversified and complete institution embracing nearly every branch of industry, mechanism and art." While in the city, Joseph made it a point to show Edna and the girls the sights, visiting Central Park, the Zoo, the Museum, the Battery and, of course, Broadway.

After an absence of over three weeks, most of which time was spent making arrangements for his daughters' schooling, he returned home with Edna on February 12, 1896. "Arrived at Salt Lake this morning at about 4 a.m.," he recorded in his journal, "and came directly home. Found all well at home, for which my heart is full of love and gratitude to God. I visited Sarah and family, Alice and family and Julina and family,

Mary, and my daughter Lenora (who was married to Joseph Nelson) and found them all well. Alvin and David went for the trunks . . . gave Andrew 05¢." The Andrew mentioned was Alice's three-year-old toddler, Andrew Kimball Smith, who was named after Alice's twin brother, Andrew Kimball, the father of President Spencer W. Kimball. A week later President Smith recorded, "Mended Andrew's hobby horse."

With the kind of love and interest these entries clearly imply, it is no wonder that President Smith and his wives created a family solidarity that was a model for the entire Church. In their family, everyone felt needed, loved, and important; the scriptures were the favorite reading material; and each day began and ended with fervent prayer.

During 1897, the Church celebrated the Jubilee anniversary of the arrival of the pioneers in the Salt Lake Valley. To commemorate the event, the First Presidency commissioned C. E. Dallin, a Utah-born sculptor, then living in Boston, to create the Brigham Young and Pioneer monument. It was dedicated by President Wilford Woodruff and placed on Temple Square. However, the venerable President, now ninety years old, was unable to read the dedicatory prayer because of general weakness and shortness of breath caused by asthma, which had afflicted him for several years. He was able to find some relief from this ailment while at sea level, and on this account he made occasional trips to the California coast, usually to San Francisco. In the late summer of 1898, President Woodruff made still another trip there, seeking relief from an asthmatic attack and from the heavy pressures of his office, which were intensified by the load of debt under which the Church groaned. It was while he was there, staying at the home of his friend Isaac Trumbo, that he passed away on September 2, 1898.

As they had done at the death of John Taylor, George Q. Cannon and Joseph F. Smith temporarily took charge of affairs, arranging for and conducting President Woodruff's funeral and overseeing his burial in the beloved valley he had gazed upon for the first time on July 24, 1847, from a carriage he was driving that carried the ailing Brigham Young. It was in the hearing of the faithful diarist that the Lion of the Lord had declared "This is the right place," and it was to him that the injunction "drive on" was addressed.

Chapter Seventeen

New Challenges and Old Solutions

Because of instructions President Woodruff gave before his death, there was no long delay in reorganizing the First Presidency as there had been following the deaths of Joseph Smith, Brigham Young, and John Taylor. The complexities of the day were too great to admit of an administration directed by a committee of twelve men. So, on September 13, 1898, eleven days after the death of President Woodruff, Lorenzo Snow was installed as the fifth president of the Church, with George Q. Cannon and Joseph F. Smith as his counselors. Facing the new presidency was a financial problem of massive proportions that ultimately was solved through a dramatic revelation given to President Snow. But in the early months of their administration, the new leaders were searching prayerfully for solutions. And in their searching, they used proven principles employed by spiritual leaders throughout the centuries. President Smith gave voice to them in a talk delivered at the general conference in April 1899. "The clouds may gather over our heads," he told the Tabernacle audience, "and, as in the past, it may seem impossible for us to penetrate them; yet there can be no clouds so dark, so gloomy or so heavy, but God will roll them away in His own time and will bring good out of threatening evil. He has done it in the past, He will do it in the future; for it is His work, not the work of man." (CR, Apr. 1899, p. 41.)

This statement breathes the sentiments of all spiritually minded people; it defines the principle of faith and underscores the reliance on God that a person of faith must have. Too often those possessing the intelligence and ability of a Joseph F. Smith are inclined to rely too much on their own powers and therefore fail, or, if they succeed, are inclined to attribute success to their own efforts.

Like Nephi of old, then, the new presidency moved forward one step at a time, confident in the knowledge that when that step had been taken, God would show them the next step.

Because of pressing obligations requiring immediate cash, the First Presidency, supported by the Twelve, decided on December 1, 1898, to issue bonds in the amount of $500,000. Later, that amount was doubled. In implementing the decision, President Smith aroused the enmity of Frank J. Cannon, a son of President Cannon, because of Joseph's urging that the bonds be sold locally rather than on the eastern markets. When President Smith's advice was followed, Frank J. Cannon became embittered, largely, it is assumed, because he stood to make a substantial fee from financial associates in the east who hoped to market the bonds. Frank J. Cannon's bitterness was vented in a book he wrote a few years later that severely and unfairly maligned President Smith. Because of his relationship to Frank J. Cannon's father, President Smith never retaliated but merely went his way, usually leaving the charges unanswered or allowing others to answer for him.

Joseph F. turned sixty just a few weeks after being sustained as President Snow's counselor. Having reached an age exceeding the life expectancy of many at that day, he appears to have felt the need for a change and an opportunity to reflect upon the past and to ponder the future. And since Sarah was convalescing from a recent serious illness, he decided that a trip away from the bustle of life in Salt Lake City would be a therapeutic blessing to both of them. It came as no surprise that in Joseph's mind the ideal place for the kind of rest he contemplated was Hawaii, where life was slow-paced and where the love and jollity of the people would have a soothing yet energizing effect upon him and Sarah. Having decided upon this plan with the family, Joseph presented the idea to President Snow. The next morning the benign president, who still carried vivid memories of his near-drowning in those islands, said to his friend and counselor, "Well, Joseph, last night when I got home and thought of your going away I felt like crying. I depend upon you to help me, you understand things and I need your help. You are not afraid to speak your mind before any one, therefore, you are a helpful counselor, and I rely upon your integrity and your judgment. Still, if you have made up your mind and feel clear that you will be all right on the sea, and the voyage will do your wife good, all right." (JFS, pp. 304-5.)

This compliment is one of the finest Joseph would receive in his role as a counselor and could well serve as a standard for anyone who serves in a similar position.

Once he knew of his leader's feelings, Joseph F.'s course was clear. He willingly delayed the trip until President Snow felt it was timely for him to leave.

In early January, after critical decisions had been made about issuing bonds to raise money for the interim financing of the Church, President Snow advised Joseph he would not object were the counselor to leave then for Hawaii. Learning this, Joseph F. and Sarah and two daughters left Salt Lake City by train on Saturday, January 7, 1899, destined for San Francisco. With them were Bishop Albert W. Davis and a daughter. In Joseph's pocket were gold coins totaling $450, the remnant of a $500 gift from his friend and fellow Hawaiian missionary George Q. Cannon. The $50 difference represented tithing President Smith had paid on the gift, to which he had added another $50 covering income from another source. While President Smith appreciated this thoughtful gesture and the much-needed financing it provided, he was more grateful for the blessing his friend conferred upon him.

The tourists steamed out of the famed Golden Gate on January 11 and a week later arrived in beautiful Pearl Harbor after a rough passage that caused even seasoned sea-traveler Joseph F. Smith to "part with his supper."

After seven days on the restless, sometimes agitated sea, the party welcomed the solidity of land, land the like of which the young girls had never seen before. It was an old and welcome sight to Joseph F. as he gazed on the rich verdure and the towering volcanic mountains that overshadowed the beautiful harbor at Honolulu. But to the three young ladies, and, to a lesser extent, to Sarah, it was a novel, almost unbelievable sensation to find themselves in the islands of enchantment about which their father had told them so much. And more impressive to them than the physical beauty all around was the unspoiled, genuine love that shone from the brown, well-scrubbed faces of the native Saints who greeted them, all attired in their Sunday best and well-ornamented with leis of the colorful, fragrant flowers that abound in the islands.

The floral offerings with which the visitors were liberally bedecked were but a prelude to the mountain of gifts bestowed upon them later—especially upon beloved Iosepa. These were presented to the apostle at a luau held later in the day. The gifts he received from two of the sisters had special meaning for the president, not as much from any intrinsic value they possessed as from the spirit with which they were given. Sister Koleha presented him with a cane, a double Waa (canoe), and an ointment made from Koa seeds. The comments this humble sister made when the gifts were presented to him affected Joseph deeply, almost moving him to tears. "Joseph F. Smith, the servant of the Most High God," Sister Koleha's prepared speech began, "the man of open heart filled with love, Greetings: Here is my little gift of love for you to hold in your hand, also my loving letter. May God bless you, amen." The other gift of special note was a handmade quilt presented to him by Ma Mahuhii, his surrogate mother of long ago who was now wrinkled with age. President Smith gratefully acknowledged these gifts from his "true friends who had stood by the truth through the long years since they joined the church, invoking the blessing of God upon them."

The luau revived fond memories of the many feasts Joseph had shared with his Polynesian friends. "I enjoyed my poi and fish—I ate nothing else, although we had sweet potatoes, boiled chicken, bread and guava jelly and many other things to tempt the appetite, with oranges and bananas galore."

As President Smith toured Oahu and other nearby islands, he was struck by the vast changes that had occurred since he was there in exile. New highways had been constructed, new buildings dotted Honolulu's skyline, and there was evidence of an invigorated business climate, caused chiefly by increased maritime trade, the development of large pineapple and sugarcane plantations, and an expanded cattle industry.

Wherever he went during this five-week stay, President Smith found friends of yesterday, most of whom had retained their commitment to the Church. He encouraged and admonished them as the circumstances required, preached to them, prayed with them, and blessed those who asked for it. He counseled the local leaders, inspected the Church holdings on the islands, and provided the young corps of missionaries, who were carrying on the traditions he and President Cannon had helped to establish almost half a century before, with ample grist for their journals. By now, Joseph F. Smith was almost a legend in Hawaii, and the impressionable young elders who heard him speak in the setting where he had commenced his ministry doubtless filled their personal records with word sketches of his appearance and demeanor and with quotations from his sermons and sayings.

But most of the time during this stay, President Smith and his family enjoyed the slow-paced life of Hawaii, with its magnificent mountains, surf, and forest; its serenity; and its loving, open-hearted people.

With a combined sense of reluctance and eagerness, President Smith ended his Hawaiian vacation on February 21, 1899, and embarked for home on the S.S. *Australia*. He was reluctant, as always, to leave the warm-hearted Saints in the islands, whom he loved as if they were members of his own family, and to leave the haunting beauty of Hawaii. But he was eager to return to his duties at Church headquarters, duties he had meditated about often during his leisure. As the ship carrying Joseph F. and his party moved slowly out of

Pearl Harbor, it passed several American warships, including the battleship *Oregon,* which the travelers had inspected just the day before and had marveled at its enormous size, at the massive armor protecting it, and at the huge guns bristling on its decks. Even prophetically attuned as he was, it is doubtful that this man of peace had any hint of the future tragic events that would occur in that same quiet harbor.

Taking the customary week for its Honolulu to San Francisco run, the S.S. *Australia* steamed through the Golden Gate on February 28. After spending a few days in San Francisco to get their land legs back, the president's party entrained for Salt Lake City, arriving there March 5.

As President Smith counseled with the brethren as they prepared for the April general conference, a principal theme was the mountain of debt the Church faced as a result of the bonds that had been issued a few months before. Frugal by nature and warned through decades of strong preaching to avoid debt, the general authorities were understandably anxious to shuck off the heavy burden and to return to a pay-as-you-go policy. These anxieties were reflected in the sermons delivered from the Tabernacle pulpit in early April. During the morning session of the last day of the conference, April 9, Franklin D. Richards, president of the Twelve, took up the theme, alluding to it as "that old, threadbare subject, that you have not heard anything new about for a long time." (CR, Apr. 1899, p. 46.) Brigham Young, Jr., the next speaker, followed suit, alluding to and endorsing President Richards's remarks and emphasizing that tithepaying is an initiatory principle of sacrifice that will help one to prepare to live the higher law of consecration. President Snow, who followed Brigham Young to the pulpit, commented on his remarks and posed the question, "How much of this tithing shall I give?" Answering his own query, the prophet suggested a formula for the payment of tithing that many have followed to advantage: "One of the best things to do under such a temptation as that [to withhold part of the Lord's share] is to give, so as to be sure, a trifle more than is required; and to think you have it wholly within yourself to do so." (Ibid., p. 51.)

That afternoon, President George Q. Cannon, in turn,

commented on and built on Elder Young's remarks. "Brother Brigham Young told us this morning," President Cannon said, "that the law of tithing was an inferior law. It is. The law of consecration is a higher law, and it was revealed to us, but we were not prepared to receive and act upon it." (Ibid., p. 65.) Showing again the keen, analytical mind he brought to every task, President Cannon provided the main theological reason behind the law of tithing and consecration: "Why does [the Lord] ask you and me to consecrate all we have and hold it subject to His will? If he is going to take us into partnership He wants to know in the first place whether we will be willing to do as He wants us and to share all that we have with Him." (Ibid., p. 65.)

Moved by the same impulse that had prompted President Richards, Elder Young, and presidents Snow and Cannon to dwell on the law of tithing, President Smith, who followed George Q. Cannon at the afternoon session, added these comments: "I believe the Lord designs in this principle to test the obedience of the people. When we come to stand before the bar of God, to be judged out of the things which are written in the books, we may find a difference between those things which are written in the books here and the things which are written in the books there. We can see this now. Who knows whether or not I pay my tithing? Do not the books show that I am a tithe payer? Certainly, they do; for all that I pay is credited to me on the tithing books of the Church. I think our system of bookkeeping in relation to the tithes of the people is so perfect that any man who has ever paid tithing may go to the books and find there his credit. But the books here do not pretend to keep an account of the tithing you owe to God. We do not keep an account of that which you should pay; we simply keep an account of that which you do pay. But there is One above us who knows; and there may be a system of keeping accounts there wherein it will be known just what every man should pay to be honest with himself and the Lord. If that be so, when we come to be judged out of the things which are written in the books, the difference be-tween that which we have paid and that which we should have paid will appear in the books, and they will show where we have been deficient in our duty." (Ibid., p. 68.)

It was against this background that President Snow and a large group traveled to Southern Utah on a speaking tour in May. President Joseph F. Smith and his wife Alice were in the party, as were Elders Franklin D. Richards, Francis M. Lyman, Abraham O. Woodruff, and Rudger Clawson of the Twelve, and Bishop William B. Preston. At a meeting held in St. George on May 17, President Snow told the audience, "My brethren and sisters, we are in your midst because the Lord directed me to come; but the purpose of our coming is not clearly shown at the present, but this will be made known to me during our sojourn among you." (Romney, *Life of Lorenzo Snow*, p. 456.) At a later meeting, President Snow "told them that he could see, as he had never realized before, how the law of tithing had been neglected by the people, also that the Saints, themselves, were heavily in debt, as well as the church, and now through strict obedience to this law—the paying of a full honest tithing—not only would the church be relieved of its great indebtedness, but through the blessings of the Lord this would also be the means of freeing the Latter-day Saints from their individual obligations and they would become a prosperous people." (*Church News*, Jan. 20, 1934.)

President Franklin D. Richards and Elder Francis M. Lyman of the Twelve and Presiding Bishop William B. Preston also expounded the principle of tithing in their addresses, thereby lending strength to President Snow's remarks on the subject and adducing different arguments and reasons supporting the principle.

With this foundation having been laid, and having received spiritual direction to do so, President Snow launched an extensive and aggressive campaign to lift the Church and its members out of debt through emphasis on this ancient law. It was decided, therefore, that the trip home would be highlighted by meetings along the way, where the Saints would be instructed and motivated to tithe.

This trip by horse and buggy was no joyride. The roads or trails were primitive, and the housing was often rustic. Joseph described one stretch of road as being "dry, dusty, rutty and rocky." On another day, "the wind blew a gale and the dust was smothering and suffocating." And after a hard day's drive, and long, spiritually draining meetings, it was sometimes upsetting not to find the domestic amenities one was accustomed to at home. Alice, for instance, was "nearly frightened out of her wits" one night when she turned down the bed covers to see a centipede resting there.

The first "tithing" meetings on the way home were held at Toquerville and Kanarra, small LDS villages northeast of St. George. Several miles from Cedar City, the third stop, the travelers were met by a brass band and twenty-seven horsemen who served as an official escort into town. There they saw a touching sight that was to be repeated at almost every stop along the way. Dozens of well-scrubbed, happy-faced children were lined up to greet the prophet, who responded by blessing them and by shaking their hands.

Joseph quoted President Snow as telling the Cedar City Saints, "The time has come for men and women to pay their tithing. The time has come for the church to prepare to go to Zion. If they don't go for a thousand years, they must prepare so that they may be ready when they are called."

After leaving Cedar City, the travelers stopped first at Parowan and then at Beaver. While it did not bear directly on the subject of tithing, President Smith was so impressed with the following statement the prophet made at Beaver that he copied it in his journal: "Never marry unless the Spirit of God bears witness that you are mating a companion for all eternity as well as for time. It is better not to marry at all than to do so contrary to this principle."

After leaving Beaver, the party held tithing meetings at Kanosh, Meadow, Fillmore, Holden, Scipio, and Nephi. At the latter place, the group disbanded, most of them taking the train for Salt Lake City. "President Snow called our company together," Joseph F. reported, "and expressed his pleasure in the association of our trip. He said that if he had offended anybody, he asked forgiveness. He urged that the spirit of exhortation on tithe paying be carried to all the stakes in Zion."

On May 30, 1899, three days after arriving in Salt Lake City, President Snow had the opportunity to give powerful impetus to the injuction he had given to Joseph and the others in Nephi when he addressed the officers of the Young Men's Mutual Improvement Association in the Tabernacle. Following this address, a resolution was unanimously adopted that committed those present to observe the law of tithing, and to do all in their power "to get the Latter-day Saints to do likewise." (CHC 6:359.) A month later, at a solemn assembly of priesthood leaders held in the Salt Lake Temple, a similar resolution was adopted by the principal priesthood leaders of the Church from throughout the intermountain area. (Ibid., p. 360.)

In this manner was launched a kind of tithing crusade, the ultimate result of which was to lift the Church out of the morass of debt in which it had been mired. Leaders, young and old, imbued with the commitment and enthusiasm generated at the special meetings held in Salt Lake City in May and July, carried the tithing message throughout the main body of the Church. And when the Saints gathered for general conference in October 1899, they were treated to another round of tithing sermons. One of the most complete and scholarly of these was delivered by President Joseph F. Smith, who spoke at the Saturday afternoon session on October 7. The essence of his message, which was buttressed by extensive quotations from the standard works, seems to be embodied in this excerpt: "We are not talking to you about paying your tithing because it is a pleasure to do so, or because we desire to harp upon that principle; but we are doing it because the necessities of the people are such that it becomes obligatory upon the leaders of the Church to say something upon this principle, that not only the people may do their duty in regard to this law, but that there may be something in the storehouse of the Lord with which to meet the necessities of the people; for the necessities of the Church are the necessities of the people." (CR, Oct. 1899, p. 41.)

The results of the tithing crusade were soon evident. During the months of June through September 1898, about $65,000 was paid in tithing, while from June 1 to September 15 in 1899, about $137,000 was paid. And in the years that followed, the impetus of that sudden upsurge in dedication to the principle of tithing was apparent, accounting in large measure for the financial strength of the Church and the general prosperity of its members today.

Two months after the October general conference, President Smith suffered the loss of three dear friends: "I heard this morning," he recorded on December 9, "first, that Prest. Franklin D. Richards died a little after 12 O'clock this morning. Second, that Sister Makanoe died this morning about 5 O'clock and, third, that Aunt Emily Partridge Smith [Young] also died this morning about 4 O'clock." He added thoughtfully, "The grim reaper has gathered, indeed, a bountiful harvest this morning."

The passing of "Aunt Emily" aroused some of Joseph F.'s memories of his boyhood days in Nauvoo and of his namesake, the Prophet Joseph Smith, to whom Emily had been sealed. After the martyrdom, she had married President Brigham Young for time and had been a mainstay of his household during all the intervening years since the exodus. Her death broke another living link with the past and must have been a reminder to sixty-one-year-old Joseph F. Smith of his own mortality. Sister Makanoe's passing doubtless reminded President Smith of his close Polynesian ties, and President Franklin D. Richards's death severed a close apostolic relationship of over three decades.

Since Elder Richards had lived in Ogden for many years while he had presided as stake president, it was decided that he would be buried there. So, on Tuesday, December 12, the day of the funeral and burial, Joseph and Sarah traveled to Ogden on the morning train with a large group of the deceased's friends and relatives. The services were held in the old tabernacle located in downtown Ogden on the block where the Ogden Temple now stands. "When the doors were opened," President Smith noted, "the tabernacle was soon crowded to its full capacity." The speakers included Joseph F. Smith and the other members of the First Presidency, and Elder Brigham Young, Jr.

This quartet represented the four senior apostles. At the

time, there was some uncertainty as to the seniority between President Smith and Brigham Young, Jr., since the latter was ordained an apostle before Joseph F., but he was inducted into the Quorum of the Twelve Apostles after him. In the interval between Elder Richards's death and the April general conference in 1900, there were many discussions about the question of seniority, the results of which were summarized by President Smith in this journal entry of April 5, 1900: "We met with the eleven apostles and partook of the Sacrament, Brigham Young blessed the emblems. It was unanimously decided that the acceptance of a member into the Council or Quorum of the Twelve fixed his rank or position in the apostleship. That the apostles took precedence from the date they entered the quorum. Thus today President Snow is the senior apostle. President George Q. Cannon next, myself next, Brigham Young next, Francis M. Lyman next, and so on to the last one received into the quorum. In the case of the death of President Snow, President Cannon surviving him, would succeed to the Presidency, and so on according to seniority in the apostleship of the Twelve; that ordination to the apostleship under the hands of any apostle other than to fill a vacancy in the quorum, and authorized by the General Authorities of the church did not count in precedence; that if the First Presidency were dissolved by the death of the President, his counselors having been ordained apostles in the Quorum of the Twelve would resume their places in the quorum, according to the seniority of their ordination into that quorum. This important ruling settles a long unsettled point, and is most timely."

President Smith took up this theme again at a stake conference in the Oneida stake, where he explained why Brigham Young had not been sustained as the president of the Twelve. He told the audience that "President Snow did not care to part with the next senior apostle, as his counselor, to take the Presidency of the Twelve. Therefore, Brigham Young was the acting senior apostle pro tem."

Reflecting the wide variety of the duties he filled as a counselor in the First Presidency, Joseph F. found himself in Old Mexico two short months after the Oneida stake conference.

His chief mission there was to investigate an expedition comprised of Church members led by Benjamin Cluff, Jr., whose destination was South and Central America and whose apparent purpose was to trace evidences of ancient American civilizations. Concerned that if nothing were said about it, the conduct of the party and its findings would be deemed to have the implied approval of the Church, President Snow had assigned Joseph F. to look into the matter and to make recommendations. This he did, sending a detailed report to President Snow by letter. In answer, he received this telegram from the Prophet: "Letter received. Unanimous mind of Council of First Presidency and Apostles today is that the Expedition disband and return home, unless reasons exist to contrary, unknown to us; but even if this be so, and Brother Cluff and others proceed, they must assume all responsibility." (JFS, p. 312.) Feeling there was merit in the trip, Benjamin Cluff, Jr., and several of his associates decided to continue their expedition, but did so with the understanding it was not under the aegis of the Church.

Having disposed of the business that had taken him to Mexico, President Smith turned to the apostolic duty that always weighed upon him—to bear testimony of the Savior and to instruct and inspire the Saints. He decided, therefore, to take a trip from Juarez to Pacheco, a distance of some thirty-five miles into the rugged Sierra Madres. With him from Salt Lake City were his wife Edna (whose turn it was to accompany her husband on a trip) and Elder Seymour B. Young of the First Council of the Seventy. With the Salt Lake visitors were stake president Anthony W. Ivins, a promising young leader who seven years later would be called to the apostleship by President Smith, and Helaman Pratt, a counselor to President Ivins and a son of Parley P. Pratt. Helaman, whose name alone clearly revealed his LDS heritage, was born at Mt. Pisgah during the exodus, and at the time of the trip with President Smith had spent almost twenty-five years laboring with the Saints in Old Mexico.

To Anthony Ivins and Helaman Pratt, the trip to Pacheco was an everyday occurrence. To Joseph F., Edna, and Elder Young, however, it was an unforgettable ordeal. Traveling through the San Diego Canyon and pass, Joseph, who was no stranger to primitive roads and travel, encountered "the roughest, rockiest, nearest impassible pass I ever passed over within the period of my remembrance. . . . The roads are indescribable." However, the beautiful scenery that opened to view as the travelers ascended higher and higher into the rugged mountains was just compensation for the abominable roads. "Pacheco is situated among the pine forests of the Sierra Madres," Joseph wrote approvingly, "is romantic and picturesque in appearance . . . is about 6100 feet above the sea and has a population of about 250."

The Smiths were the overnight guests of Henry Lunt, a former bishop in Cedar City, Utah. Because of the remoteness of Pacheco, not many General Authorities visited there. Accordingly, it was an especially significant event to have two of them visit at the same time, especially since one of them was an apostle and a member of the First Presidency. At the meeting held in the evening, the little chapel was packed. "We had a good meeting," Joseph confided to his journal, "after which we shook hands with those present."

The next day, the party traveled still farther upward to the LDS colony of Garcia, "situated in a beautiful little round valley in the Sierra Madres, 6850 ft above sea level, and surrounded by pine forests." The combination of the high altitude and the weariness from the hard travel in a buckboard caused Edna to doze off during her husband's remarks at the evening meeting. Arousing suddenly from her slumber when the speaker pounded the pulpit for emphasis, Edna exclaimed aloud, "O!, good gracious." Thinking this was a signal that he had talked too long or too loud, the president hurriedly ended his remarks and sat down, "not knowing what might come next." Seeing time was left, Brother Ivins asked if he could say a few words. Flashing the sense of humor that was often masked by a somewhat austere manner, and showing publicly the easy rapport he had with his family, Joseph answered aloud, "Yes, and if that woman interrupts *you*, we will put her out."

After returning from this trip to Mexico, President Smith barely had time to clear his desk before he was assigned to make a trip north to Canada. He and Julina and sons Hyrum Mack and Alvin Fielding left Salt Lake City on September 10, 1900, traveling by rail to Great Falls, Montana, via Butte. At Great Falls, the party joined prominent businessman E. T. Galt in his private car, which Joseph described as being "elegant," for the trip into Canada. Arriving at his destination, President Smith worked with his fellow counselor in the First Presidency, George Q. Cannon, who was also in Canada, in conducting numerous meetings in Sterling, Magrath, Lethbridge, and Cardston. Between meetings, they inspected the area's extensive canal system, which had been built by the Saints, and counseled the local brethren on ecclesiastical and temporal matters.

At the Church meetings held during this trip, President Smith frequently invited his two sons to speak or to pray. Twenty-eight-year-old Hyrum, the elder of the two by two and a half years, was most frequently called on. This able young man, who had been named in honor of his grandfather, the Patriarch, and whose middle name, Mack, honored his great-great-grandfather, Solomon Mack, doubtless would have been more nervous than he was in sharing the pulpit with his father and President Cannon had he been able to see clearly what would take place in a little more than a year. Had he been blessed with unusual prescience, he would have foreseen that on October 24, 1901, he would be ordained an apostle and inducted into the Quorum of the Twelve by the president of the Church—Joseph F. Smith, his father. Two other significant events would necessarily precede Hyrum's call to the apostleship: first, the death of George Q. Cannon on April 12, 1901, at the comparatively young age of seventy-four; and second, the passing of the benign President Lorenzo Snow on October 10, 1901, at age eighty-seven.

Returning from Canada in late September, President Smith immediately began preparing for the October general conference. Speaking at the Sunday morning session on October 7, he developed three familiar themes: unity, tithing, and home industries. As to tithing, he contrasted the voluntary nature of this principle as practiced by the Saints with the pressurized fund-raising efforts of other denominations, which "keep up their revenue by begging, by passing around the collection-box every time they assemble for worship." (CR, Oct. 1900, p. 47.) As to home industries, he deplored the failure of the Saints to patronize the woolen factory at Provo, noting with regret that 85 percent of the output of this facility was sold to markets outside Utah. (Ibid., p. 48.)

Not long after this conference, Joseph again left Salt Lake City for an extended trip through the LDS colonies in Colorado, Arizona, and Old Mexico. His main purpose was to give encouragement and instruction to the Saints residing in these remote areas where the desert was not as tamed as in the Salt Lake Valley. Alice accompanied him, taking along her five-and-a-half-year-old son, Jesse Kimball Smith, and eighteen-month-old Fielding Kimball Smith. Aside from the fact that it was her turn to accompany President Smith, Alice was especially anxious to make this trip because it would enable her to see her twin brother, Andrew, who was the stake president in the Gila Valley in southeastern Arizona. Joseph's journal entry for November 22, written in Thatcher, Arizona, noted, "We found Andrew Kimball and family all in good health. They all seemed pleased to see us and gave us a hearty welcome."

Included in Andrew's family was a ruddy-cheeked, brown-eyed, five-and-a-half-year-old boy named Spencer Woolley Kimball, who was destined to follow his Uncle Joseph into the prophetic chair as the twelfth president of the Church. At this early age, President Smith's nephew had already begun to show the qualities of loyalty, hard work, and dependability that were to characterize his adulthood. And although he was very young at the time, Spencer was old enough to appreciate the importance of the man who would soon become the president of the Church and to be aware of the humble circumstances under which the Kimballs hosted their visitors. In discussing this visit with the author seventy years after it took place, Spencer described a tent near the Kimball home that was used as an overflow bedroom. And the condition of the main residence in Thatcher is suggested by this entry made in the diary of Spencer's mother, Olive Woolley Kimball, within a few months of the Smiths' visit in late 1901: "I was sick . . . all night. It just poured down with rain. . . . All the beds and bedding got wet. Our house leaked in every room. I felt discouraged as every place but our front room was so wet but we got through the day alright and lived." (Kimball, *Spencer W. Kimball*, p. 41.)

On the return trip to Salt Lake City, President Smith visited many other LDS communities, including several on the Little Colorado River. On December 15, 1900, he made this journal entry about a meeting held in St. Johns, Arizona: "The quarterly conference convened. The choir sang. Opening prayer by Patriarch Henry J. Platt. Prest. D. K. Udall made the opening remarks, reviewing the condition of the stake. Counselor Elijah Freeman followed, expressing his feelings on the present situation and reviewing the history of the settlement of this forbidding, barren and dry country. There was a great curse on the land and it will take great faith to remove it." As a means of countering this somewhat pessimistic counsel, the next speaker urged the people "to remain on their possessions and maintain their property and their foothold, and not abandon their post." President Smith added his endorsement of these sentiments by noting, "Good counsel."

Leaving St. Johns, the president and his party traveled to Holbrook, Arizona, by way of the little town of Concho, where they caught the train to Albuquerque, New Mexico. Alice, who had been left in Thatcher to visit with Andrew Kimball and his family, was to have met her husband in Albuquerque on December 18 but did not arrive until the nineteenth. Joseph was not unduly disturbed by the delay other than showing an understandable concern for the safety of his wife and children. Having sent wires to learn their whereabouts, he spent the time reading, writing in his journal, walking about the town, and shopping. He purchased several colorful Indian lap robes as Christmas gifts for his wives.

Being reunited at last, Joseph, Alice, and the little boys traveled without incident to Salt Lake City via Trinidad and Colorado Springs, arriving on December 21, just in time to make final preparations for Christmas. Joseph took special pains to see that each family had not only suitable gifts but food for a special Christmas dinner, either turkey or "good rump roasts." On Christmas day, the patriarch noted with some satisfaction that his families were "all pleased with their 'Christmas.'" As for himself, he received a "number of hand-kerchiefs . . . and several neck ties," indicating that the staple Christmas gifts for husbands and fathers have not altered much over the years.

Chapter Eighteen

Presidential Ministry Begins

F ollowing the October general conference of 1900, George Q. Cannon obtained permission from President Snow to travel to Hawaii to attend the Jubilee anniversary of the opening of that mission fifty years before. He was received with great affection as he traveled around the islands, visiting old friends, who showered him with gifts and garlands and plied him with the special foods and entertainment usually reserved for royalty. And royalty was included in his train of admirers and wellwishers when Liliuokalani, the sister of the native king Kalakua, came to pay her respects. This regal woman, who was the last of the native rulers of the Hawaiian Islands, and who had been deposed by the revolution of 1893, paid President Cannon the ultimate compliment when she asked for and received a blessing at his hands.

This welcome and peaceful interlude among loving friends and in a balmy climate did wonders for President Cannon, who had not been in robust health for several months before his visit. He returned to Salt Lake City in January 1901, rejuvenated and ready to take up again the arduous responsibilities of his office. All went well for a while, but soon the rigors of a harsh Utah winter began to take their toll. By March, his health had deteriorated to the point that he found it necessary to seek relief at pleasant Monterey on the California coast, where he had vacationed periodically. In less than a month, the great man was dead, having passed away on April 12. Notified of President Cannon's passing by a wire from John Q. Cannon, the president's brother, Joseph F. paid his longtime friend and associate this sincere tribute: "Thus the noble career, the valiant labors, and the brilliant life of President Geo. Q. Cannon have come to a finish in this world. He was both a humble and a great man, a mighty chieftain in the councils of the brethren. All Israel will mourn his death and feel their great loss of him. But God is at the Helm!"

President Snow delayed filling the vacancy in the First Presidency until the October general conference. During the interval, Joseph's duties were multiplied as he strove to take up the slack caused by the death of his friend. When the conference convened on Friday, October 4, President Snow was not well and instructed President Smith to take charge, which he did. Not until the last session on Sunday afternoon, October 6, was President Snow able to attend. At the conclusion of his brief remarks at that session, President Snow said he had selected another counselor who he thought would be energetic and strong and would "serve the people, and help me and President Joseph F. Smith along in a proper way." (CR, Oct. 1901, p. 62.) The man selected was Elder Rudger Clawson, whom President Snow had called to the Twelve three years before and who previously had served as the president of the Box Elder stake, where President Snow had served as the presiding officer many years before. It was fated, however, that Elder Clawson would never be set apart as a counselor, as President Snow passed away on the following Thursday, October 10, 1901. The funeral services were held in the Salt Lake Tabernacle on Sunday, October 13, just a week after the deceased had spoken publicly for the last time. President Smith, who presided at these services, referred to his departed leader as "the last among the Apostles who were, in their mature years, intimately acquainted with the Prophet Joseph Smith." (CR, Oct. 1901, p. 96.) He then paid Lorenzo Snow this high compliment: "With the exception perhaps of the Prophet Joseph Smith himself, there has never stood a man upon the earth in this generation who has borne a more clear cut, positive and direct testimony of the divine mission of Joseph Smith and the divinity of this great latter day work than President Lorenzo Snow did." (Ibid.)

On October 17, a week after President Snow's death, the apostles convened in the Salt Lake Temple, where, in accordance with the established pattern, Joseph F. Smith, the senior apostle, was set apart as the sixth president of the Church. And on Sunday, November 10, 1901, a special conference convened in Salt Lake City, where the new First Presidency and the other general officers were presented for sustaining vote. At the beginning of the first session, President Smith told the large audience jammed into the tabernacle, "President Snow said to me, 'you will live to be the President of the Church of Jesus Christ of Latter-day Saints, and when that time comes you should proceed at once and reorganize the Presidency of the Church.'" (Ibid., p. 71.) He also set the tone for his administration in these words: "It is our duty to take hold of the work vigorously, with full determination and purpose of heart to carry it on, with the help of the Lord, and in accordance with the inspiration of His Spirit, as it has been done in the past. It is our privilege to live nearer to the Lord, if we will, than we have ever done, that we may enjoy a greater outpouring of His Spirit than we have ever enjoyed, and that we may advance faster, grow in the knowledge of the truth more rapidly, and become more thoroughly established in the faith." (Ibid., pp. 69-70.)

Sustained as first counselor in the First Presidency was eighty-one-year-old John R. Winder, who at the time had served as a counselor in the Presiding Bishopric for fifteen years. Bishop Winder was brought favorably to President Smith's attention in 1892 when he was placed in charge of preparing the Salt Lake Temple for dedication. During the dedicatory services, President Smith spoke highly of Bishop Winder's work and "pronounced a blessing on him for time and all eternity." (Jenson, *LDS Biographical Encyclopedia* 1:245.)

Joseph F.'s second counselor was the fifty-seven-year-old Dane, Anthon H. Lund, a native of Aalborg, Denmark, who had been an apostle for twelve years. A resident of San Pete

County after immigrating to the United States in 1862, President Lund was prominent there in Church, business, and political circles, serving as vice-president and then as president of the Manti Temple, as the manager of the cooperative store in Ephraim, and as a member of the territorial legislature elected from San Pete County. At the time of his call to the First Presidency, he was serving as the Church historian, having succeeded Franklin D. Richards in that position. It was said of Elder Lund that even his antagonists loved him. And Elder Heber J. Grant, a fellow apostle, said of him, "Erastus Snow was my ideal of an apostle of the Lord, and Brother Snow's mantle has, in my opinion, fallen upon Elder Anthon H. Lund." (Ibid., p. 167.)

The Church over which Joseph F. Smith was called to preside had grown from a membership of six in 1830 to a membership of almost two hundred eighty thousand in October 1901, divided into fifty stakes and twenty-one missions. Over one-sixth of the membership resided in the Salt Lake Valley, and until just a year before Joseph became president, this large concentration of Latter-day Saints was included in a single stake and fifty wards.

For the most part, the Latter-day Saints who comprised the Church at this time were faithful and disciplined. But as Joseph surveyed the Church when he became its president, comparing it with the Church as defined in the revelations, he found some organizational deviations. Addressing himself to these at the special meeting held on November 10, 1901, the new president said, "We cannot deny the fact that the Lord has effected one of the most perfect organizations in this Church that ever existed upon the earth. I do not know of any more perfect organization than exists in the Church of Jesus Christ of Latter-day Saints today. We have not always carried out strictly the order of the Priesthood; we have varied from it to some extent; but we hope in due time that, by the promptings of the Holy Spirit, we will be led into the exact channel and course that the Lord has marked out for us to pursue, and adhere strictly to the order that He has established." President Smith then read the portion of Doctrine and Covenants 124 that defines the duties and authorities of the general

Church officers. After doing so, the prophet added, "These are the officers of the Priesthood as the Lord has given it, and we propose to follow it as near as we know how in the future, but we will take such other measures as may be deemed proper and right in due time." (CR, Oct. 1901, pp. 71-72.)

These remarks seemed to foreshadow the main thrust of Joseph F. Smith's administration. In the years ahead, as promised in this inaugural address, he defined and emphasized the role of the priesthood. He explained the broad and enduring authority of the priesthood to act in the name of God. He outlined the relative jurisdictions of priesthood quorums and ward and stake organizations. He analyzed and cataloged the qualities priesthood bearers should cultivate. He underscored the delicate relationship between priesthood authority in the Church at large and in the individual families that comprised the Church. And he provided important insights into the place of the priesthood in the hereafter.

Three days after delivering this inaugural address, President Joseph F. Smith celebrated his sixty-third birthday. He was then at the height of his mental and spiritual powers and in his physical appearance projected the idealized image of a prophet. He carried 185 pounds on a well-proportioned five-foot-eleven-inch frame. A full beard and gray, abundant hair framed a face that reflected his dominant characteristics of willpower, persistence, and kindliness. The most striking aspect of this face was the steady gaze of his brown eyes, which had a penetrating, searching quality.

Little if any time was required to acquaint the new president with the requirements of his office. For thirty-five years he had been one of the inner circle of Church leaders. He had served as a counselor to the four previous presidents (Brigham Young, John Taylor, Wilford Woodruff, and Lorenzo Snow), and he had served with the last three throughout their presidencies. Moreover, his knowledge of Church leaders and doctrines extended to the earliest days of the Church. Moreover, he had seen Church administration from the perspective of a follower while for many years he had served on various missions.

But these impressive credentials of heritage and experience were, in a sense, overshadowed by another that vastly strengthened his new role. This was the exemplary character of his personal and family life. It would have been difficult to have found another man and his family who more convincingly portrayed the beneficial fruits of their religion. His was a family of love, unity, and achievement, comprised of the patriarch, his five living wives, and thirty-six living children who ranged in age from eighteen months to thirty-two years.

Another significant strength Joseph F. Smith brought to his office was the almost unanimous support and loyalty of Church leaders and members. From practically the beginning of his apostolic career, there was a widely held opinion that he would one day be the president. Allusion has been made already to the insight given to Lorenzo Snow in Hawaii in 1864 that the outspoken young Joseph F. Smith, not yet a general authority, would one day be president of the Church. President Snow shared that insight with Joseph F. after the death of Wilford Woodruff, telling him that he would succeed to the presidency at Lorenzo's death. (JFS, p. 324.) And Wilford Woodruff made a similar prediction at a stake conference while he was president of the Church. (Ibid.)

However, some members showed little enthusiasm for Joseph F. Smith's ascendency to the presidential office. These were generally in three categories: those who deplored his aggressive outspokenness; those who feared or were jealous of his authority; and those who felt that his call was more the result of family ties than personal merit. Some of those in the first category came at last to this conclusion: "Once stern and unrelenting, [Joseph F. Smith] has mellowed as the years go on, until he sees but the good in humanity and forgives men their trespasses." (*Goodwins Weekly*, Apr. 18, 1916.) Those in the other categories, whose biases were too deeply entrenched, never really changed, although the way in which President Smith acquitted himself in office may have given some of them pause for reflection.

Chapter Nineteen

Grappling with the Problems of Presidency

W hile the steps taken by Lorenzo Snow to solve the Church's financial problems had set it on an upward course, much was yet to be done before the goal would be reached. So President Smith picked up the baton where his predecessor had laid it down and pushed forward. This objective absorbed much of Joseph's time and energy during the early days of his administration. He continued to preach the principle of tithing aggressively, as evidenced by his keynote address at the October general conference in 1902: "We will say to the people that we have no reason to complain of the diligence of the Saints, so far as we are able to judge, in keeping the law of tithing. We believe that the Latter-day Saints are observing that law as faithfully as they have ever done, and we beseech of you that you will continue to do this until our hands shall be freed from all obligations, and until we shall have means in the storehouse of the Lord with which to accomplish greater works, which may be necessary to be done." (CR, Oct. 1902, p. 2.)

The fruits of this effort are suggested by the fact that on New Year's Eve, 1903, the First Presidency celebrated the halfway mark in paying off the Church's million-dollar bond. Three years later the balance of the bond was paid, leaving the

Church debt-free for the first time in many years. And with the principle of tithing firmly imbedded in the minds and hearts of the people, the way ahead was clear for an era of financial stability that the Church a few years before would have thought impossible.

As it turned out, Church finances were overshadowed by a problem of far greater magnitude during the early years of President Smith's administration. This was the seemingly perennial problem of polygamy, which had vexed the Latter-day Saints for many decades. Although the Manifesto had been in effect for more than ten years, there was still uncertainty in some quarters about the extent to which it was applicable and some laxity in the precise definition and enforcement of it. The difficulty lay in the misunderstanding of some that the prohibition did not extend beyond the borders of the United States, and in the comparatively wide diffusion of the authority to perform sealings. This state of affairs came to a head in the celebrated case of Reed Smoot, in which President Joseph F. Smith was deeply involved and which produced a convulsive and permanent change in the attitude of the Church toward polygamy and in the status of those who continued to practice or preach it.

At the center of this absorbing drama stood Reed Smoot, who had been called and ordained an apostle and inducted into the Quorum of the Twelve by President Lorenzo Snow on April 8, 1900. In 1902, Elder Smoot sought and obtained from President Smith a waiver of the Church's so-called political manifesto, making it possible to take a leave of absence from his position in the Twelve and to offer himself as a candidate for the U.S. Senate. His candidacy proved successful when, on January 20, 1903, the Republican-controlled Utah legislature elected him. Immediately a groundswell of opposition developed in Salt Lake City. It was generated by a group of sectarian ministers interspersed with a sprinkling of nonmember professionals and businessmen. Wasting no time, these militant critics published a document six days after Reed Smoot's election, protesting his being seated in the Senate. The essence of their protest was that the Senator-elect was a member of a "self-perpetuating body of fifteen men" who

219

shaped the beliefs and controlled the conduct "of those under them in all matters whatsoever, civil and religious, temporal and spiritual." (United States Smoot Proceedings 1:1.) Specifically, the protesters alleged that these Church leaders had exercised their influence so as "to inculcate and encourage a belief in polygamy and polygamous cohabitation" and that they had countenanced and connived "at violations of the laws of the State prohibiting the same regardless of pledges made for the purpose of obtaining statehood and of covenants made with the people of the United States, and who by all the means in their power protect and honor those who with themselves violate the laws of the land and are guilty of practices destructive of the family and the home." (Ibid.)

A separate protest was made by the Rev. J. L. Leilich; it was similar in substance but more strident and condemnatory in tone. (Ibid., pp. 26-27.) However, it lost any force it might have had by the inclusion of a false allegation that the Senator-elect was a polygamist.

Moving with customary glacial speed, the Senate Committee on Privileges and Elections did not consider these protests for a year. In the meantime, Senator Smoot was sworn in and began to function as if everything were normal. By January 1904, the committee, prodded by the protesters, was ready to wheel its ponderous investigative machinery into place. The hearings began on January 16, 1904, amidst a flurry of sensational press releases that were to continue for the nearly two years during which the committee received testimony. It was what in the present vernacular would be called a media event, with the press grinding out its daily grist of sensational stories culled from the testimony of a "veritable cloud of witnesses." Receiving the kind of press treatment routinely accorded to it, the Church found itself the butt of public ridicule and slander as biased reports focused on the sensational aspects of the testimony.

It was in this circus-like atmosphere that President Smith traveled to Washington, D.C., in early 1904 to appear before the committee as one of its principal witnesses. On March 2, 1904, he was called to the stand, where he remained for three days of intensive and sometimes belligerent questioning by the committee and its legal staff. When he first took the stand, President Smith had some feelings of trepidation, not knowing exactly what to expect. These feelings were intensified when he scanned the faces of the committee members, all of whom, with the exception of Senator Dillingham of Vermont, reflected dislike and mistrust. And when the questioning began, the witness soon perceived that the Church was on trial, not Senator Smoot. This was evidenced by the kinds of questions put to him, questions about the nature of God, the kinds of revelations he had received, his private life, his personal beliefs, and his duties as president. As the questioning continued, however, Joseph F. seemed to gain self-confidence. His years of experience as a speaker, author, administrator, and legislator came to his aid, lending an air of poise and authority that, added to his dignified bearing, his imposing appearance, and his frank responses, disarmed his questioners and put them on the defensive.

President Smith came to the witness stand realizing that he was in violation of the law because he had continued after the Manifesto to cohabit with the wives to whom he had been sealed prior to 1890. And the committee's legal staff, also being aware of that fact, apparently had hoped to use it to embarrass and discredit the witness. To their surprise, however, President Smith was perfectly open in acknowledging that he had continued to live with these wives. He explained that this conduct merely reflected the love, loyalty, and responsibility he felt toward them, but he denied that it demonstrated an intention to perpetuate polygamy. The testimony also showed that nonmembers, including federal officials, had acquiesced in this arrangement, not only as to President Smith but as to other polygamous Latter-day Saints, to gradually eliminate the practice through attrition. (United States Smoot Proceedings 1:130-33.)

However, President Smith denied that he had continued to authorize or perform polygamous sealings after the Manifesto and that any such sealings had been performed on the sole authority and responsibility of those performing them.

Among other things, the voluminous testimony in the Smoot hearings (which failed in their purpose to unseat the

Utah senator) showed that a comparatively large number of polygamous marriages had been performed after the Manifesto by some who held the sealing power. The most prominent among these was John W. Taylor of the Twelve, a son of President John Taylor, who expressed his views of the scope of the Manifesto in these words: "I have always believed that the government of the United States had jurisdiction only within its own boundaries, and that the term 'laws of the land' in the manifesto meant merely the laws of the United States." Responding to the fact that the head of the Church and others had taken the position that it applied to every part of the Church, Elder Taylor had said, "It is doubtless true that this view of the matter has been given by President Woodruff and others, but I have never taken that as binding upon me or the Church, because it [such interpretation] was never presented for adoption by 'common consent,' as was the manifesto itself, and I have disputed its authority as a law or rule of the Church." (See United States Smoot Proceedings 4:441; *In Defense of the Faith and the Saints* 2:329-30.)

Returning home from Washington, D.C., only a short time before the April general conference, President Smith, concerned about adverse publicity from the Smoot hearings and about the loose observance of the Manifesto, decided to plug the hole that had enabled John W. Taylor and others who shared his views to ignore the Manifesto beyond the borders of the United States. At the morning conference session on April 6, 1904, President Smith presented to the conference for its sustaining vote what has since been known as the Worldwide Manifesto. Before reading it to the conference, he made these comments: "Now I am going to present a matter to you that is unusual and I do it because of a conviction which I feel that it is a proper thing for me to do. I have taken the liberty of having written down what I wish to present, in order that I may say to you the exact words which I would like to have conveyed to your ears, that I may not be misunderstood or misquoted. I present this to the conference for your action." President Smith then read the following statement, which bore his signature as the president of the Church: "Inasmuch as there are numerous reports in circulation that plural marriages have been entered into contrary to the official declaration of President Woodruff, of September 26, 1890, commonly called the Manifesto, which was issued by President Woodruff and adopted by the Church at its general conference, October 6, 1890, which forbade any marriages violative of the law of the land; I, Joseph F. Smith, President of the Church of Jesus Christ of Latter-day Saints, hereby affirm and declare that no such marriages have been solemnized with the sanction, consent or knowledge of the Church of Jesus Christ of Latter-day Saints, and I hereby announce that all such marriages are prohibited, and if any officer or member of the Church shall assume to solemnize or enter into any such marriage he will be deemed in transgression against the Church and will be liable to be dealt with, according to the rules and regulations thereof, and excommunicated therefrom." (CR, Apr. 1904, p. 75.)

Francis M. Lyman, president of the Twelve, then presented a resolution committing the members of the Church to "approve and endorse this statement" and agreeing to "support the courts of the church in the enforcement thereof." Being seconded by Elder B. H. Roberts and several others, this resolution was then adopted by the unanimous vote of the conference. (Ibid., p. 76.)

President Smith's firm action was a clear signal that he intended to enforce the Manifesto with rigidity. And although the 1904 statement retained the language "the law of the land," from which John W. Taylor and others had taken license to continue to perform polygamous sealings, the inclusion of language providing for the excommunication of violators and the background of the Smoot hearings against which the 1904 statement had been presented and adopted clearly closed the loopholes in the Manifesto.

A few still refused to accept this policy because of feelings that the mandate to live polygamy given by earlier Church presidents was irrevocable. Among these were John W. Taylor and Matthias Cowley of the Twelve. These two able men, who were only forty-seven at the time, resigned from their positions on October 28, 1905. Several years later, because of continued advocacy of their views, they were disciplined by ecclesiastical courts, Elder Taylor being excommunicated and Elder Cowley being disfellowshipped. And out in the Church, the repercussions from the Official Statement were more widespread, though not as visible and dramatic as in the case of the two apostles.

While President Smith was to be troubled intermittently by the aftershocks, as in the Taylor-Cowley affair and in handling other dissidents, the Worldwide Manifesto of 1904 laid at rest the problem of polygamy as far as the Church was concerned. This left him free to pursue other projects. One of these was initiated at the same general conference that saw the curtain rung down on the polygamy drama. Joseph F. introduced the matter through his first counselor, John R. Winder, who presented a resolution that the Church erect a "suitable building or monument" to the memory of Joseph and Hyrum Smith. After the resolution had been adopted by the conference "without a dissenting vote," President Smith appointed John R. Winder as chairman of the planning committee with Francis M. Lyman, William B. Preston, and George Romney as members. (Ibid., p. 77.)

The purchase of the Solomon Mack farm by the Church in May 1905 provided the logical location for such a memorial, since it was here, at Sharon, Windsor County, Vermont, that the Prophet Joseph Smith was born on December 23, 1805. Later developments suggested the advisability of making it a memorial for the Prophet Joseph Smith alone, although in a sense it became a memorial for the entire Smith family. To dramatize the farm as the location of the Prophet's birth, it was decided that a granite monument thirty-eight and a half feet high representing the length of Joseph Smith's life would be erected there. The contract for the monument was awarded on July 24, 1805, to the R. C. Bowers Co. of Montpelier. Despite difficulty in obtaining a solid piece of granite thirty-eight and a half feet long, and the shortness of time, the shaped and polished monument was erected and a small cottage constructed near it in time to celebrate the centennial of the Prophet's birth.

President Smith and a large party left Salt Lake City on Monday, December 18, 1905, in a special train destined for

Vermont to attend the unveiling and dedication of the monument. Arriving in South Royalton on Friday, December 22, the president, with members of his family who accompanied him, made a pilgrimage by sleigh to nearby Tunbridge, where Hyrum Smith was born. Betraying both his historical bent and his family loyalty, Joseph F. took time while there to visit the town clerk to check old records. He discovered a veritable treasure trove of Smith genealogy, including entries of the marriage of his grandparents, Joseph Smith, Sr., and Lucy Mack Smith, the births of their children Alvin, Hyrum, and Sophronia, along with entries pertaining to other relatives. The long lapse of time since these progenitors had walked Vermont's green hills could not have dimmed his recollection of the family triumphs and travails during the intervening years nor the reverential love he felt for them. And on the following day, as he traveled over rock-ribbed, rolling landscape to the monument site, he could not have failed to marvel at the tenacity and fortitude of forebears who had scratched a living from such resistant and unpromising soil.

The veiled monument, standing straight and stark against the surrounding hills, presented an impressive sight as the party came in view of it. Already gathered when the president's party arrived were scores of Vermonters from nearby farms who had come out of curiosity or neighborliness, and many Latter-day Saints who had accompanied the presidential party from Salt Lake City or traveled from nearby communities or states to pay homage to their martyred prophet.

After brief services, President Smith offered a dedicatory prayer that included the customary expressions of thanks and pleadings for the protection of the monument and cottage. It also contained this unusual petition for the surrounding countryside and its inhabitants: "We ask Thee to bless the people of South Royalton, of Tunbridge and Sharon, and surrounding country. And this land being the birthplace and the nursing place of many of Thy most faithful and renowned servants, who have made their mark in the world for the uplifting and benefit of mankind, O God, wilt thou let Thy peace and blessing be upon this land. May it be prospered. May those who dwell here multiply and increase and replenish the

Joseph F. Smith with Andrew Jenson (left) and Oluf J. Andersen of the Scandinavian Mission. (Church Archives.)

earth. May all barrenness be removed from the soil, that it may be fruitful and prosperous from this time forward; that good men may gather here, and those born here find place and be happy and enjoy themselves in the midst of these everlasting hills." (JFS, p. 363.)

After the congregation sang "Praise to the Man," Edith A. Smith, the oldest female representative of the Smith family present, unveiled the huge monument which, in the rough, weighed nearly sixty tons. Adding the two granite bases on which the shaft rested, the massive monument weighed almost one hundred tons, harmonizing fittingly with the rugged Vermont landscape.

The unveiled monument revealed this commemorative inscription carved into its south face: "Sacred to the Memory of Joseph Smith the Prophet. Born here 23d December, 1805, Martyred Carthage, Illinois 27th June 1844." And on its north face was etched the Prophet's "Testimony," which included this sentence, identifying him with the martyred Patriarch and thereby fulfilling, to a degree, the original plan of jointly memorializing Joseph and Hyrum: "In his ministry he was constantly supported by his brother Hyrum Smith, who suffered martyrdom with him."

Participating in this dedication had a profound emotional effect on President Smith. Being in the locality where the earthly roots of his father and uncle had been planted, and where the Prophet and the Patriarch had been taught the religious truths that would unlock the door to the Restoration, his mind was called up to serious reflection about his past and about his family and its role in the unfolding history of the Church. The emotions evoked by these reflections boiled to the surface at a little gathering held in the cottage following the dedication ceremonies, where the President was presented with a watch chain and locket by his counselor, Anthon H. Lund. In his brief remarks of acceptance, Joseph, who ordinarily refrained from personal references in his public utterances, revealed a tender and vulnerable side of his personality that few people ever saw. "Of course, my heart has been full during the whole of the day," he told his listeners. "Yesterday, while visiting the birthplace of my father and some of his brothers and sisters, and contemplating this rugged country, filled with hills and ravines, the thought that here in this land was where my kindred had birth, that we are perhaps traversing the same roads and the same ravines, and possibly partaking of the products of the same orchard from which our ancestors two or three generations ago partook, and then the thought of dedicating this monument—[here the president broke down, his voice choked with emotion, and his eyes filled with tears; but, making an effort to control himself, he continued]—My heart is like that of a child. It is easily touched, especially with love, I can much easier weep for joy than for sorrow. I suppose perhaps it is due to some extent to the fact that all my early remembrances were painful and sorrowful. The persecutions of the Prophet and people in Missouri and in Illinois, the final martyrdom of the Prophet and my father, the expulsion of the Saints from Nauvoo, the driving out of the widows and the orphans from their homes, the journey across the plains, the hardships we endured in the settling of the valley of the Great Salt Lake, and trying to make a home there, my experiences on the plains, in standing guard herding cattle, and going to the canyons; then starting out at age fifteen on a mission to the Sandwich Islands, so far away, alone apparently, without father or mother, without kindred or friends scarcely—all this had a tendency in my youth to depress my spirit. But I had strength by the grace of God to keep myself from deadly sins. And now when I experience the expressions of confidence and love of my brethren and sisters whom I love, it goes directly to my heart. I want to thank you for the expressions made through President Lund by my brethren and sisters who are present, and to say that I appreciate and prize it more than all else in the world. I would rather die any moment than to do aught that would forfeit the confidence and the love of my friends and my brethren. I want to live so that I will be worthy, in some degree—I cannot expect to be as worthy as I should be—of the love and confidence shown toward me; but I desire to have at least some merit and to be a little worthy of the confidence and love of my brethren." (JFS, pp. 364-65.)

This remarkable statement, uttered extemporaneously, provides important insight into the motivations that impelled Joseph F. Smith through a long life of service and achievement. The obvious mainspring was his love of family, including his immediate genetic family, and the larger family comprised of his brethren and sisters in the Church. It is clear that the death of his parents and the adverse consequences that flowed from that loss were the chief sorrows of his life, which cloaked his maturing years in sable hues. And it is equally clear that the growth and maturing of his own family was the chief happiness of his later life, enabling him to give them the love, security, and sense of belonging that he so sorely missed as a lonely orphan.

The dedication of the Joseph Smith Memorial turned out to be merely the first stop in a kind of odyssey as the travelers traced the path of the Smith family across the continent. From Vermont the clan traveled to Boston, Massachusetts, where several meetings were held in Deacons Hall. These were attended by President Smith's party as well as by local Church members and by missionaries laboring in the area. On Christmas day, Joseph F. and members of his family went to nearby Topsfield and Boxford, where Robert Smith, the original progenitor of the Smith family in America, had lived, and where many of his children were born. At Boxford, the descendants of this honored ancestor refreshed themselves with a drink from the old well he reportedly had used. Joseph Fielding Smith, the president's son, who was among the drinkers, reported that the water was "clear and cool." (JFS, p. 370.)

The next stop on the itinerary was Palmyra, New York, from where they traveled to nearby Manchester Township to visit the farm and home owned by the president's grandfather, Joseph Smith, Sr., and where had occurred the fateful visitation of the Father and the Son to the boy prophet, thereby beginning the epic drama of the Restoration. Visiting in turn the Sacred Grove and the Hill Cumorah, the members of the group were reminded in a powerful and personal way of the spiritual heritage they possessed and of the divine, other-worldly nature of the work in which they were engaged. The spirituality of the occasion was richly enhanced by a moving prayer offered by President Smith atop the Hill Cumorah, following, as it did, the singing of the hymn "An Angel from on High."

Seeds planted by this visit took root within a few years, which resulted in the Church's purchasing substantial land in the area, including the Joseph Smith Farm, the Hill Cumorah, and the Sacred Grove. As developed and beautified, these today constitute one of the key links in the Church's extensive chain of visitors centers and historical attractions.

From Palmyra, the party traveled to Cleveland, Ohio, by train and then to Kirtland by team. The focal points of interest here for President Smith were the temple and the old home where his parents had lived. These buildings were of significance to him as symbols of the ecclesiastical and domestic roles played by his father in that place. While in Kirtland in the 1830s, Hyrum Smith had served successively as a member of the bishopric, as a high counselor, as an assistant counselor in the First Presidency, and finally as a counselor in the First Presidency. While serving as an assistant counselor, he was a member of the committee, chaired by Joseph Smith, that drafted the rules and regulations governing the use of the temple. Against this background, President Joseph F. Smith was both annoyed and amused to read the inscription on the front of the temple: "House of the Lord, Built by the Church of Jesus Christ of Latter-day Saints, 1834, Reorganized Church of Jesus Christ of Latter-day Saints in Succession By decision of the Court February, 1880." After reading these words and reflecting on them, Joseph F. said aloud to the group standing with him in front of the building, "No order of the court could transmit the succession of the Holy Priesthood or of the Spirit and power and religious rights of the Church established by revelation from God." (JFS, p. 371.)

President Smith showed a special interest in the Hyrum Smith home to which Mary Fielding had been taken as a new bride. Here Joseph F. Smith was conceived, his parents having left Kirtland just a few months before his birth in Far West, Missouri, in November 1838.

This trip, which ended in early January 1906 and which was so powerful in cementing family ties and so sweet in arousing pleasant memories, was, in a sense, a welcome antidote to the sour note sounded by another Smith during the previous summer. This unwelcome family discord came in the person of Frederick M. Smith, the eldest son of Joseph Smith III, then president of the Reorganized Church. Traveling to Utah under the sponsorship of ex-U.S. senator from Utah Thomas Kearns, who in February 1905 had delivered a scathing attack on Church leaders on the Senate floor, Frederick M. Smith arrived in Salt Lake City intent on capitalizing on what he mistakenly perceived as a deterioration in the unity and strength of the Church. The visitor's misconceptions arose from the fulminations of the wealthy ex-senator through the pages of his newspaper, the *Salt Lake Tribune,* which he had purchased in 1901 in the hope it would help to perpetuate a lengthy career in the Senate. Mr. Kearns had made his attack on the Church, and chiefly on President Joseph F. Smith, on February 28, 1905, just four days before the end of his term. It being apparent then that he would not be returning to the Senate, the *Tribune's* publisher, who had amassed a fortune from Utah's mines, fired a parting salvo at the Church, characterizing it as a dangerous monarchy feeding on the tithes of the people and covertly allowing its leaders to live in polygamy. "Lately no effort has been made to punish any of these people by local law," he thundered on the floor of the Senate. "On the contrary, the ruling monarch [meaning President Joseph F. Smith] has continued to grow in power, wealth and importance. He sits upon innumerable boards of directors, among others that of the Union Pacific Railway, where he joins upon terms of fraternity with the great financial and transportation magnates of the United States, who hold him in their councils because his power to benefit or to injure their possessions must be taken into account." Having thus defined what he ostensibly considered to be a grave danger, the senator prescribed a solution: "It is the duty of this great body—the senate of the United States— to serve notice on this church Monarch and his apostles that they must live within the law; that the nation is supreme; that the institutions of this country must prevail throughout the land, and that the compact upon which statehood was granted must be preserved inviolate." (Congressional Record for the 58th Congress, vol. 39, part 4, pp. 3608-13.)

Enlisting the aid of an apostate editor, Frank J. Cannon, Mr. Kearns continued his campaign in the *Tribune* after his Senate term ended, and seeing the possibility of pouring more water on that wheel, persuaded the gullible young Frederick M. Smith to join his crusade. Opening up the pages of the *Tribune* to him and providing writing assistance, Mr. Kearns used the visitor for his own purposes, caring nothing about the ecclesiastical differences that existed between the two churches except as those differences were helpful in his vendetta.

Illustrative of the spirit and substance of the attacks Frederick Smith made upon the Church in the *Tribune* is this excerpt from an article about the then proposed Joseph Smith Memorial: "I protest against such erection because it is unfair in the light of what the Reorganized Church is presenting to the world that Joseph Smith was a man who taught and practiced good morals and was an advocate of peace and good will—it is unfair, I contend, that these Mormon leaders should forestall a just consideration of the work of Joseph Smith, and thereby unjust aspersion should continue to attach to his name, because such men will attach the stigma of their law-breaking to his name by erecting monuments which shall announce that they call him their prophet. These men have great amounts of money placed in their hands by a sacrificing people, for which there is no account rendered to that people, and this money they freely spend in erecting monuments to fix the eyes of the world upon their infidelity to morals and law." (JFS, pp. 354-55.)

This article and others of similar tone, which called upon Church members to reject their leaders, were not calculated to cement the bonds of friendship between the descendants of Joseph and Hyrum. And the spirit of discord they introduced was aggravated by similarly critical articles published in the organs of the Reorganized Church by Joseph Smith III.

These unprovoked attacks engendered mixed feelings of sorrow and anger in Joseph F. and his family. It was sorrowful to consider how two families descended from the same common ancestor and bound together before the martyrdom by the love of the gospel could afterward have drifted so far apart. "It was a sorrowful condition," wrote Joseph Fielding Smith, "to see these men, who should have been valiantly defending the Gospel of Jesus Christ restored through Joseph Smith the Prophet, their ancestor, engaging with the enemies of the Church in the futile effort to destroy that work." (JFS, p. 355.)

Chapter Twenty

The President at Work, at Home, and at Play

S ome time after being sustained as Church president, Joseph F. moved with his family into the Beehive House, which had been built by his predecessor Brigham Young. Because the office of the First Presidency was housed in a small structure adjoining the Beehive House, connecting it with the Lion House to the west, the move brought about a closer relationship between President Smith's ecclesiastical duties and his domestic life.

It was necessary for President Smith to walk only a few feet across a narrow hall to move from his secluded bedroom-study in the Beehive House to his official office in the First Presidency's suite. Whether he functioned in one place or the other, he worked with the same methodical precision. Charles W. Nibley, whom President Smith called as Presiding Bishop of the Church in 1907, said of Joseph F.'s work habits, "He was the most methodical in all his work of any person I ever knew. Every letter that he received had to be endorsed by him with the date and any other information, and all carefully filed away. He could not stand for disorder. Everything in connection with his work was orderly." (IE 22:196.) And he worked not only with thoroughness but with great perseverance and tenacity. "He was a most strenuous worker," reported Bishop Nibley, "and never considered saving himself at all. You could go up to his little office in the Beehive most any night when he was well, and find him writing letters or attending to some other work. Perhaps some dear old soul had written him a personal letter, and he would work into the night answering it with his own hand." (Ibid.)

But this prophet did not work incessantly. He devoted much time to his family obligations, giving support, counsel, and love to his wives and children. And this was not a merely perfunctory service but entailed a substantial investment in time and effort. Bishop Nibley has left us this fascinating view of domestic life behind the walls of the Beehive House: "I have visited at his home when one of his little children was down sick. I have seen him come home from his work at night tired, as he naturally would be, and yet he would walk the floor for hours with that little one in his arms, petting it and loving it, encouraging it in every way with such tenderness and such a soul of pity and love as not one mother in a thousand would show." (Ibid., p. 197.)

As for his diversions, Joseph F. was fond of music, especially Church hymns. And he enjoyed sports of all kinds, either as spectator or participant. Given his preference, however, he would elect to participate rather than watch. In the vigor of youth he enjoyed jumping, wrestling, and foot-racing. And in his mature years, he was introduced to the more sedate sport of golf, which alternately pleased and exasperated him. We are indebted again to Bishop Nibley, who was a frequent golfing companion, for this vignette: "He got so that he could play a very good game, excellent indeed for a man of his years. But on one occasion, down at Santa Monica, when we were playing, we were up within about one hundred feet of the flag at the hole we were making for. A light stroke should have driven the ball nearer the flag, but the inclination to look up as one tries to hit the ball got the best of him, and the consequence was he topped the ball and it rolled only a couple of feet or so. He bent over for the next stroke . . . when he topped it again and it moved but a few feet further. The third time he went up to it and hit it a whack that sent it rolling one hundred feet beyond the flag. His son, Wesley, who was playing with us, called out, 'Why, Papa, what did you do that for? You knew it would roll away down there in the ditch!' The President straightened up and said, rather severely, 'Well, I was mad at it.'" (Ibid., pp. 194-95.)

The temper this incident suggests, which he learned to control in his maturity, no doubt contributed significantly to his success. And the compulsion to achieve and to win added a powerful impetus to that basic drive. Bishop Nibley saw this aspect of his friend's personality in their checker playing, which was a favorite pastime during the many lengthy trips they took together. The bishop readily acknowledged Joseph F. as his superior in checkers and noted that ordinarily his opponent would raise no objection were he to take a move back after seeing it was an unwise one. "But on the other hand," wrote the bishop, "if I had beaten him for a game or two and should put my finger on a checker to draw it back, even though it were on the instant, he would call out with force enough, and in that positive way of his, 'No you don't, you leave it right there.'" (Ibid.)

But this aggressive, competitive aspect of President Smith's personality was softened by a good sense of humor, which frequently surfaced to relieve tensions and add a pleasing flavor to his personal relationships. "He loved a good story and a good joke," reported Bishop Nibley. "There was a good laugh in him always. He had no patience with vile stories, but there was a fine vein of humor in him, and he could relate incidents of his early life and entertain the crowd about him as few men could." (Ibid., p. 196.)

In his prophetic role, President Smith reflected many different qualities and talents, one of the most conspicuous of which was his persuasive eloquence. He often seemed to exert an almost magnetic effect on an audience. "As a preacher of righteousness, who could compare with him?" asked Bishop Nibley. "He was the greatest that I ever heard— strong, powerful, clear, appealing. It was marvelous how the words of living light and fire flowed from him. He was a born preacher, and yet he did not set himself up to be such. He never thought highly of his own great qualities. Rather, he was simple, plain and unaffected to the last degree; and yet, there was dignity with it all which enabled anyone and everyone to say, 'He is a man among men.' As preacher, leader, teacher, husband, father, citizen and man, I ask who among our mighty ones can be likened unto him?" (Ibid., p. 196.)

At the core of his personality and talents was a deep spirituality that gave color and life to all he did. And that spirituality was never more evident than when he bore testimony of the reality and divinity of God and of the saving effect of the principles of the gospel. One can sense the fervor and conviction with which these words were spoken to a packed audience assembled in the Tabernacle for general conference: "There is no salvation but in the way God has pointed out. There is no hope of everlasting life but through obedience to the law that has been affixed by the Father of Life, 'with whom there is no variableness, neither shadow of turning'; and there is no other way by which we may obtain that light and exaltation. These matters are beyond peradventure, beyond all doubt in my mind; I know them to be true. Therefore, I bear my testimony to you, my brethren and sisters, that the Lord God Omnipotent reigneth, that He lives and that His Son lives, even He who died for the sins of the world, and that He rose from the dead; that He sits upon the right hand of the Father; that all power is given unto him; that we are directed to call upon God in the name of Jesus Christ. We are told that we should remember Him in our homes, keep His holy name fresh in our minds, and revere Him in our hearts; we should call upon him from time to time, from day to day; and in fact, every moment of our lives we should live so that the desires of our hearts will be a prayer unto God for righteousness, for truth and for the salvation of the human family." (CR, Apr. 1909, p. 6.)

The spiritual impact President Smith had on an audience is hinted at by the experience of Oscar W. McConkie, who once saw a halo of light frame the prophet as he stood at the Tabernacle pulpit. (Related to the author by Oscar W. McConkie, Jr., whose friend, on hearing the story, produced an entry from his grandmother's diary that recorded a similar incident involving Joseph F. Smith.)

And these spiritual influences had a moderating and refining effect upon President Smith, causing him to exhibit toward his friends and associates the same kind of loving concern he showed his family. This facet of the prophet's character is illustrated by an incident following a presentation made to a group of Church leaders by Elder B. H. Roberts. Addressing him, President Smith said, "Brother Roberts, the Lord God loves you. He loves you for your integrity. He loves you for your forthrightness. He loves you for your willingness to stand for principle, even when you have to stand all alone, and against the assaults of your enemies and even your brethren." As he finished, the prophet put his arm around Elder Roberts in a fatherly way, saying, "And I love you too." This show of affection, which was repeated on several occasions, had a powerful and lasting effect upon Elder Roberts, who had been deprived of the guiding influence of a father during his maturing years. Of one such incident, Elder Roberts said he cherished the memory of it more than any other experience he had ever had. (See Madsen, *Defender of the Faith*, pp. 155, 227, 238, 308.)

Incidents of this kind, which occurred with greater frequency as President Smith advanced in years, increased the love and respect the members of the Church had for him and helped to moderate any negative perceptions some may have had.

But Joseph F. never allowed his affection for his associates to rule his judgment. Charles W. Nibley, who had a close personal relationship with President Smith, learned this during a quiet railside conversation on a ship in the Atlantic. "It was a bright moonlight night," reported the bishop, "and we stood there leaning over the railing enjoying the smooth sea and balmy summer night air. The Smoot investigation, which had just occurred a little while before and which had stirred up so much controversy throughout the land was fresh in our minds, and we were talking of it. I took the position that it would be unwise for Reed Smoot to be re-elected to the United States Senate. I was conscientious in my objection, and I had marshaled all the facts, arguments, and logic, that I could; and I was well informed, I thought, on the subject, and had presented them to him in as clear and yet in as adroit a manner as I possibly could. . . . I could see he began to listen with some little impatience, and yet he let me have my say, but he answered in tones and in a way that I shall never forget. Bringing his fist down with some force on the railing between us, he said, in the most forceful and positive manner: 'If ever the Spirit of the Lord has manifested to me anything clear and plain and positive, it is this, that Reed Smoot should remain in the United States Senate. He can do more good there than he can anywhere else." (IE 22:195.)

Chapter Twenty-one

Travel and Trauma

T he conversation about Reed Smoot took place as President Smith and his party were returning from a tour of northern Europe. The travelers, President Smith, his wife Edna, and Bishop Nibley and members of his family, had left Salt Lake City on July 21, 1906. The trip had special significance for the prophet, as it was the first time an incumbent Church president had traveled to Europe. And on a personal level it was exciting, as four of his sons were then serving in the European mission: Alvin Fielding, Edna's son, and Heber Chase, Alice's son, were in England; Willard Richards, Sarah's son, was in Norway; and George Carlos, Julina's son, was in Sweden.

Traveling by transcontinental train to the east coast, the party stopped at Omaha on July 24 to visit the old campground of Israel at nearby Winter Quarters. Extending an invitation to the local Saints and to the missionaries laboring in the area, President Smith hosted a pioneer-day celebration beneath the shade of the "old historic tree said to have been planted by the hand of President Brigham Young." (CR, Oct. 1906, p. 3.) In that quiet, intimate setting, which evoked so many memories of his boyhood career as a herdsman-teamster, President Smith thrilled and inspired his small, appreciative audience with eyewitness accounts of the exodus and of the unusual men and women who had participated in it. At New York City, the travelers boarded the steamer *Vater-*

land of the Red Star Line and, after a surprisingly calm Atlantic crossing, arrived at the ancient port of Antwerp, Belgium, on August 5. At the pier to greet them was Bishop Nibley's son Alexander, who then presided over the Netherlands Mission and who was the namesake of his maternal grandfather, Alexander Neibaur, one of the first male converts of Jewish blood.

Remaining in Antwerp and its environs for two days while the president instructed and counseled the Saints and missionaries there, the visitors then moved on to Rotterdam, where they were greeted by Elder Heber J. Grant of the Twelve, who was then presiding over the European Mission with headquarters in Liverpool, England. As these two tall apostles shook hands and embraced, the onlookers, who were unaware of it at the time, were gazing at two prophets who, in consecutive terms, would direct the Church for a total of forty-four years.

Stopping only briefly in Rotterdam, President Smith and his retinue went to Amsterdam, where a conference was held, attended by members and nonmembers alike and a corps of missionaries. Having been away from active missionary work for many years, the prophet was struck by the power and enthusiasm generated by the clean-cut, handsome group of young men he saw seated before him. In reporting on the impact these and other European missionaries had on him during his tour, Joseph F. told a Tabernacle audience, "I do not think there can be found in all the world a like number of equally noble, excellent-spirited young men, as are your boys who are at present out in the missionary field, and I think this can be said of them almost as a whole—extremely few exceptions at the most." (Ibid.)

Backtracking, the party returned to Rotterdam, where the president held a conference in Excelsior Hall, the customary meeting place of the Rotterdam Saints. It was of an audience in this place that the then newly installed mission president, Heber J. Grant, had written, "With the exception of the large audience in the Metropolitan Temple in San Francisco, I never faced such an intelligent and large audience out in the world." It was just such an intelligent, discriminating, and large audience that President Smith faced in Rotterdam, a city noted for its commercial wealth derived from numerous industries and a vast maritime trade and for its cultural heritage, symbolized by its libraries and many museums, including Boymans Museum and the extensive Maritime and Ethnological Museum. But in the audience, too, were many humble people, including an eleven-year-old named John Roethoff. This boy, whose eyes were so bad he could not attend school, and whose vision was becoming progressively worse, had pleaded with his mother to be allowed to accompany her to the meeting. He had expressed the conviction that were the prophet merely to gaze into his eyes, he would be healed. The mother heeded her son's request and led him to Excelsior Hall with his eyes bandaged to shield them from the painful light of the sun. After the meeting the mother, at his urging, led John to President Smith, who greeted him in a kindly way and who, during a brief conversation, lifted the bandage and looked into the boy's inflamed eyes. In doing so, he said something in English the boy did not understand. Nothing happened at the moment, as the boy may have expected, but his faith was richly rewarded when he returned home. Removing the bandages, he called excitedly to his mother that he could see clearly both at short range and at a distance, and that the severe pain he had suffered previously had stopped. (CHC 6:422.) Soon John was able to resume his schooling, and years later he moved to the United States, where he lived a normal life.

Leaving Holland, President Smith and his party traveled to Belgium, Germany, Switzerland, and France, where meetings were held with the missionaries and Saints and where the Mormon prophet conferred with local Church and government officials. Since this was a combination business and pleasure trip, the party also enjoyed the cultural advantages of the continental cities through which they passed, the museums, art galleries, libraries, and theaters. And like other tourists, they visited the sites of historic interest and natural beauty with which Europe abounds.

In Berlin, President Smith encountered the only thing that displeased him during the entire trip. There he found a rather large colony of Latter-day Saint students, many of whom had become dilatory in attending Church meetings, ostensibly because they couldn't spare the time from their studies. So irritated was the president by the spectacle of lukewarm Latter-day Saints that he decided to warm them up, and he did so by addressing the subject at some length in a general conference talk on returning home. After describing and criticizing the tepid attitudes of these students, he then addressed their parents: "Now if any of you have children in that condition I would advise you to stimulate them to do their whole duty and set a good example before the people of the world in this direction. I really think that the sending of our children to Berlin to study for years is considerably overdone, and I do not believe that as a rule very much good will ever accrue to our children who go there." (CR, Oct. 1906, p. 4.)

It is interesting to speculate about the urgent transcontinental messages that passed between Utah and Berlin following this Tabernacle bombshell. And it is interesting, too, to visualize the sudden resurgence of student activity in the Berlin Branch or the untimely return to Zion of students who could not be shaken from their lethargy or whose parents were so disturbed by the prophet's denunciation that they summoned their sons and daughters home regardless.

After concluding the tour of continental Europe, the travelers crossed the channel to England, where, on August 26, the Smith family had a small reunion in London. Arrangements had been made for George and Willard to come to London from Sweden and Norway. With brothers Alvin and Chase, who were laboring in England, these four sons of President Smith joined with their father and Edna, Alvin's mother, in a joyous get-together. Perhaps it is misleading, from the point of view of the Smith family, to differentiate between the lineal descent of these four brothers. While Edna was the natural mother of only Alvin, the others felt a filial kinship toward her as they did toward their own natural mothers and toward the prophet's other wives. Joseph F. had inculcated this attitude among his polygamous families from the beginning, discouraging his children from using the terms half-brother or half-sister, thereby eliminating any distinction between the five branches of the common family.

Aside from the joy of seeing and visiting with their parents, the brothers had looked forward eagerly to the reunion, both to compare notes about their work and to receive firsthand reports about their loved ones at home. Alvin, thirty-two, and Chase and George, both twenty-five, who had left wives and children at home, hungered for reports about their little families. And twenty-two-year-old Willard, the youngest and the only bachelor of the quartet, may have made discreet inquiry about Heber J. Grant's daughter Florence, whom he would marry four years later.

After holding a spirited conference in London, the president and his party traveled to Scotland, where they held meetings with missionaries and members at Edinburgh and Glasgow. And from Scotland they went on to Lancashire, England, where another round of meetings was held at Blackburn, a few miles northeast of Liverpool. There can be little doubt that this place aroused powerful reflections in the mind of this missionary-minded and family-oriented prophet. Near Blackburn lay Preston, where a year before President Smith's birth, his two uncles, James and Joseph Fielding, had played leading roles in the proselyting in Great Britain. Joseph Fielding, a member of the first Latter-day Saint missionary team in England, had persuaded his brother, James, a protestant minister, to open the doors of his church to the elders. The Reverend Fielding did this once out of fraternal regard, and then as quickly shut them when he saw that the persuasiveness of the elders was leading members of his flock into the River Ribble for baptism. During the life of President Smith, that first trickle of converts, begun by one uncle and his associates at the expense of another uncle, had burgeoned into a mighty flood that had nurtured the luxuriant growth of the Church in the land of Zion. To see in Great Britain and on the continent the large congregations and the battalions of eager missionaries that had sprung indirectly from that first plantation in nearby Preston would have filled anyone, and especially one such as Joseph F. Smith, with awe and gratitude.

The prophet's keen historic sense prompted him upon his

return to the United States to make another tour of early Church landmarks, even though he had visited many of them less than a year before. "On reaching New York, the 18th of September," he reported to a Tabernacle audience, "we made arrangements as hastily as possible and visited Vermont, the birthplace of the Prophet Joseph Smith, and spent a couple of days there." (CR, Oct. 1906, p. 4.) Pleased with the progress made there in beautifying the grounds, President Smith and his party traveled on to Palmyra and then to Kirtland, where they enjoyed the same experiences the president's group had had in visiting this place the previous year.

Deviating from his earlier itinerary, the president then led his party to Carthage, Illinois, the site of the martyrdom, which he had never visited before. While inspecting the jail where his father and uncle were murdered, he was gloomy and depressed. "Charley, I despise this place," he said to Bishop Nibley. "It harrows up my feelings to come here." (POC, p. 254.) At Nauvoo, he spent some time walking its familiar streets and visiting and inspecting some of the old landmarks. "It was a source of great delight and pleasure to visit the scenes of my childhood," he told a Tabernacle audience, "and to go around the deserted city and see the various houses which I remembered from my childhood. We visited the place that was once called the 'Mansion', the home of the Prophet Joseph Smith, so altered and changed today, internally at least, and so old and dilapidated outside, that one familiar with it in the early days could scarcely recognize it as the same place. The old homestead that was first built on the bend of the river, occupied by the Patriarch Joseph (the father of the Prophet Joseph) and his family in the early days, still stands, but in a most neglected condition, almost ready to crumble to the earth.

"We visited the spot where the bodies of the Prophet Joseph and his brother were buried, after their martyrdom, and also their brothers, Don Carlos and Samuel. . . . We also visited the Nauvoo House, the place where the original manuscript of the Book of Mormon was placed by the hand of the Prophet Joseph Smith, together with a bound copy of the Book of Mormon, the Doctrine and Covenants and other

Church publications extant at that time; and with petitions to the governors of the various states, on the part of the Latter-day Saints, for redress for the wrongs they had sustained at the hand of Missouri. . . . We likewise visited the spot where once stood the house in which the revelation on plural marriage was first written by Wm. Clayton, by dictation of the Prophet Joseph Smith; and also where the Endowments were first revealed and given by him. We also visited the place where the revelation on plural marriage, given through the Prophet Joseph Smith, was first read to the high council of the stake of Zion, at Nauvoo, by Hyrum Smith, and recalled some of the historical facts that occurred within those walls." (CR, Oct. 1906, p. 6.)

While this lengthy talk was devoted almost entirely to positive themes, one statement in it cast a dark, uncertain shadow: "I do not care for and don't want to pay any heed to the ridiculous nonsense, the foolish twaddle, and the impious slurs that are being cast at me and my people, by wicked hearts and perverted minds. Let God deal with them as seemeth Him good. Don't you allow yourselves to be troubled over these things in the least." Later, the speaker, without explanation or preface, inserted another enigmatic statement. Said he, "It is not my purpose to stand here and try to make any apology or to offer any defense of my own course, of my own life and labors. I am willing to leave myself and my labors and my life in the hands of God." (Ibid., p. 7.)

In November, the meaning of these vague statements was made clear when President Smith was charged with "unlawful cohabitation" under the antipolygamy laws. The basis of this traumatic charge was the well-known, unconcealed fact that he had continued to recognize, honor, and live with the wives to whom he had been sealed before the Manifesto. He had openly acknowledged this fact in his testimony at the Smoot hearings, where it also was made clear that federal officials had moderated their enforcement policy as a means of accommodating the feelings and personal difficulties of those polygamists who had taken plural wives before 1890. This wise policy had worked well and had produced a climate of cooperation and accord in Utah. All that was changed, however, with Senator Thomas Kearns's defeat in his bid for reelection and with his media vendetta against the Church and particularly against President Joseph F. Smith. Agitated by a torrent of anti-Mormon editorials and news stories that filled the pages of the Tribune, federal officials were pressured to abandon this policy of accommodation and to return to the rigid enforcement applied before the Manifesto. It was this sudden change in tactics that resulted in the charge of unlawful cohabitation being lodged against President Smith in November 1906. The judge who heard the matter adopted a more conciliatory attitude than the prosecutors and imposed only a $300 fine, waiving a jail sentence. President Smith paid the fine willingly.

The *Tribune* trumpeted this embarrassing news, berating President Smith and other Church leaders for their alleged lawlessness and implying that they secretly continued to perform or sanction plural marriage contrary to both the Manifesto and the Worldwide Manifesto. Some color to this charge was added by the unauthorized conduct of a few dissident members or excommunicants who had rejected the Manifesto. The confusion and uncertainty created by the drumbeat of propaganda caused President Smith and his counselors to issue an "address" to the Church and the world during the general conference in April 1907. This document was a formal answer to numerous charges leveled at the Church or its leaders. It scoffed at the attempts of detractors to differentiate between the Mormon priesthood and the Mormon people by condemning the former as "the personification of all that is bad" and the latter as "good, honest though misguided folk." It rejected the charge that the Church thrived on duplicity and shunned enlightened investigation by referring to its more than seventy-year history of aggressive worldwide proselyting during which missionaries had invited critical study of all Church doctrines and practices. It disputed the idea that Church leaders exercised arbitrary power over the rank and file members by explaining the doctrine of common consent and the freedom of Church members to accept or reject the counsel of the leaders at will. And it explained that tithing was a freewill offering, not an ecclesiastical tax, and was obeyed by the members without compulsion or pressure. However, the main emphasis of the "address" was upon the problem that had enmeshed President Smith after the previous general conference and had resulted in his being charged with criminal conduct and fined. "The only conduct seemingly inconsistent with our professions as loyal citizens," began the answer to this charge, "is that involved in our attitude during the controversies that have arisen respecting plural marriage." The document then explained how this practice had been introduced by Joseph Smith in Nauvoo, Illinois; how it had been continued in Utah and published to the world as a doctrine in 1852; how Brigham Young thereafter was twice appointed as territorial governor, first by President Fillmore and later by President Pierce, both appointments being ratified by the Senate; and how the first antipolygamy law was not enacted until 1862. "Moreover [the Latter-day Saints] believed the enactment to be violative of the constitution," the document explained, "which provides that congress shall make no law prohibiting the free exercise of religion. Notwithstanding this attitude and conduct on the part of our people, no decision of the Supreme Court upon this question was secured until 1879, more than thirty years after the settlement of Utah; nor were determined efforts made to enforce the law until a further period of five or six years had elapsed."

Against this background, the document suggested that the United States was bound because of this "toleration" or that it was "bound by considerations of mercy and wisdom to the exercise of patience and charity in dealing with this question." As to the conduct of the Latter-day Saints from the time the government began to enforce the antipolygamy legislation vigorously until the Manifesto, the "address" provided these explanations: "The situation, as viewed by some of our members, developed a conflict between duty to God and duty to the government. Moreover, it was thought possible that the decision of the Supreme Court might be reversed, if what was regarded as a constitutional right were not too easily surrendered. What our people did in disregard of the law and of the decisions of the Supreme Court affecting plural marriages, was in the spirit of maintaining religious rights under constitutional guarantees, and not in any spirit of defiance or disloyalty to the government."

Finally this historic document traced the attitudes and practices of the Church and its members toward polygamy after the Manifesto: "The 'Mormon' people have bowed in respectful submission to the laws enacted against plural marriage. While it is true that for many years they contested the constitutionality of the law of Congress, and during that time acted in harmony with their religious convictions in upholding by practice, as well as by spoken and written word, a principle committed to them from God, still, when every means of constitutional defense had been exhausted, the Church abandoned the controversy and announced its intention to be obedient to the laws of the land. Subsequently, when statehood for Utah became a possibility, on the condition that her constitution provide by ordinance, irrevocable without the consent of the United States, that plural marriages should be forever prohibited, the 'Mormon' people accepted the condition by voting for the adoption of the constitution. From that time until now, the Church has been true to its pledge respecting the abandonment of the practice of plural marriage. If it be urged that there have been instances of the violation of the anti-polygamy laws, and that some persons within the Church have sought to evade the rule adopted by her, prohibiting plural marriages, the plain answer is that in every state and nation there are individuals who violate law in spite of all the vigilance that can be exercised; but it does not follow that the integrity of a community or a state is destroyed, because of such individual transgressions. All we ask is that the same common-sense judgment be exercised in relation to our community that is accorded to other communities. When all the circumstances are weighed, the wonder is, not that there have been sporadic cases of plural marriage, but that such cases have been so few. It should be remembered that a religious conviction existed among the people, holding this order of marriage to be divinely sanctioned. Little wonder then that there should appear, in a community as large as ours, and as sincere, a few over-zealous individuals who refused to submit even to the action of the Church in such a matter; or that these few should find others who sympathized with their views; the number, however, is small." (CR, Apr. 1907, p. 12 following report of sessions.)

Predictably, these explanations did not convince or silence the Church's enemies. Indeed, they had the catalytic effect of attracting and combining the rage of divergent elements of the nonmember community and focusing it upon President Smith. An unfriendly press continued to vilify and caricature President Smith, and political and ecclesiastical enemies continued to speak derogatory things about him. But these persistent attacks failed to produce the result Joseph F.'s detractors sought. They neither silenced nor intimidated him, nor did they weaken or humiliate him before his followers. Indeed, they had little personal impact other than to arouse his competitive instincts and magnify him in the eyes of the Saints. These remarks, uttered after enduring another six months of abuse, show the blend of humility and militancy in his character. Said he at the 1907 October general conference, "I feel in my heart to forgive all men in the broad sense that God requires me to forgive all men, and I desire to love my neighbor as myself; and to this extent I bear no malice toward any of the children of my Father. But there are enemies to the work of the Lord, as there were enemies to the Son of God. There are those who speak only evil of the Latter-day Saints. There are those—and they abound largely in our midst, who will shut their eyes to every virtue and to every good thing connected with this latter-day work, and will pour out floods of falsehood and misrepresentation against the people of God. I forgive them for this. I leave them in the hands of the just Judge. Let Him deal with them as seemeth Him good."

Having paid love and charity their due, the prophet added these words of qualification: "But they are not and cannot become my bosom companions. I cannot condescend to that. While I would not harm a hair of their head, while I would not throw a straw in their path, to hinder them from turning from the error of their way to the light of truth; I would as soon think of taking a centipede or a scorpion or any poisonous reptile and putting it into my bosom, as I would think of becoming a companion or an associate of such a man. These are my sentiments, and I believe that they are correct." (CR, Oct. 1907, pp. 5-6.)

President Smith alluded briefly to these antagonists at the next general conference, but quickly shifted to a positive theme: "We bring no railing accusation against them," he said. "We are willing to leave them in the hands of the Almighty to deal with them as seemeth Him good. Our business is to work righteousness in the earth, to seek for the development of a knowledge of God's will and of God's ways, and of His great and glorious truths which he has revealed through the instrumentality of Joseph the Prophet, not only for the salvation of the living but for the redemption and salvation of the dead." (CR, Apr. 1908, pp. 2-3.)

Chapter Twenty-two

The Prophet as Administrator and Preacher

A fter 1908, the agitation about polygamy progressively subsided. Now and then an isolated incident would flare up, reviving the old memories and enmities, but it would soon flicker out and die like a lone ember on the hearth. With the fire of polygamy under control, with the Church out of debt, and with the political convulsions that followed statehood having been eased, President Smith entered an era of comparative quiet during which he shifted emphasis to matters of administration and exhortation.

By this time the auxiliary organizations of the Church, the Sunday School, the Primary Association, the Mutual Improvement associations, and the Relief Society had begun to thrive. With their own publications, the *Improvement Era* and the *Young Woman's Journal*, and with their vigorous programs, the MIA organizations were especially attractive to the youth. Concerned that this trend might in time cause the auxiliaries to obscure the importance of the priesthood in the eyes of young men, President Joseph F. Smith appointed a committee in 1908 to study the problem and to make recommendations. The outcome was a major revamping of the format and direction of priesthood meetings. Until this time, priesthood quorums and groups had limited their agenda to priesthood programs and projects, leaving gospel instruction to the auxiliary organizations. Now, however, a weekly class period was scheduled to enable priesthood leaders to instruct their members in religious theory and doctrine. Moreover, the priesthood meetings were divided into the six general divisions of the Aaronic and Melchizedek Priesthood quorums, and manuals were provided to guide and facilitate consistent study programs. At the same time, greater emphasis was laid upon the fellowshipping of inactive members, especially the young members of the Aaronic Priesthood. Ward leaders began to involve the young men in numerous priesthood activities, helping widows, performing ward teaching duties, maintaining church grounds, and ushering. (William G. Hartley, "The Priesthood Reform Movement 1908–1922," *BYU Studies* 13:137-56.)

President Smith also took a lively interest in the educational programs of the Church. By 1909, there were thirty-five academies, located throughout the Mountain West, that were administered by the Church Board of Education, which President Smith chaired. These were patterned after the Brigham Young Academy in Provo and the Brigham Young College in Logan. The Logan school ultimately became a public land-grant university, and the struggling academy at Provo finally emerged as a full-blown university.

On April 1, 1901, Joseph F. Smith was appointed president of the board of trustees of that institution and bestowed upon it a paternal care, sometimes glorying in its achievements and sometimes wincing at its brashness.

In the early days of his administration as the president of the Brigham Young Board of Trustees, President Smith foresaw and enthusiastically endorsed the flowering of that school as a major university. As early as 1901, the board authorized the school's president to organize medical and law schools on campus. When the school's president explained to the board that two professional schools would cause the academy to "bristle like a university," board chairman Joseph F. Smith answered, "Well, why not?" (*Brigham Young University, the First Hundred Years* 4:246.) It would be seventy-two years before President Smith's dream of a law school on campus would be realized, and at this writing (1982) the medical school still has not come into being. But the years have not dimmed the prophet's dream nor the recollection of the high hopes he had for the school as a great university.

Reading between the lines one senses that a chief ingredient in Joseph F.'s ambition for the school was his own scanty opportunities for formal education. He was impelled, too, by the teachings of the Prophet Joseph Smith that the glory of God is intelligence and that one's salvation depends upon the acquisition and application of knowledge. Said he to a Tabernacle audience gathered in general conference, "It seems to me that it would be a very sad comment upon the Church of Jesus Christ of Latter-day Saints and her people to suppose for a moment that we are at a standstill, that we have ceased to grow, ceased to improve, and to advance in the scale of intelligence." (CR, Apr. 1915, p. 3.)

As his statement about professional schools implies, President Smith's ambition for the education of his people was broad in scope, encompassing all fields of knowledge. Yet because of the essentially rural nature of the society in which he was reared and lived, his chief emphasis was upon so-called practical education, upon manual training and agriculture. "Politics, law, medicine, trade, clerking, banking are needful and good in their place," he advised the Church in a magazine article, "but we need builders, mechanics, farmers, and men who can use their powers to produce something for the use of man." (IE 6:229.) And the Prophet sometimes drew unfavorable comparisons or painted the sedentary occupations in dark hues. "One of the things that I think is very necessary," he told a Tabernacle audience, "is that we should teach our boys mechanism, teach them the arts of industry, and not allow our sons to grow up with the idea that there is nothing honorable in labor, except it be in the profession of law, or in some other light, practically unproductive and, I was going to say, unremunerative employment, but I know of scarcely any employment more remunerative than is the practice of law, to those, at least, who are proficient. But what do they do to build up the country? What do they produce to benefit the world? There may be a few of them who have farms, there may be a few of them who have manufactories, there may be a few of them who may be interested and engaged in other productive labor, something that will build up the country and the people and establish permanence, stability and prosperity in the land; but the vast majority of them are leeches upon the body politic and are worthless as to the building up of any community. . . . We need manual training schools instead of so much book-learning and the stuffing of fairy tales and fables, which are contained in many of our school books of today. If we would devote more money and time, more energy and attention to teaching our children manual labor in our schools than we do, it would be a better thing for the rising generation." (CR, Apr. 1903, pp. 2-3.)

What on its face appears to be a conflict between President Smith's attitudes toward professionals may be explained on the basis of timing and emphasis. There can be little doubt that he approved of professional training. That is clear from his hearty endorsement of the idea of law and medical schools for the Church institution at Provo. But it was apparent that only a small percentage of his people would or could obtain such training and that the bulk of them should be encouraged to learn the manual arts and agricultural skills that comprised the backbone of LDS society. And the demeaning comments he made about professionals could have been inspired in part by the insinuating charges leveled at the Church less than three months before by a group of gentile professionals. It will be remembered that in January 1903, a group of lawyers, joined by other professionals, had filed the protest against the seating of Reed Smoot. It would not have been surprising that the prophet remembered the handiwork of this group and, having remembered, would have translated his displeasure with them into broad indictments of the whole brotherhood, whether Church members or not. Whatever the reason, President Smith intermittently reverted to the theme of encouraging manual arts and agricultural training, although he never seems to have been as condemnatory of the others as he was on the occasion of this April 1903 general conference address.

In 1910, President Smith's conservative approach toward education collided with the competing desires of some of the faculty and students on the Provo campus. Led by Professor Ralph Chamberlain and his brother, William, this group sought to elevate the academic standing of the school by introducing a series of lectures and debates on subjects within the fields of the more theoretical and speculative sciences, sociology, philosophy, psychology, and anthropology. Among these were lectures on the subject of organic evolution, the Chamberlain brothers being learned and persuasive exponents of this theory. During 1909, the year of the Darwin centennial celebration, Ralph Chamberlain delivered several lectures in which he asserted that evolution necessarily implies a rational creation. The theory, he said, demanded "an ultimate cause as much as any other held as to the mode of creation and to hold it is clearly to pay a much greater tribute to the power and majesty of the creator, for uniformity of method is an indication of strength while irregularity or discontinuity is ever a sign of weakness." (Ralph V. Chamberlain, "Darwin Centennial Speech," Feb. 12, 1909, Ralph V. Chamberlain papers, Utah State Historical Society, Salt Lake City, Utah.)

From the premise that natural phenomena grow from an evolutionary process, the Chamberlains concluded that the same process is at work in the spiritual world. "If a diverse purpose is immanent in nature," wrote William Chamberlain, "nature's forms must be thought of as evolving in a way parallel to the unfolding of the divine purpose. The use of the theory is a most important means of advancing to a realization of God's immanence in nature and life and a great remover of intellectual difficulties that hamper faith in so many." (BYU periodical *White and Blue*, Feb. 14, 1900.)

Thus, he and the others who advocated this view insisted on investigating the principles of religion by applying the empirical method of science in the spiritual realm. It was this last step that embroiled the evolutionists in a direct and losing confrontation with Joseph F. Smith and the other Church leaders. The pitfalls and uncertainties this approach entailed are illustrated by a sacrament meeting talk William Chamberlain delivered in October 1910. The thesis of his sermon was that the Bible contains some mythical stories that are not

based on fact but are fictions used by the authors merely to il-
lustrate principles. He referred to the Book of Jonah as an example, saying that to look upon it as a parable "does away
with the need of believing the fish story—as fact. It also places
beyond the reach of petty critics other stories in the book used
merely for purpose of illustration." ("Professor Chamberlain's Talk on the Book of Jonah," *White and Blue*, Oct. 25,
1910.)

The consequences of such teachings were obvious. Anything in the Bible that could not be explained on the basis of
rational and provable experience would be fair game for private analysis and interpretation. The essence of the problem
this created was captured by Annie Clark Tanner, who was a
student at the time: "One of my greatest disturbances occurred when I learned that the story of Adam and Eve and the
Garden of Eden may not be literally true. . . . Too, if the story
of the Flood came from the legends of a people the Israelites
had met in captivity, or if the Book of Jonah was a satire of
Jewish self-righteousness and written as a fable to portray
that characteristic rather than history, why accept literally the
story of creation as related in the Bible?" (*Deseret News*, 1941,
pp. 183-88.)

Under these circumstances, it was necessary that President Smith and the board of trustees take action to prevent chaos on campus. Accordingly, the board appointed a
committee to study the matter, consisting of Francis M.
Lyman, Heber J. Grant, Hyrum M. Smith, Charles W. Penrose, George F. Richards, George H. Brimhall, and Horace H.
Cummings. On February 11, 1911, the committee conducted
a hearing in Salt Lake City, to which were invited three professors, Ralph Chamberlain, Joseph Peterson, and Henry
Peterson. When the hearing was concluded, the committee
recommended that the services of the three professors be ter-
minated unless they altered their teachings. ("Special Committee Report Relative to Religious Teachings," BYU Board
Minutes, February 11, 1911.) The board of trustees approved
this recommendation. And when the trio refused to change,
they were dismissed.

Since several other professors who had been teaching the

same concepts were not dismissed, it is apparent there were other reasons for the dismissal of these three. N. L. Nelson, who shared the Chamberlain-Peterson views on evolution, confirmed this in a letter he wrote to George H. Brimhall on January 6, 1912: "My understanding at the time was that he [Henry Peterson] was held to account for his interpretation of the creation as not being literally seven days and of the Jonah episode as possibly being a parable rather than a historical event—and for like interpretations of the scriptures. I did not dream that it was for the Spirit of his opposition that he was called to account." (See Brimhall Presidential Papers.)

Whatever the reason for these dismissals, they created a great stir both on and off the campus. A group of students signed a petition supporting the professors and urging a continuation of the controversial classes. And both the *Salt Lake Tribune* and the *Provo Daily Herald* chimed in with critical articles or editorials. (See *Provo Daily Herald* of February 21, 1911, and the *Salt Lake Tribune* of March 12, 1911.)

During the same period, President Smith published in the *Juvenile Instructor* an article explaining the action taken by the Church Board of Education. Wrote he, "Some of our teachers are anxious to explain how much of the theory of evolution, in their judgment, is true, and what is false, but that only leaves their students in an unsettled frame of mind. They are not old enough and learned enough to discriminate, or put proper limitations upon a theory which we believe is more or less a fallacy." The Prophet then brought the issue into proper focus by questioning its relevance and by giving emphasis to weightier and more enduring matters: "In reaching the conclusion that evolution would be best left out of discussions in our Church schools we are deciding a question of propriety and are not undertaking to say how much of evolution is true, or how much is false. . . . The Church itself has no philosophy about the *modus operandi* employed by the Lord in His creation of the world, and much of the talk therefore about the philosophy of Mormonism is altogether misleading. God has revealed to us a simple and effectual way of serving Him, and we should regret very much to see the simplicity of these revelations involved in all sorts of philosophical speculations."

(*Juvenile Instructor*, Apr. 1911, p. 209.) As to man's identity and origin, the president was content with the statement of the First Presidency published in the November 1909 issue of the *Improvement Era*, the last two paragraphs of which read, "The Church of Jesus Christ of Latter-day Saints, basing its belief on divine revelation, ancient and modern, proclaims man to be the direct and lineal offspring of Deity. God Himself is an exalted man, perfected, enthroned, and supreme. By His almighty power He organized the earth, and all that it contains, from spirit and element, which exist co-eternally with Himself. He formed every plant that grows, and every animal that breathes, each after its own kind, spiritually and temporally—'that which is spiritual being in the likeness of that which is temporal, and that which is temporal in the likeness of that which is spiritual.' He made the tadpole and the ape, the lion and the elephant; but He did not make them in His own image, nor endow them with Godlike reason and intelligence. Nevertheless, the whole animal creation will be perfected and perpetuated in the Hereafter, each class in its 'distinct order or sphere,' and will enjoy 'eternal felicity.' That fact has been made plain in this dispensation (Doctrine and Covenants, 77:3).

"Man is the child of God, formed in the divine image and endowed with divine attributes, and even as the infant son of an earthly father and mother is capable in due time of becoming a man, so the undeveloped offspring of celestial parentage is capable, by experience through ages and æons, of evolving into a God."

At the April general conference in 1911, following the evolution blowup on campus, President Smith added this footnote to the controversy: "I believe the Latter-day Saints . . . have sufficient knowledge and understanding of the principles of the gospel that they know the truth, and they are made free by its possession—free from sin, free from error, free from darkness, from the traditions of men, from vain philosophy, and from the untried, unproven theories of scientists, that need demonstration beyond the possibility of doubt. We have had science and philosophy through all the ages, and they have undergone change after change. Scarcely a century has passed but they have introduced new theories of science and of philosophy that supersede the old traditions and the old faith and the old doctrines entertained by philosophers and scientists. These things may undergo continuous changes, but the word of God is always true, is always right." (CR, Apr. 1911, pp. 7, 8.)

The prophet then proceeded to teach the Saints an important lesson in tact and judgment and to reaffirm the basic principles of their religion. He made no attempt to challenge directly the teachings of the evolutionists. Nor did he jump into the arena of that debate to affirm the literalness of the book of Jonah or to discuss the Lord's methods of creation. It was sufficient to indicate that these teachings were based upon theories that lacked clear "demonstration beyond the possibility of doubt." And the implication was clear that if this or any other theory were so proven or demonstrated, it would be embraced by him and the Saints without question.

In the meantime, the prophet reverted to basic gospel principles as to which there were no uncertainties or debate: "I want to say to you that the principles of the gospel are always true—the principles of faith in God, of repentance from sin, of baptism for the remission of sins by authority of God, and the laying on of hands for the gift of the Holy Ghost; these principles are always true and are always absolutely necessary for the salvation of the children of men, no matter who they are or where they are. . . . These principles are indispensable, for God has declared them. Not only has He declared them, not only has Christ declared them by His own voice, but His disciples . . . have taken up the same testimony and declared these things to the world. They are true today as they were then, and we must obey these things." (Ibid.)

These were principles from which the prophet could not be dislodged. And it was in the enumeration of them and related concepts that Joseph F. Smith accomplished his most notable work. Aside from the important administrative duties he performed, he was essentially a preacher of righteousness. We have already noted the appraisal of Charles W. Nibley as to his unmatched oratorical ability, an appraisal shared by most of his contemporaries. He not only had the skill to inform and entertain his listeners, but more importantly, he had the uncommon ability to motivate them and to inspire faith and confidence in them.

At the root of his effectiveness as an orator was the knowledge he possessed of the divinity of Jesus Christ and of the latter-day work the Savior had founded through the Prophet Joseph Smith. Testifying of that knowledge was a favorite theme. While it is impossible to appraise the full impact of a speaker from the cold type on a page, it is possible to get a glimpse of it from this testimony borne to a general conference audience: "My brethren and sisters, I desire to bear my testimony to you; for I have received an assurance which has taken possession of my whole being. It has sunk deep into my heart; it fills every fibre of my soul; so that I feel to say before this people, and would be pleased to have the privilege of saying it before the whole world, that God has revealed unto me that Jesus is the Christ, the Son of the living God, the Redeemer of the world; that Joseph Smith is, was, and always will be a prophet of God, ordained and chosen to stand at the head of the dispensation of the fulness of times, the keys of which were given to him, and he will hold them until the winding-up scene—keys which will unlock the door into the kingdom of God to every man who is worthy to enter, and which will close that door against every soul that will not obey the law of God. I know, as I live, that this is true, and I bear my testimony to its truth. If it were the last word I should ever say on earth, I would glory before God my Father that I possess this knowledge in my soul, which I declare unto you as I would the simplest truths of heaven. I know that this is the kingdom of God, and that God is at the helm. He presides over His people. He presides over the President of this Church, and has done so from the Prophet Joseph down to the Prophet Lorenzo; and He will continue to preside over the leaders of this Church until the winding-up scene. He will not suffer it to be given to another people, nor to be left to men. He will hold the reins in his own hands; for He has stretched out His arm to do His work, and He will do it, and have the honor of it. At the same time God will honor and magnify his servants in the sight of the people. He will sustain them in righteousness; He will lift them on high, exalt them into his presence, and they will partake of His glory forever and ever." (CR, Apr. 1901, pp. 72-73.)

As one reads these words, he is reminded of Bishop Nibley's analysis of Joseph F.'s speaking style as being strong, powerful, clear, and appealing. And as the bishop said, it was marvelous how the words of living light and fire flowed from him.

While this preacher of righteousness was at his best while bearing testimony of the divinity of the Savior and of the work He restored through the Prophet Joseph Smith, his inspired eloquence illuminated dozens of other subjects during an apostolic career that spanned more than half a century. His pulpit offerings ranged from the first principles of the gospel to life in the hereafter. He felt equally at home treating profound gospel themes like free agency, eternal life and exaltation, and the atonement, or expounding the everyday virtues of hard work, honesty, and frugality. He was quick to reprove his people of conduct he thought was improper and unworthy of a Saint. So, he frequently spoke out against card playing, pleasure hunting, gambling, improper fashions, and questionable amusements. On the other hand, he extolled the virtues of good books, proper entertainment, and healthy activities. He occasionally treated political or business themes as they impinged on his ecclesiastical responsibilities. And he regularly inculcated the usual concepts common to all Christian sects as embodied in the Ten Commandments and the Sermon on the Mount.

But the subject he treated most exhaustively and to which he returned most frequently was the holy priesthood. He took pains to differentiate between the priesthood and the keys of the priesthood: "The Priesthood in general is the authority given to man to act for God. Every man that has been ordained to any degree of the Priesthood, has this authority dedicated to him. But it is necessary that every act performed under this authority shall be done at the proper time and place, in the proper way, and after the proper order. The power of directing these labors constitutes the *keys* of the

Priesthood. In their fulness, these keys are held by only one person at a time, the Prophet and President of The Church. He may delegate any portion of this power to another, in which case that person holds the keys of that particular labor. Thus, the president of a temple, the president of a stake, the bishop of a ward, the president of a mission, the president of a quorum, each holds the keys of the labors performed in that particular body or locality. His Priesthood is not increased by this special appointment, for a seventy who presides over a mission has no more Priesthood than a seventy who labors under his direction; and the president of an elders' quorum, for example, has no more Priesthood than any member of that quorum. But he holds the power of directing the official labors performed in the mission or the quorum, or in other words, *the keys* of that division of that work. So it is throughout all the ramifications of the Priesthood—a distinction must be carefully made between the general authority, and the directing of the labors performed by that authority." (IE 4:230.)

He also made it plain that the power exercised by the priesthood is a derivative power, emanating from God, to whom priesthood bearers owe their allegiance and their acknowledgment of anything achieved through the priesthood: "I am not leading the Church of Jesus Christ, nor the Latter-day Saints," President Smith told a general conference audience, "and I want this distinctly understood. No man does. Joseph did not do it; Brigham did not do it; neither did John Taylor. Neither did Wilford Woodruff, nor Lorenzo Snow; and Joseph F. Smith, least of them all, is not leading the Church of Jesus Christ of Latter-day Saints, and will not lead it. They were instruments in God's hands in accomplishing what they did. God did it through them. The honor and glory is due to the Lord and not to them. We are only instruments whom God may choose and use to do his work. All that we can do we should do to strengthen them in the midst of weaknesses, in the great calling to which they are called. But remember that God leads the work. It is his. It is not man's work. If it had been the work of Joseph Smith, or of Brigham Young, or of John Taylor, Wilford Woodruff, or Lorenzo Snow, it would not have endured the tests to which it has been subjected; it would have been brought to naught long ago. But if it had been merely the work of men, it never would have been subjected to such tests, for the whole world has been arrayed against it. If it had been the work of Brigham Young or Joseph Smith, with such determined opposition as it has met with, it would have come to naught. But it was not theirs; it was God's work. Thank God for that. It is the power of God unto salvation, and I want my boys and girls to take my testimony upon this point." (GD, pp. 138-39.)

On another occasion, President Smith defined with more particularity this "instrumental" relationship between God and man that is inherent in the concept of priesthood. "And what is the Priesthood," he asked. "It is nothing more nor less than the power of God delegated to man by which man can act in the earth for the salvation of the human family, in the name of the Father and the Son and the Holy Ghost, and act legitimately; not assuming that authority, not borrowing it from generations that are dead and gone, but authority that has been given in this day in which we live by ministering angels and spirits from above, direct from the presence of Almighty God, who have come to the earth in our day and restored the Priesthood to the children of men, by which they may baptize for the remission of sins and lay on hands for the reception of the Holy Ghost, and by which they can remit sin, with the sanction and blessing of Almighty God. It is the same power and Priesthood that was committed to the disciples of Christ while He was upon the earth; that whatsoever they should bind on earth should be bound in heaven, and whatsoever they should loose on earth should be loosed in heaven." (CR, Oct. 1904, p. 5.)

While the prophet frequently emphasized the power and authority of the priesthood, he as often counseled about the need to exercise it with restraint and without arrogance: "There is not a man holding any position of authority in the Church who can perform his duty as he should in any other spirit than in the spirit of fatherhood and brotherhood toward those over whom he presides. Those who have authority should not be rulers, nor dictators, they should not be arbitrary, they should gain the hearts, the confidence and the love of those over whom they preside, by kindness and love unfeigned, by gentleness of spirit, by persuasion, by an example that is above reproach and above the reach of unjust criticism. In this way, in the kindness of their hearts, in their love for their people, they lead them in the path of righteousness, and teach them the way of salvation, by saying to them both by precept and example: Follow me, as I follow our head, the Redeemer of the world. This is the duty of those who preside." (CR, Apr. 1915, p. 5.)

And the duties of the priesthood here alluded to were emphasized as much if not more than its rights, authorities, and prerogatives. Said he, "The Lord here especially demands of the men who stand at the head of this Church, and who are responsible for the guidance and direction of the people of God that they shall see to it that the law of God is kept. It is our duty to do this." (CR, Oct. 1899, p. 41.) He later specified those who are subject to the duty to expound the gospel: "It is the duty of this vast body of men holding the Holy Priesthood, which is after the order of the Son of God, to exert their influence and exercise their power for good among the people of Israel and the people of the world. It is their bounden duty to preach and to work righteousness, both at home and abroad." (CR, Oct. 1901, p. 83.)

It was at the April general conference in 1906 that President Smith gave instructions about the duties of priesthood quorums that have been so extensively quoted over the years. "We expect to see the day," he began, "if we live long enough (and if some of us do not live long enough to see it, there are others who will), when every council of the Priesthood in the Church of Jesus Christ of Latter-day Saints will understand its duty, will assume its own responsibility, will magnify its calling, and fill its place in the Church, to the uttermost, according to the intelligence and ability possessed by it. When that day shall come, there will not be so much necessity for work that is now being done by the auxiliary organizations, because it will be done by the regular quorums of the Priesthood. The Lord designed and comprehended it from the beginning, and He has made provision in the Church whereby every need may be met and satisfied through the regular organizations of the Priesthood. It has truly been said that the Church is perfectly organized. The only trouble is that these organizations are not fully alive to the obligations that rest upon them. When they become thoroughly awakened to the requirements made of them, they will fulfill their duties more faithfully, and the work of the Lord will be all the stronger and more powerful and influential in the world." (CR, Apr. 1906, p. 3.)

President Smith also defined the specific responsibilities of the various offices or quorums of the Church as the circumstances required. He explained his own duties as the president of the Church in this way: "I have the right to bless. I hold the keys of the Melchizedek Priesthood and of the office and power of patriarch. It is my right to bless; for all the keys and authority and power pertaining to the government of the Church and to the Melchizedek and Aaronic Priesthood are centered in the presiding officers of the Church. There is no business nor office, within the Church that the President of the Church may not fill, and may not do, if it is necessary, or if it is required of him to do it. He holds the office of patriarch; he holds the office of high priest and of apostle, of seventy, of elder, of bishop, and of priest, teacher and deacon in the Church; all these belong to the Presidency of the Church of Jesus Christ of Latter-day Saints, and they can officiate in any and in all of these callings when occasion requires." (CR, Oct. 1915, p. 7.)

Earlier, Joseph F. had defined the relationship between the Church president and his counselors: "I will call your attention to the fact that the Lord in the beginning of this work revealed that there should be three High Priests to preside over the High Priesthood of His Church and over the whole Church. He conferred upon them all the authority necessary to preside over all the affairs of the Church. They hold the keys of the house of God, and of the ordinances of the Gospel, and of every blessing which has been restored to the earth in this dispensation. This authority is vested in a Presidency of three High Priests. They are three Presidents. The Lord himself so calls them. But there is one presiding President, and his counselors are Presidents also. I propose that my counselors and fellow Presidents in the First Presidency shall share with me in the responsibility of every act which I shall perform in this capacity. I do not propose to take the reins in my own hands to do as I please; but I propose to do as my brethren and I agree upon, and as the Spirit of the Lord manifests to us. I have always held, and do hold, and trust I always shall hold, that it is wrong for one man to exercise all the authority and power of presiding in the Church of Jesus Christ of Latter-day Saints. I dare not assume such a responsibility, and I will not, so long as I can have men like these (pointing to Presidents Winder and Lund) to stand by and counsel with me in the labors we have to perform and in doing all those things that shall tend to the peace, advancement and happiness of the people of God and the building up of Zion." (CR, Oct. [special] 1901, p. 82.)

As to the duties of the Twelve, he said, "The duty of the twelve apostles of the Church is to preach the gospel to the world, to send it to the inhabitants of the earth and to bear testimony of Jesus Christ, the Son of God, as living witnesses of his divine mission. That is their special calling and they are always under the direction of the presidency of the Church of Jesus Christ of Latter-day Saints when that presidency is intact, and there is never at the same time two equal heads in the Church—never. The Lord never ordained any such thing, nor designed it. There is always a head in the Church, and if the presidency of the Church are removed by death or other cause, then the next head of the church is the twelve apostles until a presidency is again organized of three presiding high priests who have the right to hold the office of first presidency over the Church, and, according to the doctrine laid down by President Wilford Woodruff, who saw the necessity for it, and that of President Lorenzo Snow, if the president should die, his counselors are then released from that presidency, and it is the duty of the twelve apostles to proceed at once, in the manner that has been pointed out, to see that the First presidency is reorganized, so that there may be no deficiency in the working and order of the priesthood in the Church." (CR, Apr. 1913, pp. 4-5.)

And he defined the role of the Seventy in this way: "The

Seventies are called to be assistants to the Twelve Apostles; indeed they *are* apostles of the Lord Jesus Christ, subject to the direction of the Twelve, and it is their duty to respond to the call of the Twelve, under the direction of the First Presidency of the Church, to preach the Gospel to every creature, to every tongue and people under the heavens to whom they may be sent. Hence they should understand the gospel. . . . They should take up the study of the Gospel, the study of the scriptures and the history of the dealings of God with the people of the earth, in their own quorums, and make those quorums schools of learning and instruction, wherein they may qualify themselves for every labor and duty that may be required at their hands." (CR, Apr. 1907, pp. 5, 6.)

A few years later, he commented on the role of the Presiding Bishopric: "Before we get through with the Conference, we expect to hear some reports from the Presiding Bishopric, who are the temporal custodians of the means of the Church and whose duty it is to account for the receipt and disbursement of these funds." (CR, Apr. 1912, p. 6.)

And earlier, he had discussed the role of patriarchs, saying it was their duty "to bestow blessings upon the heads of those who seek blessings at their hands. . . . They hold the evangelical office in the Church. It is their business and right to bestow blessings upon the people, to make promises unto them in the name of the Lord, as it may be given them by the inspiration of the Holy Spirit, to comfort them in the hours of sorrow and trouble, to strengthen their faith by the promises that shall be made to them through the Spirit of God, and to be fathers indeed of the people, leading them into all truth." (CR, Oct. 1904, p. 4.)

Of the duties of high priests, he said, "Every man who holds the office of High Priest in the Church, whether he is called to active positions in the Church or not—inasmuch as he has been ordained a High Priest, should feel that he is obliged,—that it is his bounden duty to set an example before the old and young worthy of emulation, and to place himself in a position to be a teacher of righteousness, not only by precept but more particularly by example—giving to the younger ones the benefit of experience of age, and thus becoming individually a power in the midst of the communities in which they dwell. Every man who has light should let that light shine that those who see it may glorify their Father which is in Heaven, and honor him who possesses the light and who causes it to shine forth for the benefit of others. In a local capacity, there is no body of Priesthood in the Church who should excel, or who are expected to excel, those who are called to bear the office of High Priest in the church. From among those who hold this office are chosen the presidents of stakes and their counselors, and the High Councils of the fifty-six stakes of Zion which are now organized; and from this office are chosen the bishops, and the bishops' counselors in every ward in Zion; and heretofore, of this office are those who have been called to take charge of our stake Mutual Improvement organizations. Those holding this office are, as a rule, men of advanced years, and varied experience, men who have filled missions abroad, who have preached the Gospel to the nations of the earth, and who have had experience not only abroad but at home. Their experience and wisdom is the ripened fruit of years of labor in the Church, and they should exercise that wisdom for the benefit of all with whom they are associated." (CR, Apr. 1908, pp. 5, 6.)

Speaking of the elders, he told a general conference audience, "It is the duty of this body of men to be standing ministers at home; to be ready at the call of the presiding officers of the Church and the stakes, to labor in the ministry at home, and to officiate in any calling that may be required of them, whether it be to work in the temples, or to labor in the ministry at home, or whether it be to go out into the world, along with the Seventies, to preach the Gospel to the world." (CR, Oct. 1904, p. 4.)

As to the duties of a bishop, he said, "It is expected that the bishop of a ward with his counselors will understand the necessities of every member of his ward. . . . It devolves upon the Bishopric of the ward to look after the poor, to minister unto the sick and the afflicted and to see that there is no want nor suffering among the people in these organized divisions of the Church. It is also the duty of these presiding officers in the Church to look after the spiritual welfare of the people, to see that they are living moral, pure and upright lives, that they are faithful in the discharge of their duties as Latter-day Saints, that they are honest in their dealings with one another, and with all the world. It is their business to see that spiritual light exists in their hearts, and that the people under their presidency and direction are living the lives of Saints, as far as it is possible for men and women, in the mortal body, beset by the weaknesses and imperfections of mankind, can be Saints." (CR, Oct. 1904, pp. 2, 3.)

He had this to say about the duties of the Aaronic Priesthood: "Then we have the Lesser Priesthood, which attends to the different temporal matters of the Church, consisting of Priests, Teachers and Deacons, who labor under the direction of the Bishopric in the various wards in which they dwell, for the work of the ministry, for the edifying of the body of Christ, the unifying of the people and bringing them up to the standard of righteousness that they should reach in the flesh, according to the light they possess and the ability and talent which the Lord has given them." (CR, Oct. 1904, p. 4.)

So frequently did President Smith return to the theme of the priesthood, and so detailed and explicit were his remarks on the subject, that this aspect of his public speaking overshadows all others. Indeed, his whole ministry was characterized by a deliberate effort to strengthen and magnify the priesthood, which he recognized as the key factor in the effective administration of Church affairs.

Chapter Twenty-three

On the Move

J oseph F. Smith's life was marked by an extraordinary mobility, beginning with his pioneer trekking at age eight. And despite advancing age and serious physical disabilities, that propensity was still evident during his early and mid-seventies.

In the first week of July 1910, he and his wife Mary T. left Salt Lake City for the East Coast with a party that included the president's perennial traveling companion, Bishop Charles W. Nibley. Their ultimate destination was Europe, where Joseph would interweave some sightseeing and recreation with a crowded schedule of Church meetings and ceremonial visits.

In New York City the party was met by the president of the Eastern States Mission, Ben E. Rich. It was this able and outspoken man who once had responded to a request for an accounting of certain funds with the crisp answer, "I spent them." With the mission president was an intelligent young assistant, Arthur V. Watkins, who later in life was to distinguish himself as a stake president, a trial judge, and a United States senator from Utah. This pair was the first of a host of Latter-day Saints the president would encounter during this trip who had already gained prominence or who would later do so.

What had been projected as a joyful, rewarding interlude for President Smith turned into a painful ordeal. The seventy-two-year-old prophet's difficulty came from an irritated sciatic nerve. Even before reaching New York City on the outward journey, he got a taste of what was in store for him. "Sorely tried with sciatica," he recorded on July 7, en route to Manhattan.

Boarding the S.S. *Vaderland*, the party embarked for Dover, England, in hot, humid weather on a sea "like glass." President Smith found as the *Vaderland* reached the open sea that there was "not a breath of air." While this condition was to alter somewhat as the voyage wore on, still it was, for the most part, an extremely calm and, because of the heat, unpleasant trip. Adding to the unpleasantness was the president's lame leg, the pain from which was intense and frequent. "In bed all day," he recorded on July 16. "The first time any such a thing has happened in all my sea-faring experience."

Two days later, Joseph's spirits were lifted when, on reaching Dover, his son Franklin Richards Smith joined the party. Franklin, Sarah's boy, was an exuberant, strong-minded twenty-two-year-old who had been in England for almost two years, laboring intermittently in Birkenhead, Preston, and Leyland. Occasionally, President Smith found it necessary to curb the overflowing spirits of this likable young man. "I am sorry you were not a little more discreet in responding to President Penrose," the father had written to his son on February 19, 1910. "Boys on missions should cultivate amity with all, and more especially with their file leaders and presidents. I hope you will keep on the good side of President Penrose [whom President Smith would call as his second counselor in a little over a year] and all your companions. Missionaries should all be as members of one family and each should strive to make it pleasant for all the rest. Strife, or differences, or any degree of the spirit of dissension existing among them just so much weakens their influence and impairs their usefulness and efficiency. Avoid carefully giving offense to any, but always be ready to show kindness and sympathy."

Franklin's presence greatly enlivened President Smith's entourage as it crossed the channel to Rotterdam, where a conference was held with about eleven hundred members and friends, who crowded into a rented hall. Sharing the pulpit with President Smith was Elder Rudger Clawson of the Twelve, who a month earlier had succeeded Charles W. Penrose as the president of the European Mission. Also present to speak were Bishop Nibley; Brigham G. Thatcher, president of the Netherlands Mission; and, of course, Joseph's son Elder Franklin R. Smith.

While in the low countries, the president exposed Mary and Franklin to some of the cultural and historical treasures to be found there—the museums and the Old Pilgrim Church in Rotterdam; the battlefield at Waterloo, where Napoleon suffered defeat by Wellington's army; and the world's fair at Brussels, which was then in progress. Because of the large crowds that had swarmed to Brussels for the fair, the president's party had difficulty finding suitable hotel accommodations.

From Rotterdam, the travelers went to Copenhagen via Hamburg and thence to Sweden, where, among other things, President Smith and Bishop Nibley attended an international peace conference at Stockholm as delegates from Utah. Leaving Sweden, the party went to Berlin, where they met the wealthy Utah businessman David Eccles and his wife, who were touring Europe. Also in Berlin the president met twenty-one-year-old Henry D. Moyle, who years later would be called as an apostle and as a counselor in the First Presidency.

In Zurich, Switzerland, where the group traveled next, Joseph and Mary were greeted by their twenty-year-old son, Calvin, who was serving as a Swiss missionary. A few months later, the prophet gave wise advice to this missionary son, as he had previously advised Franklin R. Concerned that Calvin was spending too much time composing letters, he wrote to him on November 11, 1910, "I have before me four long interesting letters written by you on the following dates: September 22nd, and 30th, and October 7th and 16th. All of which I was glad to receive and have read with very much pleasure and interest. I have also read your letters to Mamma and Samuel and James and also to Sister Lucy, all written within a very short period of time. While it is very interesting to get long letters from you, it must be considerable of a labor for you to write so many *long* letters and keep up with your other labors and duties in the field. I hope you will be prudent and not undertake to do too much, nor overdo yourself. It was a rule of your late kinsman, President George A. Smith, to make short prayers, but fervent ones, short sermons and to the point, and short letters well digested. It is often much more of a labor to write a short letter well composed and digested than a very lengthy rambling one." Lest his son take offense at this mild rebuke, the kindly father, who loved his children enough to take the time to counsel and correct them, added this bit of droll humor, "I think you are a very good letter writer, only that your hand writing appears rather small for so large a boy."

Enjoying the magnificence of the Swiss countryside with its fertile, narrow valleys; its towering peaks; and its neat, well-kept houses and barns, the party traveled on through Lausane and Basil to Paris. There, as if to reproach the city that never sleeps, President Smith remained in bed most of the time, nursing a painful sciatica attack. The only redeeming feature of this Paris visit, as far as the President was concerned, was that his grandson Joseph Smith Nelson joined the party there. "Our little Joseph" was a special joy to his grandfather, who doubtless saw in him, as he did in his other progeny, the prospects of an eternal increase.

Crossing the channel back to Great Britain, the Prophet held a series of meetings at London, Glasgow, and Liverpool. At London he again encountered Mr. and Mrs. Eccles, who were still on their "grand tour." And at Glasgow, he met and was impressed by a tall, forthright missionary with a booming voice; his name was Alma Sonne. The Prophet doubtless saw great potential in this fine young man. It is likely, however, that he failed to see the illustrious future that lay ahead of him as a banker in Cache Valley, Utah, and as a general authority, Elder Sonne being among the first group of men called as assistants to the Twelve in 1941.

At Liverpool, Joseph F. was caught up in a nostalgic reverie when he visited the old Church building at 42 Islington.

273

There, in the distant past, he had spent so many hours counseling and instructing missionaries, studying, writing sermons or articles, weeping with joy or sadness over letters and pictures received from his family in far-away Utah, or battling respiratory ailments.

The measured pace of British life had not altered the general appearance of the surrounding neighborhoods, where Joseph F. had been accustomed to take his constitutionals, although here and there could be seen buildings that did not exist before or vacant spaces where buildings once stood. But the pierhead on the River Mersey, with its cathedral-like buildings and bustling wharves, was essentially unchanged. There Joseph had seen hundreds of missionaries or converts come and go.

Any recollection of pain or discomfort President Smith had while visiting Liverpool scarcely could have equaled the agony of his sciatica attacks. And he was in almost constant pain as he traveled to London and thence to Dover, where he and his party had bookings for a return voyage. Boarding the ship on August 20, Joseph promptly went to bed, seeking relief from the severe pains that resembled a mammoth toothache centered in his hip and thigh. Not given to self pity or grousing, he brushed off his infirmity with the exclamation, "Oh what a task."

Noting the discomfort of his passenger, the ship's captain sought to apply some practical psychology by giving him a book about the trials and tribulations of Helen Keller, who, though blind and deaf, surmounted her physical disabilities to become a woman of high accomplishment. The prophet failed to note the effect of this remedy. But his notation of the incident implies a sense of gratitude for the captain's concern.

After an unpleasant Atlantic crossing, the president's ship docked at a Manhattan pier on August 29. There to meet him was President Ben E. Rich, who shepherded the party to the mission home at No. 33, 126th Street, where they remained for a day.

On the thirtieth, President Rich deposited the travelers at the New York Central Railway station, where they boarded the *Independence*, a private car provided by Judge Lovett, an influential railroad executive. The crew included a butler, a porter, and a cook, whose sole duties were to care for the needs of President Smith and his party.

Ordinarily, Joseph's deprived background made it difficult for him to accept such luxurious treatment with good feelings. However, worn out by an exhausting travel schedule and by the severe pain in his leg, he accepted the judge's offer with alacrity. Anxious to board the car where he could relax and rest his leg, the president did something he ordinarily would not have done: "A young lady n. paper reporter wanted my photo for a n.p. report but I declined. We came near having a scene. Mary T. got mad. We were soon on our way in one of the most elegant private cars I ever saw with every convenience & comfort with through transportation without change to Salt Lake City." As the train that included President Smith's luxury car left Omaha, he was caught up again in a reverie that brought to mind events of long ago: "We are crossing the plains, which first I crossed in 1848: 64 years ago, on the 23rd of the month, we landed in Salt Lake Valley, after a journey of over four months; now we cross in about one day and two nights." But the realities of the moment soon crowded in upon him, evoking this comment: "My sciatica does not let up on us at all."

Considering the red-carpet treatment he had been accorded at each stop during his trip, the reception he received on arriving in Salt Lake City on Saturday morning, September 3, must have been something of a letdown: "We reached Salt Lake at about 7:30 this morning. No one to meet us. Joseph Nelson's auto came to our relief and we all piled in and started for the 'Beehive.' We met David A., with Agnes and Silas coming in an auto on our way up."

Neither pain, fatigue, nor a two-months accumulation of work on his desk could deter Joseph from promptly performing his patriarchal duties. "After breakfast and a rest," he recorded as the last entry of the bittersweet European tour, "I drove down & called on Sarah, Edna and Alice and at Mamies, Donnies and Josephs."

Having performed what to him was the most essential duty at the moment, the prophet went to bed, where he was to remain for over a month. His first effort at public speaking following his convalescence was at the opening session of the general conference on October 6, 1910. "I do not feel I should occupy very much time this morning," he told his Tabernacle audience. "I have just got out of my bed, where I have lain for more than a month, with very little exercise, and I feel the effects of the inertia, the inactivity to which I have been subjected—not willingly but unwillingly—for the last thirty days or more." With that cursory explanation of his long illness, the prophet then bore his testimony and endeavored to counteract the flood of abuse that had again begun to pour forth regularly from a hostile press and, unfortunately, from some members of the Church. President Smith said, "I feel in my heart to say to this congregation that I love the gospel, I love the truth that has been revealed anew to the children of men in these latter days, more, if possible, today than ever I did in my life. . . . I stand before you today . . . on the ground that I have tried to be true to God, to the utmost of my knowledge and ability; that I have tried to be true to my people, . . . and I have been true to the world in every pledge and promise that I have made to the world, notwithstanding there have been men who have shown a disposition to make it appear that I was a hypocrite, that I was two-faced: that I was one thing to the world and another thing in secret. I want it distinctly understood that those who have conveyed such an idea as this to mankind have been wilfully injuring me, wronging me, and falsifying me and my character before the people; and I want it distinctly understood those things must stop. They must stop at least among men that profess to be members of the Church of Jesus Christ of Latter-day Saints. I can endure to be maligned and persecuted by my enemies, who are also enemies of the Kingdom of God, but I do not want to be maligned . . . by men who profess to be members of the Church of Jesus Christ of Latter-day Saints, neither intentionally or otherwise." (CR, Oct. 1910, pp. 2, 3.)

By June, the Prophet felt well enough to take to the road again. Accompanied as usual by his friend Charles W. Nibley, he traveled to Washington, D.C. At the depot to meet the Utah visitors was Senator Reed Smoot, who took them immediately to his home on the outskirts of Washington, a home Joseph characterized as "elegant."

The main purpose of this trip was to enable the president and Bishop Nibley to testify before a congressional committee that was considering legislation that would markedly affect the Church's agricultural holdings. Since the committee was behind schedule and unable to receive the president's testimony in the afternoon of June 26 as was originally planned, he napped briefly and then in the "cool of the evening" took a scenic drive along the Potomac with the senator. Those acquainted with Washington's weather in late June will appreciate Joseph's brief account of this outing: "A very close, muggy, hot night—but quite pleasant riding in the auto."

President Smith was before the committee for over three hours the next morning. During the afternoon, while Bishop Nibley was testifying, Senator Smoot took the prophet to meet President William Howard Taft. This jolly, rotund man, who had a brain to match his giant physique, greeted President Smith warmly, chatting amiably with him for some time about government and Church matters of mutual interest and concern. Later that day, and during the next day, too, President Smith was introduced to other Washington functionaries, senators, military men, and bureaucrats, including the president's secretary of state. In the office of the latter, the visitors also were introduced to the British foreign minister, who doubtless was surprised at President Smith's intimate knowledge of his native England, extending back almost fifty years.

Everywhere President Smith went during this short visit to the nation's capital, he found the doors to the seats of political power were readily opened to him. Always he was received with courtesy and in some instances with deference, a reaction that contrasted sharply with the mean and petty treatment he continued to receive from his implacable enemies in Utah. And, accompanied by Reed Smoot, he could not have failed to recall the controversy that had swirled around the senator a few years before nor the distasteful hearings where he was made to feel that he and the Church, not the senator, were on trial. While the passage of time had failed to eradicate completely the hostility and bigotry that ran rampant during the Smoot hearings, it had moderated them and had given the Church and its president a status and prestige never enjoyed before. Moreover, through hard work and steady integrity, Senator Smoot had made significant contributions to the work of the Senate, thereby earning the respect of his associates and, in a sense, thereby vindicating President Smith's judgment in authorizing him to enter politics.

On the return trip, Joseph indulged in another of the nostalgic detours that became more frequent as he grew older. Stopping at Omaha, he went to nearby Florence, the new name of the old pioneer community of Winter Quarters. After riding thoughtfully through the streets of this familiar yet strange place, and after reflecting at the site of the lonely cemetery where hundreds of Latter-day Saints lay buried, he decided on an impulse to visit the herd grounds where as a boy he had tended the family livestock. Now seventy-three years old and with but a few remaining years to live, he gazed upon the familiar landmarks, which time had not erased, and recalled the happy and the frightening events that had occurred there to a fatherless, relatively unknown boy, not yet ten, who in the long years between had matured into the prophetic leader of a worldwide church whose membership then exceeded four hundred thousand. Like most people in their twilight years, President Smith savored these moments of reflection, which aroused gratitude for past fortune and courage to face an uncertain future.

The president arrived home on July 2 and eleven days later left for the Pacific Northwest on a long-planned trip. Accompanying him was his wife Alice and her four younger children, Lucy Mack, Andrew K., Jesse K., and Fielding K., who ranged in age from twenty-one-year-old Lucy Mack to eleven-year-old Fielding K., the life of the party. Also along were seven other children, Rachel and Edith, daughters of Julina, who were twenty-one and seventeen; Sarah's daughters Jeanetta and Asenath, twenty and fifteen; Edna's daughter Zina, twenty-one, who had married Ambros John Greenwell the previous December; and Martha, age fourteen. Also from the president's family was granddaughter Alice

Nelson, whose mother, Leonora, had died four years before. Joining this happy, noisy throng were John Henry Smith, the president's second counselor, and members of his family; Presiding Bishop Charles W. Nibley and members of his family; and Elder Seymour B. Young of the First Council of the Seventy.

There was an abundance of chattering and good-natured fun in the private car that carried these congenial travelers first to Pocatello, Idaho, and then to Huntington, where the brethren held a meeting with the Saints in that area. The slim attendance there was offset by a large crowd that attended an open-air meeting in Walla Walla, Washington, two days later.

Passing through Portland, the party moved on to Seattle, where on Friday, July 21, they boarded the S.S. *Princess Charlotte* for a voyage to Victoria, British Columbia. Returning the following day on the S.S. *Princess Adelaide*, the party traveled to Portland, where successful meetings were held in which the president felt he had "good liberty" in speaking. While in Portland, the party took a river ride to Oregon City and back.

Leaving Portland Monday night July 24 by a fast mail train, the party returned to Pocatello, where they caught a train to the Yellowstone station near the park. There they hired two large stages that carried them into the heart of one of the most extraordinary public parks to be found anywhere. This side trip was made chiefly for the benefit of the many young people in the party whom the President wanted to expose to the grandeur of a vast, essentially untamed, wilderness area. Their acquaintance with the eighty-acre Liberty Park in Salt Lake City had hardly prepared the Smith children for this gigantic park, which embraces over two million acres and is surrounded by the Gallatin, Shoshone, Teton, and Targhee national forests, which, at that day, were hardly less primitive than the park itself. One can imagine the indulgent pride with which the seventy-three-year-old, bearded and benign prophet introduced his children, especially the irrepressible eleven-year-old Fielding K., to the wonder of this vast fairyland—to the wide varieties of plants, including microscopic algae and giant evergreens; to the animals, including bison, bear, elk, moose, deer, and bighorn; and to the thousands of hot springs, with their surface manifestations as colorful hot pools, mud caldrons, steam vents, paint pots, hot rivers, and, most spectacular and impressive of all, the geysers.

This trip, as much as any other he ever took, illustrated two important aspects of President Smith's travels. First, whenever feasible, he always took one or more members of his family with him, both for companionship and for their education. Second, he never took a trip merely for the sake of sightseeing or vacationing. There was always a framework of meetings or business around which his trips were arranged. Yet, so long had he carried a heavy load of responsibility, from which he could never escape and which never abated, he had learned to carve out moments or days in the midst of hectic schedules to revive his energies and to build his family relationships.

One can better comprehend President Smith's mobile lifestyle by following him through a few months of his seventy-fifth year. On April 27, 1913, he traveled to Payson, Utah, with his thirty-four-year-old son, David Asael, who was then second counselor in the Presiding Bishopric, a position he had occupied for six years. At this time, David A., who was one of Julina's sons, still had twenty-five years of service in the Presiding Bishopric ahead of him, twenty of which would be in the role of first counselor. In Payson, father and son joined in dedicating a new chapel.

Four days later, Joseph F. and Sarah left for Los Angeles with the president's cousin, George Albert Smith, who at the time had been a member of the Twelve for ten years. There the Smith cousins held a district conference, and the president dedicated a new building, one of the few in the area, which foreshadowed the first stake in California, which would be organized in Los Angeles a decade later. This building cost "a little more than $20,000.00" and was paid for "mostly by the Trustee in Trust."

Following the dedicatory service, one of the local Church members, Eddie South, drove the president and his party down to the beach, where they were staying in a cottage. Affirming the rapid proliferation of automobiles even at that

early day, Joseph wrote, "We met more than 300 autos returning from the beach," a notation from which one also may infer
a gentle criticism of Sabbath breakers. Reflecting the comparative novelty of the automobile, President Smith recorded on
the following day that the fifteen-mile trip to the city took
thirty-eight minutes. He also reported with some satisfaction
that the return trip that evening was negotiated in only thirty-
seven minutes.

During the day, lengthy meetings were held with the
Southern California missionaries, who had been invited to attend the dedication of the chapel. During the noon break, the
president and George Albert Smith "took lunch with Bro.
George Romney & family, Mexican refugees." Among the
children who gathered around the table that day was sixteen-
year-old Marion G. Romney, who never would forget that
President Smith kindly patted him on the head and said, "My
boy, never be ashamed that you are a Mormon." (As related
to the author.)

The perceptive prophet, whose background made him
keenly aware of the fears and needs of deprived youth, may
have sensed the emotional turmoil of this fine young man,
whose parents and family had been stripped of everything
but their faith and the clothing on their backs and driven from
their comfortable homes during the Mexican revolution. Marion, who grew into a respected attorney, an apostle, and a
member of the First Presidency, always heeded that prophetic admonition and implanted it in the minds of numerous
associates over the years.

Following the usual pattern of sandwiching a little relaxation between his Church duties, Joseph enjoyed watching
and listening to the restless sea, napping, reading, and visiting with family members who then lived in Los Angeles.
These included his daughter Donette, fondly called Donnie,
who had married Alonzo Pratt Kesler and who was living in
Los Angeles.

On Wednesday, May 7, the prophet participated in one of
those family events that always gave him satisfaction; he confirmed his "little grandson A. P. Kesler Jr, he having been
baptized on his birthday." Despite some reservations Joseph

F. had about lawyers, this grandson was to become one, and he ultimately would be elected attorney general of the State of Utah.

Back home, the prophet presided at a special meeting of all Salt Lake Temple workers on Friday, May 23, when they commemorated the twentieth anniversary of work in that temple. The next day found him in Helper, Utah, where he had traveled in a private car to transact business at Uncle Jesse Knight's Spring Canyon coal mine. The next day in Helper he organized a ward comprised mostly of the miners who worked in the area and their families.

On June 15, the president, aided by his son David A., dedicated another new chapel, this one at Morgan, Utah. In July, he took a swing through Wyoming and Montana into Canada, where, at Cardston, on Sunday, July 27, he dedicated the site for the temple that was later constructed there. Earlier in the day he had attended three separate meetings, speaking in each one. Moving on to Raymond, he held a midweek conference where he blessed and admonished the Saints and stimulated support for the temple.

September found the prophet in St. George, where he held a two-day conference on the thirteenth and fourteenth. Sharing the pulpit with him were his counselor Anthon H. Lund and his son David A., who, with their wives, had accompanied him, Julina, and daughter Rachel. Also in the party was son Wesley and his wife, Mary.

Later in the month, President Smith went to Lehi in Utah County to attend to pressing water problems; and a week later, on November 2, he dedicated a new chapel in Chicago. Accompanying him on this trip were George Albert Smith and Bishop Charles W. Nibley.

Soon after his return from Chicago, the president traveled to Los Angeles again, this time with Sarah and cousin George Albert. The latter accompanied the prophet on this trip to balmy southern California, as he had on an earlier one, not only because of his relationship to the president and his position in the Twelve, but also because of his frail health, which always was improved by the lower altitude, the warmth, and the exhilarating sea air.

A few days after returning from Los Angeles, the president embarked on a three-week tour to Arizona, where meetings were held with Saints all along the way. Traveling by train via Colorado and New Mexico, and connecting with the Santa Fe line at Albuquerque, he detrained at Holbrook, Arizona, and was driven by coach to Snowflake, the LDS community that was first presided over by his kinsman Jesse N. Smith.

After holding a stake conference there, he backtracked to Holbrook and went on by train to the south rim of the Grand Canyon via Flagstaff. After spending two pleasant days at the lodge near this scenic wonder, he traveled on to Phoenix, where, in addition to holding meetings with the handful of Saints there, he met with Arizona's first governor, George W. P. Hunt, who had taken office only the year before when Arizona was admitted to the union as the forty-eighth state. While in this area, the prophet also visited Mesa, east of Phoenix, where there was a much larger concentration of Latter-day Saints, and from there he went to inspect the Roosevelt Dam on the upper reaches of the Salt River, whose impounded waters meant life and wealth to those who occupied the fertile desert lands of the Salt River Valley.

Traveling southward again, the president visited the Saints in the Gila River Valley, holding a stake conference in Thatcher, where he renewed acquaintances with Alice's relatives the Kimballs. And finally, he went to Tucson, an ancient Spanish city near the border, where Church influence was minimal. There he met and encouraged the small group of Latter-day Saints who had settled there.

Deciding to close the loop, the party entrained for Los Angeles, where President Smith was again able to visit with the members of his family who lived there.

Returning to Salt Lake City on December 15, the prophet noted that on the sixteenth he "had to work in the office all day." On the twenty-first, he made his last trip of the year when he traveled to nearby West Point, where he dedicated still another new chapel.

Thus, at age seventy-five, when most of his contemporaries were in their graves, bedridden, or wearing out their last years in easy retirement, Joseph was actively engaged in his apostolic ministry, traveling throughout the Church and remaining at home only long enough to keep in touch with his large, fast-growing family; to recharge his physical energy; and to check with his able associates on the administrative affairs of the Church.

Chapter Twenty-four

Love of Family

President Smith and his associates laid special emphasis on the quality of the moral lives of the Latter-day Saints. And since they conceived that the main instrument in teaching moral principles was the family, they gave much admonition and instruction about family roles and responsibilities. President Smith repeatedly emphasized that the family is a divine, not a man-made, institution. "I want the young men of Zion to realize that this institution of marriage is not a man-made institution," he wrote. "It is of God; it is honorable, and no man who is of marriageable age is living his religion who remains single. . . . There are great consequences connected with it, consequences which reach beyond this present time, into all eternity, for thereby souls are begotten into the world, and men and women obtain their being in the world. Marriage is the preserver of the human race. Without it, the purposes of God would be frustrated; virtue would be destroyed to give place to vice and corruption, and the earth would be void and empty." (IE, Jul. 1902, pp. 713-14.)

Having thus affirmed the divine origin and purpose of the family, President Smith defined the rights and duties of its various members. Of the father, he said, "There is no higher authority in matters relating to the family organization, and especially when that organization is presided over by one holding the higher priesthood, than that of the father. This authority is time honored, and among the people of God in all dispensations it has been highly respected and often emphasized by the teachings of the prophets who were inspired of God. The patriarchal order is of divine origin and will continue throughout time and eternity. There is then a particular reason why men, women, and children should understand this order and this authority in the households of the people of God, and seek to make it what God intended it to be, a qualification and preparation for the highest exaltation of His children. In the home the presiding authority is always vested in the father, and in all home affairs and family matters there is no other authority paramount. . . . The father presides at the table, at prayer, and gives general directions relating to his family life whoever may be present. . . . This authority carries with it a responsibility, and a grave one, as well as its rights and privileges, and men cannot be too exemplary in their lives, nor fit themselves too carefully to live in harmony with this important and God-ordained rule of conduct in the family organization." (*Juvenile Instructor* 37:146-47.)

As to mothers, President Smith wrote, "Motherhood lies at the foundation of happiness in the home, and of prosperity in the nation." (*Juvenile Instructor* 50:290.) And again, "In the home the mother is the principal disciplinarian in early child life, and her influence and discipline determine in a great measure the ability of her children to assume in manhood and womanhood the larger governments in church and state. In addition, however, to home government, women often stand with their husbands in responsible places and share in some measure the success or failure which characterizes their husbands' administration of affairs. . . . The word and the law of God are as important for women who would reach wise conclusions as they are for men; and women should study and consider the problems of the great latter-day work from the standpoint of God's revelations, and as they may be actuated by his Spirit, which it is their right to receive through the medium of sincere and heartfelt prayer." (*Juvenile Instructor* 38:371-72.)

The prophet reemphasized these responsibilities of parents in the training and discipline of their children: "It is the duty of Latter-day Saints to teach their children the truth, to bring them up in the way they should go, to teach them the first principles of the Gospel, the necessity of baptism for the remission of sins, and for membership in the Church of Christ; teaching them the necessity of receiving the gift of the Holy Ghost by the laying on of hands, which will lead them into all truth, and which will reveal to them things that have passed and things which are to come, and show to them more clearly those things which are present with them, that they may comprehend the truth, and that they may walk in the light as Christ is in the light; that they may have fellowship with Him, and that His blood may cleanse them from all sin." (CR, Apr. 1912, p. 135.)

A few years later, he took up this subject again, admonishing parents in their duty to teach their children: "Another great and important duty devolving upon this people is to teach their children, from their cradle until they become men and women, every principle of the Gospel, and endeavor, as far as it lies in the power of the parents, to instil into their hearts a love for God, the truth, virtue, honesty, honor and integrity to everything that is good. That is important for all men and women who stand at the head of a family in the household of faith. Teach your children the love of God. Teach them to love the principles of the Gospel of Jesus Christ. Teach them to love their fellowmen, and especially to love their fellow members in the Church, that they may be true to their fellowship with the people of God. Teach them to honor the priesthood, to honor the authority that God has bestowed upon His Church for the proper government of His Church." (CR, Apr. 1915, pp. 4-5.)

Not only did the prophet admonish parents to teach their children and to give special emphasis in their teaching to the first principles of the gospel, but he provided a veritable catalog of other things important for parents to teach and children to learn: "We are a Christian people," he told a Tabernacle audience just a year before he died. "We believe in the Lord Jesus Christ, and we feel that it is our duty to acknowledge him as our Savior and Redeemer. Teach it to your children. Teach them that the Prophet Joseph Smith restored again to earth the priesthood that was held by Peter and James and John, who were ordained under the hands of the Savior himself. Teach them that Joseph Smith, the Prophet, when only a boy, was chosen and called of God to lay the foundations of the Church of Christ in the world, to restore the holy priesthood, and the ordinances of the gospel which are necessary to qualify men to enter into the kingdom of heaven. Teach your children to respect their neighbors. Teach your children to respect their bishops and the teachers that come to their homes to teach them. Teach your children to respect old age, gray hairs, and feeble frames. Teach them to venerate and to hold in honorable remembrance their parents and help all those who are helpless and needy. Teach your children, as you have been taught yourselves, to honor the priesthood which you hold, the priesthood which we hold as elders in Israel. Teach your children to honor themselves, teach your children to honor the principle of presidency by which organizations are held intact and by which strength and power for the well-being and happiness and upbuilding of the people is preserved. Teach your children that when they go to school they should honor their teachers in that which is true and honest, in that which is manly and womanly and is worth while; and also teach them to avoid the bad examples of their teachers out of school and the bad principles of men and women who are sometimes teachers in schools. Teach your children to honor the law of God and the law of the state and the law of our country. Teach them to respect and hold in honor those who are chosen by the people to stand at their head and execute justice and administer the law. Teach them to be loyal to their country, loyal to righteousness and uprightness and honor, and thereby they will grow up to be men and women choice above all the men and women of the world." (CR, Apr. 1917, pp. 5-6.)

And in still another general conference talk, the prophet described the special need to protect and train children because of their helplessness at birth and their slow maturing process. He also noted their susceptibility to the influences of their environment and touched on the most important thing to give and teach children—love: "It does not need argument to convince our minds that our children will be just about what we make them. They are born without knowledge or understanding—the most helpless creatures of the animal creation born into the world. The little one begins to learn after it is born, and all that it knows greatly depends upon its environment, the influence under which it is brought up, the kindness with which it is treated, the noble examples shown it, the hallowed influences of father and mother, or otherwise, over its infant mind. And it will be largely what its environment and its parents and teachers make it. . . . You will observe that the most potent influence over the mind of a child to persuade it to learn, to progress, or to accomplish anything is the influence of love. More can be accomplished for good by unfeigned love, in bringing up a child, than by any other influence that can be brought to bear upon it. A child that cannot be conquered by the lash, or subdued by violence, may be controlled in an instant by unfeigned affection and sympathy. I know this is true; and this principle obtains in every condition of life. . . . I would have it understood that I believe that the greatest law and commandment of God is to love the Lord our God with all our mind, might and strength, and our neighbors as ourselves; and if this principle is observed at home the brothers and sisters will love each other, they will be kind and helpful to one another, showing forth the principle of kindness and being solicitous for each other's good. Under these circumstances the home comes nearer being a heaven on earth, and children brought up under these influences will never forget them, and though they may be in trying places their memories will revert to the homes where they enjoyed such hallowed influences, and their better natures will assert themselves no matter what the trials or temptations may be." (CR, Oct. 1902, pp. 92, 93.)

While President Smith's admonitions about family life customarily were practical, they always had as their goal spiritual objectives. "We expect to have our wives and husbands in eternity," he said. "We expect our children will acknowledge us as their fathers and mothers in eternity. I expect this: I look for nothing else. Without it I could not be happy. The thought or belief that I should be denied this privilege hereafter would make me miserable from this moment. I never could be happy again without the hope that I shall enjoy the society of my wives and children in eternity. If I had not this hope, I should be of all men most unhappy; 'for if in this life only we have hope in Christ, we are of all men most miserable.' All who have tasted of this influence of the Spirit of God, have had awakened within them a hope of eternal life, cannot be happy unless they continue to drink of that fountain until they are satisfied, and it is the only fountain at which they can drink and be satisfied." (*Deseret News Weekly* 33:131.)

In large measure, President Smith discerned the "hope of eternal life" referred to in this statement in the sweetness of his earthly family associations. The quality and intensity of these are best understood from his personal correspondence. In a letter to one of his wives, he extolled the virtues of mothers and motherhood: "Oh my God, how I love and cherish true motherhood! Nothing beneath the celestial kingdom can surpass my deathless love for the sweet, true, noble, soul who gave me birth—my own, own, mother! O she was good! . . . A royal daughter of God! To her I owe my very existence as also my success in life, coupled with the favor and mercy of God! And next to her I hold in my heart of hearts the Mothers of my own children. I love them with an imperishable love. I honor them as the Mothers of my children! I cherish them as the dearest partners of my greatest joys, the sweetest, best ministers to my earthly pleasures and happiness. My wives! My companions in joy, in sorrow, in poverty or plenty, in time and throughout all eternity! I love them for I have confidence in them. I know them; they are clean and sweet and pure." (JFS, p. 452.)

In another letter, he traced how the bonds of matrimony were strengthened and altered as the years wore on: "My Dear Companion: I congratulate you on attaining your 39th birthday, with such favorable prospects before you and such a goodly record behind. No one can appreciate better, the blessings of the past, or more fondly hope for the good promises of the future on your behalf than I. While we cannot return to our youth, live over again the happy past, or retrace

Joseph F. Smith and his family (Church Archives)

the journey we have travelled together, save in memory, the future is as full of hope, as fraught with joyous anticipation, and as big with faith in our destiny as it ever was. Our position grows stronger as we near the end of life's voyage. I think better of you, prize you higher, you are nearer to me and I love you more today than I did then or twenty years ago. Every hour, week, month and year, strengthens the bond of our union and each child cements it with an eternal seal. My only regret is my inability to express in a more substantial manner my affection and good will. If I possessed wealth by the millions I could only feel rich in the enjoyment it would afford to my family. For myself, I want nothing but my family and their weal, and food and covering." (JFS, pp. 453, 454.)

In a sense, the tender feelings he bore toward his wives intensified his feelings for his children. These parental feelings never were more powerfully felt or more poignantly expressed than at the death of one of his children. A letter written shortly after the passing of his eldest child, Mercy Josephine, who died at age three, reflects the love and tenderness the father felt toward her, a love and tenderness that extended equally to all his family: "I scarcely dare to trust myself to write, even now my heart aches, and my mind is all chaos; if I should murmur, may God forgive me, my soul has been and is tried with poignant grief, my heart is bruised and wrenched almost asunder. I am desolate, my home seems desolate and almost dreary, yet here are my family and my little babe; yet I cannot help but feel that the tenderest, sweetest and yet the strongest cord that bound me to home and earth is severed, my babe, my own sweet Dodo is gone! I can scarcely believe it and my heart aches, can it be? I look in vain, I listen, no sound, I wander through the rooms, all are vacant, lonely, desolate, deserted. I look down the garden walk, peer around the house, look here and there for a glimpse of a little golden, sunny head and rosy cheeks, but no, alas, no pattering little footsteps. No beaming little black eyes sparkling with love for papa; no sweet little inquiring voice asking a thousand questions, and telling pretty little things, prattling merrily, no soft little dimpled hands clasping me around the neck, no sweet rosy lips returning in childish innocence my fond embrace and kisses, but a vacant little chair. Her little toys concealed, her clothes put by, and only the one desolate thought forcing its crushing leaden weight upon my heart—she is not here, she is gone! But will she not come back? She cannot leave me long, where is she? I am almost wild, and O God only knows how much I loved my girl, and she the light and the joy of my heart.

"The morning before she died, after being up with her all night, for I watched her every night, I said to her, 'My little pet did not sleep all night.' She shook her head and replied, 'I'll sleep today, papa.' Oh! how those little words shot through my heart. I knew though I would not believe, it was another voice, that it meant the sleep of death and she did sleep. And, Oh! the light of my heart went out. The image of heaven graven in my soul was almost departed. . . . Thou wert a heavenly gift directly to my heart of hearts. I loved thee more than tongue can tell, more than the soul can speak through mortal agency. Thou didst make me a better man; for thy sake I loved humanity, earth, and heaven, more; thine image drew me nearer unto God, and caused heaven to bless and flourish in my home. Thy bright spirit lightened all my cares and made all the earth seem better. O thou wert all in all to my most fervent love; for thee I could brave life or death. More precious than the apple of mine eye. More dearly loved than life. Dodo, how I miss thee; but sleep my babe, in peace." (JFS, pp. 455-57.)

These are the words of a thirty-two-year-old father who had just suffered through the first major tragedy involving his children. It is true he had lost a child previously when Sarah's firstborn, a little girl named Sarah Ella, died February 11, 1869, six days after her birth. But traumatic as it was, that incident could not compare in its impact with the loss of Mercy Josephine—not that he loved the one more than the other, but that three years of life with the elder girl had forged special bonds of affection and understanding that were most painful to sever.

Over the years, the prophet was to suffer the trauma of laying other children to rest. Heber John, Alfred Jason, Rhoda Ann, and John Schwartz died in their infancy in 1874, 1878,

1879, and 1889. Alice died in 1901 at the age of nineteen, in the prime of young womanhood. Albert Jesse died in 1883 at age two; and Robert was buried in 1886 at age three. Ruth passed away in 1898 in her midteens. Joseph suffered these losses in his immediate family and buried many of his other relatives and friends. He was thoroughly indoctrinated in the principles of life, death, and the resurrection, which he expounded eloquently over the years, so one would have expected that his grief at death would have moderated. But it was not so. Despite his advancing age, the death of each loved one produced the same anguish and the same fervent expressions of love and loneliness.

Consider this eulogy seventy-seven-year-old Joseph F. Smith wrote in his journal at the death of his wife Sarah, who passed away March 21, 1915: "We were greatly pained and grieved to see that she had taken a sudden change for the worse and was sinking. Dr. S. L. Richards was present and expressed the fear that she could not endure through the night. But we watched and prayed every moment and every hour throughout the day and into the night. Seeing her gradually growing weaker and shorter of breath, doing everything possible to prolong vitality until 5 mts after midnight, when without a sign of movement, or the slightest struggle she softly ceased breathing and for the first moment in three weeks fell to rest! And her Sweet Spirit took its flight. But Oh! with that parting our own heart swelled with bitter grief. Not for our lovely companion but that we could not keep her with us. Oh! how I loved! Oh! how I love that sweet and lovely soul. My darling wife! My lovely and beloved companion for more than 47 years! Mother of four of my beloved sons and seven of my beauteous daughters. My home maker in very deed. An undying part of my own life; a maker of my purest joy and greatest happiness. Oh! how I thank my Father in heaven for her, and for her children. My Mamma darling! No words of mine can express my love for you; my longing for a life eternal with you. My joy is our eternal union and the determination of my soul to try to live worthy of you. Just now it seems that the very essence, center and core of my happiness has fled with you and I cannot yet sense that you are not here.

O God be merciful to me! for my heart is broken. And my soul is sad. But yet, I *know* I shall claim her as my wife, mother of my children, companion of my bosom, a most beauteous star in my crown of glory for ever and ever. It must be so! else I would be a miserable wreck stranded upon the shore of eternity, imperfect and incomplete without her. What I say of her applies to all of those sweet souls whom God has given to me."

And, moved upon by a poetic impulse, he composed this following the death of his infant son Albert Jesse, one of Edna's children:

Gone to join his noble kindred
In their bright and happy home;
Gone where mortal ills are ended
And no death can ever come.

Where his sweet angelic spirit
Bright as pure celestial light,
Sped, his blessings to inherit
Whence from earth he took his flight.

O how choice to us his visit;
Tenderly to him we clung,
But our earthly joys exquisite
Faded when they'd just begun.

O our Albert, how we loved him!
Swelled our hearts with ample joy;
Now on earth we e'er shall miss him—
Miss our pretty infant boy!

Eyes that flashed with diamond brightness,
Hair like silken threads of gold,
Perfect form; how rare his likeness—
Beauty cast him in her mould!

Time can ne'er efface a feature;
Years may come and go apace;
Ne'er will see more beauteous creature;
Ne'er behold more lovely face.

Richer for his mind's adornments;
Comelier his spirit's grace;
Promising in life's attainments
Foremost rank amid his race.

When our trials came upon us,
Bowed beneath the chastening rod,
Mingling tears of grief and praises,
Voiced our thanks for him to God.

Sleep thou with thy darling brothers;
Rest thou with thy sisters sweet,
Weep we now for thee and others,
But ere long in bliss we meet. (JFS, pp. 459, 460.)

This small sampling from the voluminous writings of Joseph F. Smith reveals an unbroken consistency between his preachings and his practices pertaining to the family. What he enjoined upon the members of the Church as to their parental responsibilities, he demonstrated by his own conduct. And this demonstration was not meant only for show. Indeed, the public image of the prophet's family, which was positive in every respect, failed to show the depth and intensity of the love he felt for each member, which only these intimate writings reveal. It was this love for family, shared by all his colleagues in the leading councils of the Church and inculcated in the general membership, that held out the promise of millennial peace to a troubled world.

Chapter Twenty-Five

Light and Shadow

T he murder of Austrian Archduke Francis Ferdinand at Sarajevo on June 28, 1914, did not make a significant impression on President Smith and the other Church leaders. But a month later, the event and its aftermath absorbed their interest when Austria-Hungary declared war on Serbia in retaliation. Serbia then appealed for aid to its ally and protector, Russia, which ordered a partial mobilization on its southern front. This aroused Russia's ancient enemy, Germany, whose Imperial Court then decided on war against both Russia and France. By August 1 an actual state of war existed between Russia and Germany, and on the following day, German troops entered French territory. Thus World War I had erupted on a sleepy public.

Although in its inception the war seemed remote to most Americans, to President Smith and his associates it was a dangerous reality because of its interruption of the Church's proselyting effort. Most of the missionaries serving in the European countries affected by the war were from the United States, which necessitated their being transferred to other fields of labor.

Aside from the dislocations in the missionary effort caused by the war, President Smith and his associates were concerned because of the needless loss of life that would result and because it would set member against member. These matters weighed heavily on President Smith at the general conference held following the outbreak of the war. Anxious to ease the minds of those who had loved ones serving as missionaries in Europe, he explained to his Tabernacle audience, "I think it will be safe for me to say that every precaution has been taken that could be taken for the protection of our elders in those foreign missions where war exists. In Germany, France, Austria, and portions of other countries so dreadfully involved in war, our elders have all been invited to withdraw . . . and so far as we know our German missionaries have largely and almost entirely withdrawn from that country, and also from France. Some of them are located temporarily in Holland and in Scandinavia, and a few of them, quite a number indeed, have come across the Atlantic and have been distributed to the various missions in the United States, while those who had practically completed their missions in Europe have been honorably released to return home." (CR, Oct. 1914, p. 2.)

The prophet went on to report that the affairs of the Church in the warring countries had been left in the charge of local members and that the upset and uncertainty created by the war had turned the minds of many Europeans toward spiritual matters, thereby increasing interest in the gospel message.

Later in his sermon, the prophet touched on some of the philosophical aspects of war and expounded the only real solution to this reoccurring scourge. He pointed out the incongruity of warring peoples praying to the same God for victory. Said he, "The condition of the world today presents a spectacle that is deplorable, so far as it relates to the religious convictions, faith and power of the inhabitants of the earth. Here we have nations arrayed against nations, and yet in every one of these nations are so-called Christian peoples professing to worship the same God, professing to possess belief in the same divine Redeemer, many of them professing to be teachers of God's word, and ministers of life and salvation to the children of men, and yet these nations are divided one against the other, and each is praying to his God for wrath upon and victory over his enemies and for his own preservation." (Ibid., p. 7.)

He also drew the distinction between God's foreknowl-
edge of wars and the idea that they are predestined according
to His will: "Thus they contend and strive one against
another, and at last nation rises up against nation in fulfilment
of the predictions of the prophets of God that war should be
poured out upon all nations. I don't want you to think I believe that God has designed or willed that war should come
among the people of the world, that the nations of the world
should be divided against each other in war, and engaged in
the destruction of each other! God did not design or cause
this. It is deplorable to the heavens that such a condition
should exist among men, but the conditions do exist, and
men precipitate war and destruction upon themselves because of their wickedness, and that because they will not
abide in God's truth, walk in His love, and seek to establish
and maintain peace instead of strife and contention in the
world." (Ibid., pp. 7-8.)

President Smith then prescribed the only true and lasting
remedy for the evils of war: "We want peace in the world. We
want love and good will to exist throughout the earth, and
among all the peoples of the world; but these never can come
to the world that spirit of peace and love that should exist until
mankind will receive God's truth and God's message unto
them and acknowledge His power and authority which is
divine, and never found in the wisdom only of men." (Ibid.)

In brief remarks delivered at the end of this conference,
which contained many condemnations of war and prescrip-
tions for peace, the prophet reiterated the theme propounded
in his keynote address. Said he, "We will never have peace
until we have truth. We will never be able to establish peace
on earth and good will until we have drunk at the fountain of
righteousness and eternal truth, as God has revealed it to
man." (Ibid., p. 129.)

After following the progess of the war for three years
and after seeing the United States enter the conflict in April
1917, President Smith offered the readers of the *Improvement
Era* a clinical analysis of the causes of war. He wrote, "Worldly
ambitions, pride, and the love of power, determination on
the part of rulers to prevail over their competitors in the

national games of life, wickedness at heart, desire for power, for worldly greatness, have led the nations of the earth to quarrel with each other and have brought them to war and self-destruction. I presume there is not a nation in the world today that is not tainted with this evil more or less. It may be possible, perhaps, to trace the cause of the evil, or the greatest part of it, to some particular nation of the earth; but I do not know." (IE 20:823.)

While distressed about the war and its causes, President Smith was optimistic about the future and confident that the influences of God would prevail to bring about improved conditions. "This I do believe, with all my heart," he wrote, "that the hand of God is striving with certain of the nations of the earth to preserve and protect human liberty, freedom to worship him according to the dictates of conscience, freedom and the inalienable right of men to organize national governments in the earth, to choose for themselves their own leaders; men whom they may select as standards of honor, of virtue and truth, men of wisdom, understanding and integrity, men who have at heart the well-being of the people who choose them to govern, enact and execute the laws in righteousness." (Ibid.)

While he was confident that better conditions ultimately would prevail, he frankly recognized the obstacles that stood in the way, not the least of which was the perversity of men: "I believe that the Lord's hand is over the nations of the world today, to bring about this rule and this reign of liberty and righteousness among the nations of the earth. He has some hard material to work with, too. He is working with men who have never prayed, men who have never known God, nor Jesus Christ whom he has sent into the world, and whom to know is life eternal. God is dealing with nations of infidels, men who fear not God, and love not the Truth, men who have no respect for virtue or purity of life. God is dealing with men who are full of pride and ambition; and he will find it difficult, I fear, to control them and lead them directly in the channel that he would have them pursue to accomplish his purposes; but he is striving to uplift. God is striving to bless, to benefit, to happify, to ameliorate the conditions of his children in the world, to give them freedom from ignorance and a knowledge of him, to learn of his ways and to walk in his paths, that they may have his Spirit to be with them always, to lead them into all truth." (Ibid.)

After the United States entered the war, a principal concern of President Smith and his associates was the conduct of the Latter-day Saints who inevitably would be drawn into the armed services. Realizing that military life and killing were so foreign to the training most of them had received from infancy, the prophet took special pains to steel them against the sordid conditions they would find in the service and to emphasize the need for them to use the tools of their religion as never before. "Will those men who go out from Utah, from the Church of Jesus Christ of Latter-day Saints, forget their prayers?" he asked rhetorically. "Will they forget God? Will they forget the teachings that they have received from their parents at home? Will they forget the principles of the gospel of Jesus Christ and the covenants that they have made in the waters of baptism, and in sacred places? Or will they go out as men, in every sense—pure men, high-minded men, honest men, virtuous men, men of God? That is what I am anxious about. I want to see the hand of God made manifest in the acts of the men that go out from the ranks of the Church of Jesus Christ and from the State of Utah, to help to defend the principles of liberty and sound government for the human family. I want to see them so live that they can be in communion with the Lord, in their camps, and in their secret places, and that in the midst of battle that they can say: 'Father, my life and my spirit are in thine hand!'

"I want to see the boys that go away from here in this cause, to go feeling just as our missionaries do when sent out into the world, carrying with them the spirit a good mother feels when she parts with her boy, on the morning of his departure for his mission. . . . I would say 'My boy, my son, and your son, when you go out to face the disasters that are now afflicting the world, go out as you do on a mission, be just as good and pure and true in the army of the United States as you are in the army of the Elders of Israel that are preaching the gospel of love and peace to the world. Then, if you unavoidably fall a prey to the bullet of the enemy you will go pure as you have lived; you will be worthy of your reward; you will have proved yourself a hero, and not only a hero, but a valiant servant of the living God, worthy of his acceptation and of admission into the loving presence of the Father!'" (Ibid., p. 825.)

This was not mere rhetoric, but the pleading of a concerned parent who had a host of able-bodied sons who were eligible for military service. Several of those sons were inducted into the armed forces, serving in the different branches of the military. However, because of the relatively short period during which the United States was involved in World War I, only one of them, Calvin, saw service overseas. He was the chaplain for the ninety-first division, which was engaged in some of the most bitter fighting. As a result, he was wounded several times but in each instance returned to duty after a brief convalescence.

Although he was not in the military service, another son, Hyrum M. of the Twelve, was in Europe during the war in connection with his duties as the president of the European Mission. He arrived in his field of labor in 1913 near the outset of hostilities and remained there until 1916. Much of his labor had to do with the location and transfer of missionaries from danger. This necessitated frequent trips to the continent and entry into actual war zones. On one such trip, he was imprisoned in Germany as an English spy because of his initials H.M.S., a sure sign to the Germans that he was in the royal service.

Having written to his father in graphic terms of the zeppelin attacks on England, he received this answer under date of February 19, 1916: "I trust and pray that you and all our people may escape from the terrible raids of the zeppelins that are occasionally made on the defenseless cities and towns of Great Britain. It seems to me that the only object of such raids is the wanton and wicked destruction of property and the taking of defenseless lives. No such thing as that was ever known, so far as my understanding goes, in any so-called civilized country before the present time. It appears that the spirit of murder, the shedding of blood, not only of combatants, but of anyone connected with the enemy's country, seems to have taken possession of the people, or at least the ruling powers in Germany. What they gain by it, I do not know. It is hardly possible that they expect to intimidate the people by such actions, and it surely does not diminish the force of the opposition. By such unnecessary and useless raids in the name of warfare, they are losing the respect of all the nations of the earth."

He concluded this gloomy letter on an upbeat note, reminding his son that these troubles had been foreseen by ancient prophets and admonishing him to remain faithful and to be diligent: "Well, my son, we pray that you and all who are under your direction may escape these calamities. Preach the Gospel, be faithful, teach the Elders and the Saints to put their faith and trust in the Lord, for indeed these are days of trouble and calamity which have been spoken of by the prophets, and it behooves all men to repent and to turn to the Lord before their day of repentance is past and destruction overtakes them."

The prophet's prayer for Hyrum's safety was answered, and he returned home safely within a few months, having completed his three-year mission. But in less than two years, he was dead from peritonitis, caused by a ruptured appendix. The death of this exemplary son, coming at age forty-six as he approached the height of his powers, was a crushing blow to his aged father, who had foreseen the possibility that one day he would occupy the prophetic office. Weighed down with grief, he gave vent to his feelings in still another mournful eulogy: "My soul is rent asunder," wrote he. "My heart is broken, and flutters for life! O my sweet son, my joy, my hope! O I love him still. I will love him evermore. And so it is and ever will be with all my sons and daughters, but he is my first born son; the first to bring me the joy and hope of an endless, honorable, name among men. He ever was from very infancy the soul of honor and of reason, principle and truth. From the depths of my soul I thank God for him! But I needed him more than I can express. His mind was quick and bright and correct. His judgment was not excelled, and he saw and comprehended things in their true light and meaning. When he spoke, men listened and felt the weight of his thoughts and words. O I needed him! We all needed him. He was most useful to the Church. He was indeed a prince among men. Never in his life did he displease me or give me cause to doubt him. I loved him through and through. He has thrilled my soul by his power of speech, as no other man ever did. Perhaps this was because he was my son, and he was filled with the fire of the Holy Ghost. And now, what can I do? O what can I do! My soul is rent, my heart is broken. O God, help me!" (JFS, p. 474.)

But amidst the shadows of war and death during the last few years of his life, the aged prophet enjoyed frequent intervals of light and joy. As always, these were centered around his family and work. In the spring of 1914, he purchased and furnished a home in pleasant California at Santa Monica. Following a usual practice, he dedicated this home to the Lord and conferred upon it the name *Deseret*, thereby perpetuating in California the symbolism of the Beehive House, his main Salt Lake City residence.

About the same time, he purchased a new Reo automobile, which was one of the most fashionable cars of the day. So, at age seventy-six, the prophet was beginning to enjoy the fruits of his labors. While he was never a wealthy man, he was well-to-do in his later years because of his frugality and the wise investment of his surplus means. Bishop Nibley, who had great business acumen, was a principal financial advisor to the president, and this enabled him to realize the maximum return from his investments. Certainly, Joseph's modest affluence at this stage of life was not assignable to the small stipend received from the Church, which always has followed a policy of benign thriftiness in providing living allowances for its general authorities.

So, during this period of the prophet's life, we find him enjoying more leisure and a more elaborate life-style than he had ever known before. He made frequent trips to his Santa Monica home, especially during the months of inclement weather in Salt Lake City. The Christmas of 1914 was a particularly memorable one. By then Deseret was completely and comfortably furnished; and, accompanied by a number of his ever-growing brood of grandchildren, President Smith spent an idyllic holiday there.

Christmas afternoon found him on the beach watching over some of the grandchildren. At the home were good food and conversation interspersed with singing, piano playing, resting, and checkers. On December 28, he noted that the "big boys walked over the hills to the sea." And, on New Year's day, the family piled into the Reo for a drive to Pasadena, where they witnessed "the flower show and parade." President Smith's appraisal of what since has become known as the Rose Bowl Parade has been shared by many over the intervening years. It was, in his own words, "so extensive it was tiresome."

It would be a gross caricature, however, to portray President Smith at this time of life as a coupon-clipping retiree. He was still the head of an international Church and bore the ultimate responsibility for the policies that governed the conduct of hundreds of thousands of Latter-day Saints around the world. He could never lay this responsibility aside. It followed him everywhere, whether to Church or business meetings, to the beach or to the flower show. And he was always conscious of the impact his conduct or words would have on others, whether members or nonmembers. Therefore, he was guarded in his ways both in private and in public, making sure that what he said and did conformed with the high standards of the gospel and the dignity of his office.

It was typical that the relaxed Christmas holiday he enjoyed at Santa Monica in 1914 was preceded by one of those arduous tours for which he had become noted. His party left Salt Lake City on November 19 with Independence, Missouri, as the first stop. With the president were Julina, President Charles W. Penrose, and George Albert Smith and Joseph Fielding Smith of the Twelve. The only reason Bishop Nibley wasn't along was his absence from the city. But he joined the president and the others later.

The main purpose in visiting Independence was to dedicate a new chapel. With the work running behind schedule, the local leaders recruited the full-time missionaries to help with the finishing touches so that everything would be ready when President Smith arrived. Among the missionaries who helped lay sod, install benches, and scrape and wash windows was the prophet's nephew from Arizona, Spencer W. Kimball. Originally, Elder Kimball's call was to the Swiss German mission. But the outbreak of the war had necessitated a change in assignment.

The dedicatory service was held on November 22, and the following day the prophet held a special meeting with the hundred elders who were serving in that mission under President Samuel O. Bennion, who, nineteen years later, would be called as a member of the First Council of the Seventy.

Afterward, Joseph F. greeted each missionary separately, shaking his hand and giving him words of blessing and encouragement. As he greeted Spencer, who doubtless received the customary embrace and fatherly kiss reserved for the president's relatives and close friends, one cannot but wonder whether he saw in this brown-eyed, open-faced nineteen-year-old a future president of the Church.

Between meetings on the day of the dedication, the prophet paid a courtesy call on Joseph Smith III, the president of the Reorganized Church. These cousins, who had not been close in recent years, had a fine time visiting and reminiscing. It was the last time they were to see each other in mortality. Joseph III was ailing at the time and passed away quietly on December 10, 1914. Joseph F., receiving word of his cousin's death after returning to Salt Lake City from his tour, sent a wire of condolence to Frederick M., another cousin, who succeeded his brother as president of the Reorganized Church. He also wired the news to his cousin Ina Coolbrith in California. As death visited the Smith cousins, doctrinal and personal differences evaporated among the survivors, leaving a feeling of unity and gratitude for their common heritage.

From Independence, the president's party traveled to Memphis, Tennessee, and from there to Chattanooga, Tennessee; Atlanta, Georgia; Jacksonville, St. Augustine, and Pensacola, Florida; San Antonio and El Paso, Texas; Tucson and Yuma, Arizona; and Los Angeles, California, and thence home. At all these places, President Smith held meetings or at least interviewed local leaders during brief stopovers.

After returning from his California holiday, President Smith spent four busy months at home before departing for another trip to Hawaii. These were filled with family joy and sorrow, with the usual round of Church activities, and with anxious watching of the war developments abroad. He was made happy on March 18 when he performed a temple sealing for his daughter Lucy and a fine young man, Ralph C. Carter. And the next day he was overwhelmed with feelings of despair because of the illness of Sarah, who apparently had suffered a stroke and was speechless. He noted that she was in a "state of constant unrest" and lamented the condition of his "precious Mama." He spent a good part of the next day at Sarah's bedside, and the day following that, she passed away. The prophet vented his grief in another lengthy diary entry in which he extolled the virtues of this remarkable woman to whom he had been married for forty-seven years. Sarah gave birth to eleven children, five of whom preceded her in death.

The gloom caused by Sarah's death was heightened by discouraging news from abroad about the progress of the war. The prophet expressed his shock at the sinking of the *Lusitania* on May 8 and the loss of over thirteen hundred among the crew and passengers, which included "many outstanding people including Elbert Hubbard."

The following day the prophet and his party departed for still another trip to his beloved Hawaiian Islands.

Chapter Twenty-six

The Twilight Years

President Smith never seemed to tire of traveling to Hawaii, the land where he began his ministry as a teenage orphan. It was with excitement and anticipation, therefore, that he and Julina and Bishop and Sister Nibley left Salt Lake City on May 12 bound for Honolulu via San Francisco. Three days later, these seasoned travelers found themselves aboard the S.S. *Manchuria* as it steamed through the Golden Gate toward Pearl Harbor.

During the six-day passage on this his seventh visit to Polynesia, Joseph went through the customary cycle familiar to Pacific voyagers destined for Oahu: one day to acquire sea legs; five days of relaxed enjoyment; and one day anticipating the landfall at Diamondhead. After unwinding and adjusting to the ship's constant motion, the prophet indulged in the simple pleasures of shipboard life—watching the graceful albatross and the flying fish, reading, napping, and sampling the ship's excellent cuisine. Unlike many passengers who enjoyed the more active pastimes of swimming, dancing, and shuffleboard, President Smith was content with his favorite sedentary sport—checkers. After several days at sea, he noted with obvious satisfaction, "Passed part of time beating the Bishop at checkers."

An interesting diversion came on Sunday: "This morning to our surprise the chief steward invited us to lead the Sabbath service this morning." Although the brethren were given short notice, they responded willingly in the best volunteer fashion. It must have reminded this pair—the president and the presiding bishop—of their missionary days, as they provided the entire program except for the accompanist, a Mrs. Lucas, whom they pressed into service. The prophet conducted, spoke, and offered the benediction, while the bishop opened with prayer, led the singing, and spoke. At the captain's request, they passed the hat at the end of the service to receive contributions for the Sailors Home at San Francisco. Afterward, as he mingled with the other passengers, President Smith received the customary reward for such service in the form of thanks and congratulations. One admirer from Chicago, who for lack of anything better to say, enthusiastically offered his hand with the comment, "I want to shake hands with the preacher."

Docking at Honolulu on May 21, the visitors received the traditional Hawaiian welcome from the Polynesian Saints, who showered them with welcoming music and leis. The following day, the president's party was driven across the island to the Church colony at Laie. As the prophet traversed the familiar route, he was struck by the pervasive changes that had occurred in the more than sixty years since he first visited Hawaii. He wrote, "Our ride to Laie was most pleasant and presented a vast contrast between now and the last time I passed through that route. Now we have excellent paved roads and autos [instead of] dry dusty roads and slow horses and carriages; and still earlier than that on foot and on horse back."

At Laie, the Saints outdid themselves in hospitality and gourmandism with a banquet that Iosepa pronounced to be "the most extensive, elaborate and bounteous feast that I have ever attended."

Always interested in new things, President Smith visited the recently installed "Marconi Wireless Station," which, he reported, consisted of twenty-four steel towers from 300 to 480 feet high, and which could transmit wireless messages to as far away as Japan and England. In awe of this scientific and engineering marvel, he confided to his journal, "I have no knowledge or power of language to describe or express my surprise at what we saw."

Both temporal and ecclesiastical considerations had drawn President Smith to Hawaii at this time. On the temporal side, he was interested in persuading leaders in the sugar industry to establish mills at or near Laie to provide ready employment for the many Latter-day Saints who had settled in that area. It also would enhance the value of the plantation. Toward this end, the President and Bishop Nibley, along with Senator Reed Smoot, who had joined them in Hawaii, met with sugar magnate Andrew Adams on June 1 to discuss moving his sugar mills to Laie. While the results of the talks were inconclusive at the time, President Smith seemed to feel satisfied with them.

In recording the events of this day, Joseph was reminded that it was the birthday of his early mentor, Brigham Young, whom he always held in honored remembrance. And later that same day occurred an ecclesiastical event of historic significance. "This evening," he wrote, "Brothers Smoot, Nibley and myself walked over to the meeting house & had some conversation on the subject of recommending that a small temple or endowment house be erected here at Laie. We were agreed and I offered prayer and dedicated the meeting house site for a temple provided the counsel of the First Presidency & 12 shall approve it."

This incident typifies the restraint with which President Smith exercised his authority. Holding the key of ultimate earthly authority in Church affairs, he rightfully could have acted unilaterally in this matter. Instead, he yielded to the principles of unity and common consent, deferring a final decision until the matter had been considered and approved by the First Presidency and the Twelve.

Three days later, the brethren attended a meeting of a group of planters held in the prestigious Pacific Club at Honolulu, where Elder Smoot, wearing his political hat, urged those present to support the Republican Party. And the next day, the travelers boarded the S.S. *Sierra*, docked at Pearl Harbor. There they experienced again the friendliness and hospitality that endeared the Polynesian Saints to President Smith and drew him again and again to their islands. "When we came to the Sierra," he wrote, "we were met by dozens of the Saints who loaded us down with leis until we could scarcely see out. We received an ovation on our arrival May 21 on the SS Manchuria and now a double ovation as we take our departure on the SS Sierra today."

On the mainland, the Prophet spent two days in the San Francisco Bay area, where again he contacted his reclusive cousin, Josephine D. Smith, who had hidden herself under the pseudonym Ina D. Coolbrith. From there, he traveled north to Portland, Oregon, to dedicate a "beautiful new meeting house." At the depot to meet him was the vigorous young mission president Melvin J. Ballard, who, a few months after President Smith's death, would be called to the apostleship by President Heber J. Grant.

The day following his return to Salt Lake City, the Prophet presented to the First Presidency and the Twelve the matter that seemed uppermost in his mind: "I sprung the proposition to build a small temple at Laie in the interests of our people of the islands of the Pacific and it met with a warm approval by the entire council." It was only two years before this that President Smith had dedicated the site of the first temple outside the United States, at Cardston, Alberta, Canada. Now the temple on Oahu would be the first one to be constructed beyond the mainland of North America. These important initiatives toward the internationalization of temples and temple work, begun by President Smith, were not concluded during his lifetime. These temples were completed and dedicated by his successor, Heber J. Grant, the Hawaiian Temple being dedicated on Thanksgiving day, November 27, 1919, a little over a year after President Smith's death; and the Cardston temple being dedicated on August 26, 1923.

President Smith spent the remainder of 1915 in Salt Lake City attending to his usual duties, except for trips to dedicate buildings in Idaho Falls and Malad, Idaho, and a recreational trip to California in November and December.

During this period, he suffered intermittent, painful attacks of lumbago, which sometimes kept him in bed. He fought off these attacks as best he could, never complaining

Joseph F. Smith (Church Archives)

about them and recording them only in the most cursory way. As usual, he interspersed his ecclesiastical duties with business appointments and public relations contacts. Of the latter, the most significant during the period was the president's involvement in meetings held with leaders of the bar from all parts of the country who assembled in Salt Lake City during August. Among the distinguished visitors was former president of the United States William Howard Taft, who was then serving as the Kent Professor of law at Yale University and who several years later would be appointed as chief justice of the United States Supreme Court. The prophet received this brainy, rotund man with the walrus moustache in a private interview on the eighteenth, during which the pair enjoyed a "pleasant visit" off the record. The following day, a large delegation of the visiting lawyers called on the president in the Beehive House and were shown pictures of Joseph's family and given a personally guided tour of the home. In turn, the visitors urged their host to attend the final banquet session of their convention in the new Hotel Utah. Joseph agreed and that night found himself seated on the speakers' stand in the LaFayette Ballroom between Senator Smoot and Governor Baldwin of Connecticut. He reported that the banquet was "gorgeous and protracted," an obviously accurate characterization since it wore on until two in the morning. And he found the speakers, anchored by President Taft, to be "brilliant and witty."

"The good feeling for Utah was unrestrained and lavish," he said of the speakers, "as also the flow of champaigne & cigars and cigarette smoke." It is a mark of Joseph's humanity and humility that his private record of the event is devoid of any condemnation of the different life-style of these men, while it speaks approvingly of their intelligence, eloquence, and humor.

In arranging for functions of this kind, and in handling the numerous other duties connected with his office, President Smith had ample assistance. Not only was there an able and experienced clerical staff upon which he could call, but he had his counselors as well as the other general authorities who were always available and pleased to help. But of all these, he relied most heavily on the members of his family who occupied positions of high responsibility. His sons Hyrum and Joseph Fielding, both of whom were members of the Twelve, were called upon often. Joseph Fielding was especially helpful in handling the president's voluminous correspondence, taking dictation, or helping edit sermons and writings. David A. helped his father handle personal matters, often acting as chauffeur, purchasing agent, or traveling companion. Cousin George Albert Smith of the Twelve was a frequent traveling companion, now and then pressed into service to perform secretarial duties. And, of course, prior to his death, cousin John Henry Smith was used as a confidant and sounding board, even before he was called as a counselor in the First Presidency.

President Smith's frequent use of relatives served a dual purpose. It lifted a heavy burden from his shoulders, and it also enabled him to personally instruct them in the skills of Church administration. This produced rich dividends for the Church in the years ahead when two of those who had been specially tutored by him, cousin George Albert and son Joseph Fielding, became presidents of the Church, bringing with them a wealth of important insight and knowledge they would not otherwise have had.

The prophet's love for family these illustrations suggest was the source of alternating joy and sorrow. In October, his twenty-seven-year-old daughter, Zina, the wife of John Greenwell, suddenly took ill. Reacting as if this mature woman was still a small child under his personal charge, the prophet canceled his meetings in order to be available to help if necessary. "This sad news worried me and greatly disturbed my peace of mind," he recorded in his journal. "All I could do was to appeal to the Lord in prayer for help. How helpless we are!" Three days later the concerned father "spent the evening and night until 11:30 p.m. mostly in prayer." And a week later, Zina passed away, leaving another void in her father's earthly diadem and bringing on another sad lamentation. As Joseph advanced in years, it seemed that his feelings of melancholy at the death of a loved one grew ever more intense.

The prophet's spirits brightened perceptibly a fortnight later when his wives, children, in-laws, and grandchildren, 120 strong, gathered in the upper hall of the Bishop's Building to celebrate his seventy-seventh birthday. With good food and pleasant conversation, interspersed with musical numbers and entertaining toasts, the benign patriarch spent a memorable evening of happy relaxation among those he loved most.

As the Salt Lake City weather began to turn cold the latter part of November, President Smith decided on another visit to Santa Monica and Deseret. Traveling via San Francisco to visit the fair in progress there, Joseph and his party entrained for Los Angeles on November 28. His diary entry describing the trip reveals a keen perception of the beauty and fertility of the countryside through which they passed: "Found ourselves about 8:30 this morning running along near the sea shore. There appeared to be an unusually heavy surf rolling in which made the scene grand and interesting. Our course lay along the shore principally until about noon when we turned toward the hills, coming out into the San Fernando Valley about 1:00 p.m., where we had our lunch. Passing through this fertile valley was delightful. Many fields were covered with the fruits of vines left in full view by late frosts, ungathered and almost ungatherable for multitude. Large fields of squash, pumpkins, melons, and other products literally covered the ground."

At Deseret, the president settled into the relaxed holiday routine he usually followed at this pleasant hideaway. However, because of the intermittent attacks of lumbago he had suffered in recent months, he did not play golf during this two-week visit. So he occupied himself with walks, rides, reading, and writing, interspersed with the handling by mail or telegraph of Church and business matters that could not await his return home.

During one outing, Joseph and members of his family visited Ocean Park; on another they attended a performance of the famous Harry Houdini; and during another, they took a leisurely drive through a pleasant suburban community called "Holliwood." One accustomed to the Hollywood of today with its bustle, tinsel, overreaching, publicity hype, and inflated prices will appreciate this contrasting view as seen through the eyes of the seventy-seven-year-old patriarch who visited the place during its infancy: "We had a delightful ride through Holliwood. This is an ideal day, warm, clear and balmy. We got some lemons by the wayside, 3 doz. for 15¢."

The year 1916 was almost a replica of the preceding year with the usual grist of Church administration, visits to Deseret, family anniversaries and celebrations, and yet another trip to Hawaii. This was made to follow up on the plans for the temple and to check on affairs pertaining to the Church plantation. The president and Bishop Nibley and their wives arrived in Honolulu on February 29 and departed for home on March 8. During this short interval, the prophet managed to sandwich a nostalgic pilgrimage into his schedule when he visited the place where his departed friend George Q. Cannon had commenced the work in Hawaii many years before. Driving from Laie to Honolulu on the sixth, the party encountered the beginning stages of a Kona storm with high winds but no rain. That evening a meeting was held with some of the Saints, during which "rain began to fall and increased rapidly and before bed time it pounded in torrents." Typically, however, it cleared the next morning, when the president set out with Bishop Nibley for a tour of some of the landmarks Joseph had come to love: Waikiki, Diamond Head, and Pacific Heights along the ridge between the Nuuanu and Pauoa valleys. There, at an elevation of over a thousand feet, they had a magnificent view of both valleys as well as Honolulu and Pearl Harbor. Carried back in memory to his earliest visit to this hauntingly beautiful place, the prophet reminisced in his journal: "It was on this ridge where Geo. Q. Cannon & others met in prayer and made the opening start of the Hawaiian Mission in 1850 or 51." So enthralled was Joseph with the spectacular scenery and the memories it evoked that he and the bishop drove back to Honolulu to get their wives, Edna and Julia, to allow them to share the experience.

There is a sense of wonder in President Smith's account of this incident, wonder at the inspiring beauty of Oahu, his second home, and at the results that had flowed from the inconspicuous beginning of the work in Hawaii less than seventy years before. And as they boarded their ship for the return home the next day, he would have been reminded even more forcefully of the fruits of those labors when a throng of

Hawaiian Saints appeared at dockside to wish them bon voyage with their leis, their laughter, and their unbounded love. "We have had most loving and lovely treatment every day of our seven days of visit among the Latter-day Saints of Oahu at Honolulu and Laie," the Prophet recorded appreciatively.

So often had Joseph made the return voyage from Honolulu to San Francisco that he had little new to comment on. One noteworthy thing that found its way into his diary, however, was the report of a disturbing change in the tide of his friendly competition with Bishop Nibley at the checkerboard. He recorded after two days at sea: "Played the Bish today. He got three out of nine games. He is gaining."

One aspect of sea travel that troubled the prophet was the immodest dress of some of the female passengers. This reflected the change in clothing styles and the relaxed atmosphere aboard ship. His reaction was prompt and unequivocal when he saw the same thing creeping in among his own people. At the MIA conference in June, he unburdened himself of his strong feelings on the subject: "I laid down the law pretty tight on women's dress and the bawdy fashions of today and hurt the feelings of one or two."

One of the most distinguishing features about 1916 for President Smith was his keen interest in politics. Convinced that the Church and the nation would be benefited by the high tariff policies of the Republican Party, he supported the candidacy of the Republican standard bearer, Charles Evans Hughes, against the incumbent democrat, Woodrow Wilson. President Wilson had been one of the chief architects of the Underwood Tariff Act, which had sharply revised tariff rates downward and had levied a federal income tax to counterbalance the resulting loss of revenue. The Republicans had keyed on the issues raised by this and other legislation sponsored by President Wilson, issues the prophet adopted as his own and in which he became emotionally involved.

Following a customary policy, however, he seldom expressed his political views in public, leaving Church members to vote their own convictions. But in private, he was a strong partisan, lending his support to the candidate of his choice where that seemed appropriate. So, October 25 found him attending a Republican rally where the main speaker was William E. Borah, Republican U.S. senator from neighboring Idaho. "I attended the Republican Rally at the theatre," wrote the prophet "and heard Senator Borah deliver one of the best and most masterly compaign addresses that I ever heard from any speaker. The house was packed from pit to dome and hundreds could not get in. He was given absolute attention and much sincere applause." And on Monday, November 6, the night before the election, he attended another rally: "Jos. F. Jr. and I attended the Republican rally at the Salt Lake theatre. Senator Geo. Sutherland was the principal speaker and his address was masterly and unanswerable."

The hopes and expectations Joseph had for a Republican victory were dashed the next day when Utah went democratic. And on the eighth he noted, "A pall of gloom hangs over the city and the republican party of Utah."

The annoyance and disappointment at the outcome of the election were soon submerged by the constant flood of private and Church affairs. Four days later, the president was afflicted with intense chest pains that put him in bed. These were the harbingers of a deteriorating physical condition that would accelerate until his death two years later. He managed to get out of bed on the thirteenth for a birthday party in the Bishop's Hall in the afternoon and a reception in the Beehive House in the evening. And, having forced himself into motion, he continued to shoulder his heavy administrative responsibilities without letup during the remainder of the year, intermingling them with needed interludes of rest and relaxation.

He was saddened by the deaths of two old friends, Francis M. Lyman, president of the Twelve, who died November 18 and whom Joseph characterized as "a stalwart in the ranks of Zion's teachers," and William McLachlan, president of the Pioneer Stake, who died in early December, "a most excellent man" with whom the prophet crossed the plains in 1863 in Captain John Woolley's company.

In an effort to build his strength and to ward off other physical disabilities, on December 1 President Smith played a game of golf with his son Joseph and Franklin S. Richards.

One must wonder at the effectiveness of this remedy in view of President Smith's notation that there was "too much snow."

Throughout 1917, many entries found their way into the prophet's diary that clearly signalled that his physical machine was wearing out. The diary includes such entries as "My heart was throbbing with rapid violence"; "I had a very painful, restless night"; "I passed a most sleepless and uncomfortable night, with great difficulty to get full breath."

In an effort to mend his tattered health, the prophet went to Deseret in February 1917. There he was flattered to receive an invitation to enjoy the privileges of the exclusive Brentwood Country Club during his stay. In thanking the board of directors for this courtesy, the prophet noted, "Having only started on the links as a member of the Salt Lake Country Club at the age of 78, I can hardly hope ever to become an expert, but I enjoy the exercise which I find to be physically beneficial to me."

Joseph returned home in late March in time to prepare for the April general conference and for the move into the newly completed Church Administration Building at 47 East South Temple. On April 3, he observed that "the brethren are getting moved into their new quarters," and two days later he recorded his own move with this succinct entry: "Moved into the new office and opened and passed upon the mail." That lean sentence announced what was, in effect, the end of one era and the beginning of another. It announced the transition of the Church from a comparatively obscure and much maligned sect into an international organization of stature and influence. And it moved the Church from the backwater of pioneer isolation into the mainstream of world affairs. One cannot inspect the plain, compact annex that connects the Beehive and Lion Houses and that served so long as the executive offices of the First Presidency and then visit the spacious, ornate building next door without sensing the symbolic significance of this move. And to enter the front door of 47 East South Temple and walk through the ornate outer and inner foyers and the onyx room into the First Presidency's council room initially conveys a sense of grandeur and opulence that seems inconsistent with the humble beginnings of the Church and the humble beginnings of Joseph F. Smith, who built the new headquarters. But it was a change in form, not in substance. The Church and the man who directed it remained essentially the same.

Three weeks after the general conference, when the move to the new building had been completed and when his desk had been cleared of matters pending at headquarters, the prophet again departed for Hawaii. Both business and Church matters drew him there. Of the latter, his concern about the progress of the new temple was paramount. Joined by Alice and daughters Jeanetta, Asenath, and Agnes and by Bishop Nibley and three of his daughters, the prophet left Salt Lake City on April 30, arriving at Honolulu May 8 aboard the S.S. *Maui*.

The day after reaching Oahu, Joseph made his way to Laie and immediately delved into the matter that was uppermost in his thoughts: "We visited the temple & found the workmen all around. We did not approve of Bro. Ramsay's coloring in his water scenes and we ordered a change." Five days later, after making side trips to other islands, the prophet returned to Oahu to inspect the temple again. A combined sense of urgency and irritation may be inferred from this entry of the fourteenth: "Visited the temple this morning. Workmen still busy and to all human appearance the finish is by no means nearby. Bro. Ramsay is trying to improve his colors by our suggestion."

Two days later, President Smith and his party sailed for the mainland from picturesque Pearl Harbor. Intermixed with his yearnings to see the temple completed and to return for the dedication was a vague feeling that he would never see Hawaii again. As the familiar silhouette of Diamond Head receded into the distance, he gave voice to this indistinct impression as he recorded the events of the day in his journal: "Commenced this morning to pack up. And at about 9 o'clock started for the pier and the SS Maui, where we met many of our friends, and smothered with leis and gifts of fruits, nuts and candy we boarded the ship and bid good by to our friends and Honolulu, perhaps for the *last time*."

Joseph F. Smith, about 1917 (Church Archives)

The emphasis given to this statement by the underlining, a practice he seldom followed, implies a depth of feeling not fully expressed in his words. The progressive deterioration of the prophet's health that followed lends credence to this view. During his keynote address at the October general conference, the president sandwiched this revealing comment between certain doctrinal themes and a recitation of recent temporal achievements: "I begin to feel that I am getting to be an old man, or rather a young man in an old body. I think I am just about as young as I ever was in my life in spirit. I love the truth today more than I ever did before in the world. I believe in it more firmly now than I ever did before, because I see it more clearly, I understand it better from day to day by the promptings and inspiration of the Spirit of the Lord that is vouchsafed to me; but my body gets tired, and I want to tell you, sometimes my poor old heart quivers considerably." (CR, Oct. 1917, pp. 6-7.)

Three months later the emotional stress caused by the death of his son Hyrum M. added still another layer to the heavy physical burden the prophet carried. Progressive accumulations of these physical and emotional woes prompted the prophet to make this observation at the general conference held in April 1918: "It is an unusual thing for me to attempt to make any apology for myself, but I am in a condition of health just at this time which may prevent me from taking so active a part at this session of our conference as I have usually taken." (CR, Apr. 1918, p. 2.)

Chapter Twenty-seven

The Vision

Gauged by the events of the last several months of his life, the prophet's declining physical strength was accompanied by a corresponding strengthening of his spiritual perceptions. Indeed, during the same sermon, he made this significant, confirming statement: "I may have physical ailments, but it appears to me that my spiritual status not only remains steadfast as in times past, but is developing, growing, becoming more thoroughly established in the faith of the gospel, in the love of truth, and in a desire to devote all the energy, time, wisdom and ability the Lord may give to me to advance his cause in the earth and to help all I can to build up Zion in these latter days." (Ibid.)

Unable to keep up with the fast physical pace he had set in his earlier years, President Smith spent most of his time during the months just preceding his death in quiet prayer and meditation. He shared the results of his experience with the Saints assembled in the Tabernacle during the keynote address of the October 1918 general conference: "I will not, I dare not, attempt to enter upon many things that are resting upon my mind this morning, and I shall postpone until some future time, the Lord being willing, my attempt to tell you some of the things that are in my mind, and that dwell in my heart. I have not lived alone these five months. I have dwelt in the spirit of prayer, of supplication, of faith and of determination; and I have had my communication with the Spirit of the

Lord continuously; and I am glad to say to you, my brethren and sisters, that it is a happy meeting this morning for me to have the privilege of joining with you in the opening of this eighty ninth Semi-annual Conference of the Church." (CR, Oct. 1918, p. 2.)

Doubtless, the most significant thing that rested on the prophet's mind was an extraordinary experience he had had the day before. As he had sat in his comfortable study in the Beehive House, pondering over the scriptures in preparation for the conference, he had been impressed as never before, with the great themes of the atonement, the redemption, and the exaltation of mankind through their obedience to the principles and ordinances of the gospel. These reflections called to his mind the writings of the Apostle Peter, and to refresh and sharpen his memory, he re-read the third and fourth chapters of First Peter, which recount the Savior's ministry among the spirits in prison. The focused intensity of his mind upon these themes, against the background of months of inner delvings and strugglings, resulted in the most startling and refulgent spiritual experience of Joseph's life: "The eyes of my understanding were opened," he wrote of the incident, "and the Spirit of the Lord rested upon me, and I saw the hosts of the dead, both small and great." Among those the Prophet saw in vision were an "innumerable company of the spirits of the just" who had been faithful and diligent in mortality and who had died in the hope of a "glorious resurrection" through the grace of the Father and the Son. These "were filled with joy and gladness and were rejoicing together because the day of their deliverance was at hand." And these, he wrote, were visited by the Savior, who "preached to them the everlasting gospel, the doctrines of the resurrection and the redemption of mankind from the fall, and from individual sins on condition of repentance."

Seen also in Joseph's vision were the wicked, the ungodly, the rebellious, and the unrepentant "who had defiled themselves while in the flesh." To these the Savior did not go; nor did they hear his voice. Seeing the great multitudes of the ungodly who thronged the spirit world, and realizing the Savior's visit there was limited to three short days during which he personally visited only the just, the prophet wondered about the meaning of Peter's statement that the Master preached to the disobedient spirits who lived in the days of Noah. In this quandary, he was shown that this was accomplished through the principles of agency and delegation: "From among the righteous he organized his forces," wrote Joseph in his account of the vision, "and appointed messengers, clothed with power and authority, and commissioned them to go forth and carry the light of the gospel to them that were in darkness, even to all the spirits of men."

As one would have expected, the message carried to the ungodly by these spirit-world emissaries was harmonious with the message carried to the nations by God's earthly ministers: "These were taught faith in God, repentance from sin, vicarious baptism for the remission of sins, the gift of the Holy Ghost by the laying on of hands, and all other principles of the gospel that were necessary for them to know in order to qualify themselves that they might be judged according to men in the flesh, but live according to God in the spirit."

So it was that the organization and instruction of his agents occupied all of the Savior's time during his three-day visit to the spirit world—the period during which his body lay in the tomb. And the composition of the group that was so instructed and the qualities and characteristics of its individual members attracted President Smith's special attention: "Among the great and mighty men who were assembled in this vast congregation of the righteous were Father Adam, the Ancient of Days and father of all, and our glorious mother Eve, with many of her faithful daughters who had lived through the ages and worshipped the true and living God. Abel, the first martyr, was there, and his brother Seth, one of the mighty ones, who was in the express image of his father, Adam. Noah, who gave warning of the flood; Shem, the great High Priest; Abraham, the father of the faithful, Isaac, Jacob, and Moses, the great law giver of Israel, Isaiah, who declared by prophecy that the Redeemer was anointed to bind up the broken hearted, to proclaim liberty to the captives, and the opening of the prison to them that were bound were also there."

President Smith went on to name other Old Testament prophets or patriarchs whom he saw, to allude generally to Nephite prophets who were there, and to name some of the prophets of the last dispensation who were among the company, including the Prophet Joseph Smith and his brother Hyrum. Moreover, it was shown to him "that the faithful elders of this dispensation, when they depart from mortal life, continue their labors in the preaching of the gospel of repentance and redemption, through the sacrifice of the Only Begotten Son of God, among those who are in darkness and under the bondage of sin in the great world of the spirits of the dead. The dead who repent will be redeemed through obedience to the ordinances of the house of God, and after they have paid the penalty of their transgression, and are washed clean, shall receive a reward according to their works, for they are heirs of salvation."

Soon after the conference, President Smith reduced the vision to writing and on October 31, 1918, presented it to his counselors and the Quorum of the Twelve Apostles and the Church patriarch, who unanimously accepted it as a revelation from God. On April 3, 1976, the general conference of the Church, on motion unanimously approved, formally accepted this vision and authorized it to be included as section 138 of the Doctrine and Covenants. (CR, Apr. 1976, p. 29.)

This unusual vision, which underscored the universal application of the gospel and demonstrated the thinness of the veil and the spiritual link between earth and the world beyond, was a fitting climax to an exceptional career. And it was a fitting prelude to the final scenes of Joseph F. Smith's mortal life, which, as one acquainted with him would have expected, was set in the midst of his family.

Chapter Twenty-eight

The End and the Beginning

On November 10, ten days after President Smith's vision was accepted by the apostles and the patriarch, his family honored him at a celebration commemorating the anniversary of his sustaining as president of the Church. And being only three days before his eightieth birthday, both events were celebrated at the same time. Moreover, because the day fell on Sunday, those who attended came fasting, which heightened the spiritual tone of the gathering.

As the aged prophet stood to address his family, his white beard and hair gleaming in the sunlight, he was only nine days away from death. Yet he appeared strong and virile; he spoke with firmness and conviction; and he imparted an extraordinary sense of spiritual power and perception, a sense that had grown apace as he matured in age. There was rapt attention as the prophet spoke quietly yet distinctly about a theme he had brooded over through the years as he had seen his family multiply and prosper: "I cannot help reflecting a little on the fact that over sixty years ago I had to start out in the world without father or mother, but one brother . . . and four sisters. My brother has passed and three of my sisters have also passed away, there being one left. Without anything to start with in the world, except the example of my mother, I struggled along with hard knocks in early life. . . . And so I have passed along more than sixty years with no one

Joseph F. Smith with Junius F. Wells, organizer of the Young Men's Mutual Improvement Association, at the dedication of the Hyrum Smith Memorial, Salt Lake City Cemetery, June 27, 1918. (Church Archives.)

to care for me or take one thought of me except the servants of the Lord; some of them having been my kinsmen, and they were always kind to me and to mine. I was fortunate to be left among them, but I have had to watch my step, my 'P's' and 'Q's', so to say, for fear I would do something that would diminish my standing and involve my honor and my word. If there is anything on earth I have tried to do as much as anything else, it is to keep my word, my promises, my integrity, to do what it was my duty to do."

The patriarch then traced the tortuous financial path he had trodden from poverty to a modest security. The formula is familiar: "I have saved my means whenever I could. I never failed, whenever it was possible, to put away a fraction of my earnings where it would be safe and where it might accumulate a few cents interest." He talked about his frugality, observing that the only items of jewelry he owned had been given to him. And predictably, he then focused upon the jewels that he treasured above all others: "But when I look around me and see my boys and girls, whom the Lord has given to me, and I have succeeded, with His help, to make them tolerably comfortable, and at least respectable in the world, I have reached the treasure of my life, the whole substance that makes life worth living. I have a family I am proud of, every individual member of it I love." Then followed tributes to his wives and to his children, of whom he said, "As far as I know all [are] faithful in the Church and all willing to do their duty under all circumstances."

In concluding this last address he was to deliver in mortality, the prophet expressed his gratitude for all the Lord had given him. He affirmed that his head and heart were "just as good as they ever were" but hinted at the physical weakness that would soon lead to his death. Said he, "I want to say to my children that my body isn't what I would like it to be." (JFS, pp. 477-79.)

A week later the prophet was seized with a painful attack of pleurisy that put him in bed. This, added to his advanced age and weakened condition, soon degenerated into pleuropneumonia. Two days after the pleurisy attack, he was dead.

Aside from the loneliness of a temporary separation, President Smith's family and friends could find little to mourn about in his passing. He had surpassed by a decade the customary three-score-and-ten allotted to man. He left behind a life filled with achievement and growth, a stainless reputation, and an extraordinary family. And the purity and rectitude of his conduct foreshadowed a preferred status in the spirit world beyond.

And so it was a solemn but peaceful audience that gathered around the prophet's open grave for his memorial service. A raging epidemic of influenza had prevented the customary public service in the Tabernacle. Instead, the casket carrying his body was taken directly from the Beehive House to the cemetery in a cortege that passed thousands of onlookers who lined the streets to pay their last respects to the venerable leader. These included the thoughtful priests of the Catholic Church who stood in front of the Cathedral of the

Madeleine on East South Temple and ordered the tolling of the cathedral's mournful bells as the cortege passed.

The graveside services were brief but impressive. The invocation was offered by cousin George Albert Smith of the Twelve and the dedicatory prayer and benediction by counselor Charles W. Penrose. The speakers, counselor Anthon H. Lund, who also conducted, Bishop Charles W. Nibley, and President Heber J. Grant traced the prophet's life and ministry and extolled his virtues and achievements.

Numerous editorials, letters, and cards of sympathy heaped praise on the deceased leader and extended condolences to the family. None of these was more generous or unexpected than the one that appeared in the *Salt Lake Tribune*. In a revealing statement, this once implacable foe traced the metamorphosis of its views of the deceased prophet: "In his earlier days he was fiery, fearless, impetuous and uncompromising, and was therefore looked upon as a fanatic intolerant of moderation and irreconcilable to opposition. But with the coming of age, the assumption of authority, the increase of responsibility and the consequent contact with his fellow men, came a broadening of vision and a softening of his nature which gained for him a recognition of those sterling qualities for which he will be remembered longest and best. . . . In later years he made many friends in every walk of life, in every circle of society, in every cult or congregation with which he came in contact. He was a preacher of the gospel as he understood it, and an orator of exceptional power and eloquence. He was a leader upon whom his people leaned because of the simplicity of his character and the frankness of his disposition."

And the obituary in the *Deseret News*, reflecting a different perspective, stressed the patriarchal qualities of the deceased leader: "No trait of his resplendent character was more beautiful and conspicuous than this tender attachment which he ever manifested toward all those who had claim upon it. No man ever held more truly the key to that love which 'is the secret sympathy, the silver link, the silken tie, which heart to heart and mind to mind in body and in soul can bind.' In this parting from him, therefore, there is not only the sense of bereavement for a wise and righteous leader taken away, there is also among tens of thousands the feeling of personal sorrow in the separation from a genuine friend, a compassionate father, a kind and patient brother. These relationships President Smith desired to sustain to his people, and did sustain, in every sense of the word."

So, member and nonmember alike observed the passing of this remarkable man, revealing in their expressions of condolence the varying perceptions they had of him and his work. And the applause that accompanied the descent of the curtain on his mortal life doubtless was echoed by applause through the veil as the curtain rose on a new phase of the life and eternal quest of Joseph F. Smith.

Bibliography

Bancroft, Hubert Howe. *History of Utah*. Salt Lake City: Bookcraft, 1964.

Brimhall, Dean R. Papers. Special Collections Department, Marriott Library, University of Utah, Salt Lake City, Utah.

Corbett, Don Cecil. *Mary Fielding Smith, Daughter of Britain: Portrait of Courage*. Salt Lake City: Deseret Book Company, 1966.

Jenson, Andrew. *Latter-day Saint Biographical Encyclopedia: A Compilation of Biographical Sketches of Prominent Men and Women in the Church of Jesus Christ of Latter-day Saints*. Salt Lake City: The Andrew Jenson History Co., 1901.

Journal of Discourses. 26 vols. London: Latter-day Saints' Book Depot, 1854-86.

Madsen, Truman G. *Defender of the Faith: The B. H. Roberts Story*. Salt Lake City: Bookcraft, 1980.

Nibley, Preston. *The Presidents of the Church*. Salt Lake City: Deseret Book Company, 1947.

Roberts, B. H. *A Comprehensive History of The Church of Jesus Christ of Latter-day Saints, Century One*. 6 vols. Salt Lake City: The Church of Jesus Christ of Latter-day Saints, 1930.

———. *Defense of the Faith and the Saints*. 2 vols. Salt Lake City: Deseret News Press, 1907, 1912.

———. *The Life of John Taylor*. Salt Lake City: George Q. Cannon and Sons, 1892.

Romney, Thomas Cottam. *The Life of Lorenzo Snow*. Salt Lake City: Deseret News, 1955.

333

Smith, Eliza R. Snow. *Biography and Family Record of Lorenzo Snow.* Salt Lake City: Deseret News, 1884.

Smith, Joseph. *History of The Church of Jesus Christ of Latter-day Saints.* 7 vols. 2nd ed. rev. Edited by B. H. Roberts. Salt Lake City: The Church of Jesus Christ of Latter-day Saints, 1932-51.

Smith, Joseph F. *Gospel Doctrine.* 5th ed. Salt Lake City: Deseret Book Company, 1939.

Smith, Joseph Fielding. *Essentials in Church History: A History of the Church from the Birth of Joseph Smith to the Present Time.* Salt Lake City: Deseret News, 1922.

———. *Life of Joseph F. Smith.* Salt Lake City: Deseret Book Company, 1938.

United States. Congress. Senate. Proceedings before the committee on privileges and elections of the US Senate in the matter of the protests against the right of Hon. Reed Smoot, a Senator from the State of Utah, to hold his seat. Washington, Government Printing Office, 1906.

Wilkinson, Ernest L., ed. *Brigham Young University: The First One Hundred Years.* 4 vols. Provo, Utah: Brigham Young University Press, 1975.

Index

335

Nauvoo: peaceful period in, 7-8;
exodus from, 11; Joseph F.
returns to, 49-50, 244-45
Nauvoo Legion, 44-46
Nibley, Charles W., 26; tells of
Joseph F.'s reunion with
nurse, 39-40; writes
impressions of young Joseph
F., 85; friendship of, with
Joseph F., 109; on Joseph F. at
work and play, 233-36; on
Reed Smoot, 237-38
Nibley, Preston, 58
Nuttall, L. John, 95, 159, 173

Obedience, 94
Opposition to Church: in
Missouri, 2; in Illinois, 11, 52;
from Protestant ministers in
Hawaii, 37. *See also*
Antipolygamy laws
Oxen: lost, Mary prays to find,
13-15; Joseph F.'s love for,
17-18; priesthood blessings
given to, 20-21; death of
captain's, 22

Pake, Elder, 36, 149
Palmyra, New York, 12, 229
Partridge, Edward, 42, 139-40
Patriarchal order, 286
Patriarchs, 267
Peace, 299
Pearson, C. E., 151
Penrose, Charles W., 159, 169,
256
People's Party, 185-87
Peterson, Alfred William, 90
Peterson, Henry, 256
Peterson, Joseph, 256
Poi, 33
Political Manifesto, 188
Politics: Joseph F.'s involvement
in, 89-90, 130; John T. Caine's
activity in, 160; and People's
Party, 185-87; Church denies

affiliations with, 186-88;
involvement of general
authorities in, is discouraged,
188-89
Polygamy: rejection of, by
Reorganized Church, 50,
113-14; laws passed against,
90, 127; first criminal conviction
for, 127; Saints contend for
rights of, 129-30; fasting and
prayer concerning, 175-76;
ending of, through Manifesto,
177-78; continuing problems
with, 219, 245-46; address
clarifying Church's position
on, 246-50
Poverty: of Saints at Commerce,
5; of Mary after Hyrum's
death, 10
Pratt, Helaman, 206
Pratt, Orson, 110, 111, 113;
interview of, with David
Whitmer, 115-18
Pratt, Parley P.: as missionary, 1;
arrest of, at Far West, 3; sets
apart Joseph F., 27; leads
missionary company, 28,
29-30; first editor of *Millennial
Star*, 55
Prayer: to find lost oxen, 14-15;
concerning nation's attitudes
toward polygamy, 175-76
Presiding Bishopric, 267
Preston, William B., 224
Priesthood: administrations of, to
oxen, 20-21; selling offices of,
73; format change in meetings
of, 251-52; authority and keys
of, 261-63; exercising, with
proper spirit, 263-64; duties of,
264-65; of First Presidency,
265-66; of Twelve, 266; various
offices in, and their duties,
266-69
Prostitution, arrest of officials for,
151

Index